IMAGES
of America

SAN DIEGO'S KENSINGTON

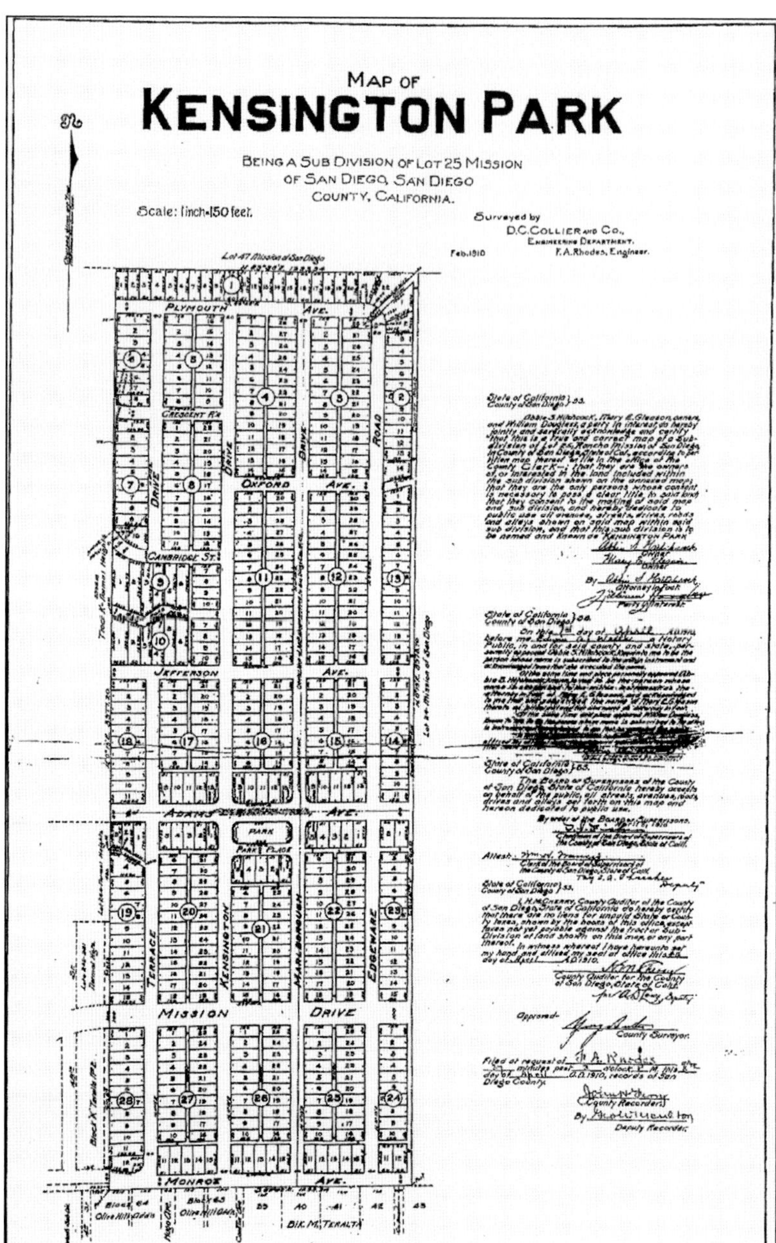

The map for Kensington Park was filed on April 8, 1910. The surveyors did not seem to notice the canyons that would make some of the plots implausible, and when in 1913 the Kensington Park Land Company bought the subdivision rights from the owners, Abbie Hall Hitchcock and Mary Gleason, a new map was filed for the next subdivision, Kensington Manor, and streets were laid out in a curvilinear fashion following the contours of the land. (Courtesy of Ron V. May.)

On the Cover: In 1926, George Forbes hired the Davis-Baker Company to develop the land in the Kensington Heights subdivision. One scheme for promoting the subdivision was a sham contest announced in the newspaper. For the prize of $100, readers were asked to design a Spanish-style home for a Kensington Heights lot. Margaret Fickiensen was the declared prize winner, but the actual model home was the work of architect Richard Requa. In this photograph, from left to right, Richard Davis, Harrison Baker, and George Forbes stand on the site of the future "Prize Spanish Home." (Courtesy of San Diego History Center.)

IMAGES
of America

San Diego's Kensington

Alexandra Wallace, Kiley Wallace,
and Margaret McCann
Foreword by Robert Sedlock

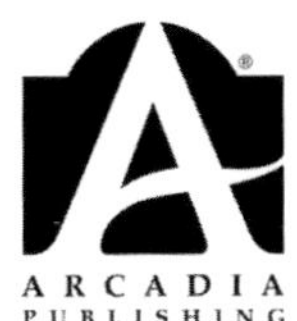

ARCADIA
PUBLISHING

ISBN 978-1-4671-2672-4

Published by Arcadia Publishing
Charleston, South Carolina

Printed in the United States of America

Library of Congress Control Number: 2017932809

For all general information, please contact Arcadia Publishing:
Telephone 843-853-2070
Fax 843-853-0044
E-mail sales@arcadiapublishing.com
For customer service and orders:
Toll-Free 1-888-313-2665

Visit us on the Internet at www.arcadiapublishing.com

We dedicate this book to our fellow preservationists, photographers, hoarders, and family genealogists, without whom many of these images and the stories they tell would be lost.

Contents

Foreword

Kensington is a neighborhood that was ahead of its time due to the careful planning of the developers. Their efforts combined to create the ambiance of a village, still apparent today in 2017.

In the early 1950s, my family moved to Kensington. Because of my interest in this area and its architecture and real estate, I wrote a research paper on the development of Kensington for a class at San Diego State College. I was fortunate to be able to interview two of the primary developers who were still residents of Kensington in 1957.

In 1909, the Santa Fe Railway sent G. Aubrey Davidson to find a suitable area in San Diego for "the development of a luxury subdivision." He became one of our city's most prominent and visionary citizens. He found the large area of undeveloped land surrounded by valleys and canyons that had been part of the San Diego Mission Rancho and was to become Kensington.

Mr. Davidson, only months before his death in December 1957, accepted a college student's request to interview him about the development he had spearheaded in 1910. I met with him in his home on Braeburn Road. Though gravely ill, he still showed great enthusiasm for his beloved Kensington and shared his experiences with me. He felt strongly that the Kensington District had the best climate in all of San Diego County. He was not surprised at the lasting popularity of the district, and told me that Kensington had become all that he and his group had dreamed.

Kensington Heights in the north end was developed by the Davis-Baker Company of Pasadena. George Forbes was the president of the Kensington Heights Company. He was generous with his time and gave me insight into the development. It was promoted extensively with contests, furnished model homes, and aggressive advertising such as "You Who Are Planning a Home—do not fail to see beautiful Kensington Heights!" Mr. Forbes gave me his library of photographs of homes under construction, completed homes, aerial photographs of the lots, subdivision maps, and promotional materials.

These two men, along with several original residents of Kensington who provided historical anecdotes, provided me with personal information for my 1957 report, "The History of Kensington."

I am grateful that Alexandra Wallace, Kiley Wallace, and Margaret McCann are publishing *San Diego's Kensington*, to inform a widespread audience of the history and unique qualities of this beautiful neighborhood in San Diego, California.

—Robert P. Sedlock Jr.
Kensington

ACKNOWLEDGMENTS

The authors wish to thank our many friends and neighbors who provided us with a trove of photographs, making this book a neighborhood effort.

We also wish to recognize Robert Sedlock for his 1957 report, *The History of Kensington*, which forms the basis for much of what we know about the history of the development of Kensington. Bob's work was brought into the light by the late Dr. Thomas Baumann in his subsequent book, *Kensington-Talmadge, 1910–1985*.

We also thank the many historic researchers, in particular Ron May and the late Dale Ballou May, who unearthed drawings, photos, and stories through their process of aiding Kensington residents in obtaining historic designation for their homes.

Our work was made much easier by Carol Meyers and Natalie Fiocre at the San Diego History Center. We also thank the staff and volunteer archivists at Benjamin Franklin Elementary School, Herbert Hoover High School, the Kensington–Normal Heights Branch Library, the Kensington Community Church, the Pacific Southwest Railway Museum, and the Lambda Archives of San Diego. As always, we are grateful to Winnie Hanford for steering us to the right people for photographs and for supporting both this book and the community at large.

INTRODUCTION

> Picture to yourself a tract of 150 acres of high level land, 14.4 miles from the center of the city. (Absolutely the best soil in the whole country.) Separated from all surrounding additions by a deep, broad canyon spanned by a $6,000 bridge over which the Street Cars (5 cent fare) run into the very center of Kensington Park. Kensington Park will absolutely and undoubtedly become the fine residential section of San Diego. We say to you in all sincerity, buy now if you possibly can.
>
> —William Douglas

Real estate agent William Douglas waxed poetic about the potential of the newly mapped Kensington Park subdivision in a 1910 advertisement in the *San Diego Union*. Located on a mesa near the south rim of Mission Valley, surrounded on three sides by canyons, this was the first of several subdivisions to materialize on scrub land that would eventually expand to become a San Diego neighborhood called Kensington.

Prior to the arrival of Spanish colonists in 1769, native Kumeyaay families lived in this general area on a nomadic basis, following food resources as they became seasonally available. Spanish explorers and missionaries were the first Europeans to settle on the land, which Spain claimed for itself, and large tracts were parceled out by the Spanish crown to soldiers and missionaries. After the Mexican war of independence from Spain ended in 1821, Alta California, as it was known, became a Mexican territory. The Mexican government secularized the mission lands and redistributed them; one such large tract, called ex-Mission Rancho, was awarded to Santiago Arguello. Arguello was a soldier in the Spanish army of the Viceroyalty of New Spain, and in 1846 was granted Rancho Ex-Mission San Diego from the secularized Mission San Diego de Alcalá lands. The 1848 Treaty of Guadalupe Hidalgo ended the Mexican-American War and brought California into the United States. By the 1870s, land surveyors began extending the boundary of the city of San Diego. Real estate speculators bought raw land and then began the process of mapping it for development. One such purchase was made by Massachusetts native Edmund Billings Hall, who had come west with his parents and sister after the Civil War and, along with his father, was listed in the 1880 census as a farmer in El Cajon valley.

Edmund Hall purchased two tracts of 160 acres each of the former Mexican land grant, the "Partition of Rancho Mission San Diego" belonging to Santiago Arguello at a land auction held in July 1881. Hall paid $160 for each tract. Shortly afterward, Edmund Hall, his mother, and sister Abbie returned to Massachusetts after the death of his father, Maj. Theron E. Hall. The unfortunate Edmund died in 1882 at age 28 when his horse bolted, dragging his carriage into a pond, where he drowned. Edmund's land was ultimately inherited by his two sisters, one of whom, Abbie, returned to San Diego around 1904 to marry realtor David Hitchcock. Hitchcock's brother, George N. Hitchcock, was a real estate attorney, and rubbed elbows with other town fathers through his membership on the boards of the San Diego Public Library, San Diego Floral Association, the Lyceum of Natural Sciences, the San Diego Humane Society, The Young Men's Christian Association, and his position as county and city superintendent of schools.

Hitchcock's prominence put him in the sphere of men such as G. Aubrey Davidson, who is likely the force behind the mapping of Ex-Mission Rancho Lot 25, and subsequent improvement of the land. Davidson was not only the president of the Southern Trust and Savings Bank, but also the president of the Panama-California Exposition and the San Diego Chamber of Commerce. His influence showed. Before the first house was built, the San Diego Electric Railway extended the Adams Avenue line across a new wooden trestle bridge over Ward Canyon into the center of Kensington Park. Water distribution was provided by the Cuyamaca Water Company, and by the time the subdivision was open for sale of lots on Thanksgiving Day in 1910, the streets had been paved with decomposed granite; the sidewalks, curbs, and gutters were poured with the finest Colton cement; pepper trees were planted in the parkways; and a landscaped "Pleasure Park" with a pond greeted potential homebuyers and speculators alike. Electricity and telephone service was provided, and the only modern amenity missing was a sewer system; the earliest homes relied on septic tanks.

By the time the 1915 Panama California Exposition opened in Balboa Park, bringing hundreds of thousands of visitors to San Diego, new houses with all the amenities had been constructed in Kensington Park, and agent William Douglas's advertisements touted the exclusiveness of the neighborhood with pronouncements such as, "Everything that money and brains can do has already been done to make Kensington the most complete and perfect residence district in San Diego. . . . The elevation is 375 feet where fog and cold wind is unknown." All throughout 1910, 1911, and 1912, Douglas breathlessly peddled the exclusiveness and desirability of the new neighborhood in a series of newspaper advertisements, ensuring the public that "never before has such an offer been made in the history of California" and "That Kensington Park is now, at this present time, the most beautiful residence section in San Diego is absolutely without question." Periodically, his newspaper advertisements would display drawings or photographs of completed houses, with pronouncements such as "Forty One Homes in Fifty Two Weeks" that aimed to show the furious building pace.

Two world wars and the Great Depression caused the build-out of Kensington to ebb and flow. Eventually, scrub land to the north was mapped and developed, becoming Kensington Manor and Kensington Heights. The neighborhood expanded eastward to include Kensington Park Annex and Talmadge Park, as well as a few smaller developments like Kensington Point, Evelyn Court, and Castle Court. Tastes changed in the 1920s, and the original Craftsman houses were supplanted by Spanish Colonial and Spanish Eclectic architecture. The Deeds of Restrictions for Kensington Park, which allowed residential buildings only, expired in 1926, allowing commercial building to begin along Adams Avenue. A second commercial district was built at the intersection of Marlborough Drive and Hilldale Road. Houses became larger, grander, and definitely more Spanish in style, encouraged in part by the popularity of the architecture in Balboa Park. Notable architects and builders, such as Richard Requa, Cliff May, Louise Severin, the Bathrick brothers of Pasadena, Chris Cosgrove, Ray Perrigo, the Dennstedts, and Benjamin Torgerson made their mark on greater Kensington. A school, a church, and a library complemented the conveniences that came from a location on the streetcar line. A neighborhood identity formed, and it fit the description from one of William Douglas's early advertisements: "For Kensington is exclusive as to 'class,' not to 'cost.' No one shall ever ask, 'Does that unkempt child and frowsy woman live in Kensington?' "

Kensington residents take pride in their historic houses, walkable streets, excellent weather, lovely gardens, convenient small businesses (many locally owned), and small-town coziness. Many houses are handed down through the generations, with more than one house still in the hands of the family of the first owners. As first described by William Douglas, Kensington remains, "without a doubt, the finest subdivision in San Diego."

One

In the Beginning

In 1910, the map of Kensington Park was filed, improvements commenced, and lots were advertised for sale for $500, with mortgages available for $25 down and $10 per month. The first houses to be built in Kensington Park were of American Craftsman design, featuring low-pitched, gabled or hipped roofs, deeply overhanging eaves, exposed rafters, a front porch with tapered columns, and multi-light windows. Much of the building material used was locally sourced, including "river rock" or cobblestone, bricks from local kilns, and glass cut on site. Lumber came from large log rafts of old-growth fir that were floated down the West Coast from Oregon and Washington State. Interior materials included quarter-sawn oak flooring and hand-crafted fir or gum wood built-in cabinetry and seating. This architectural style continued to dominate Kensington houses into the early 1920s before it fell out of favor.

The original deeds restricted building to residential only, and required a builder to spend a minimum of $2,000 on construction of a house, the suitability of which was judged by "the company's architect." Because of the residential-only nature of the subdivision, the first residents of Kensington had to do their shopping elsewhere, either in downtown San Diego or along Adams Avenue in neighboring Normal Heights.

World War I brought a shortage of material and manpower, and a general slowdown in building everywhere, including Kensington Park. Very few homes were built between 1914 and 1921. Ownership of the remaining unbuilt lots was transferred to the Kensington Park Land Company.

By the 1920 census, 106 homes in Kensington Park were occupied. Some residents were retired, and some were recent immigrants from England, Canada, Germany, and Ireland. Those who worked covered the gamut of occupations, which included electrician, bookkeeper, florist, grocery store manager, post office worker, dentist, newspaper advertiser, orange grove manager, insurance agent, musician, saleslady, building contractor, real estate agent, civil engineer, teacher, nurse, cattle broker, chicken rancher, attorney, mining assayer, steam engineer, elevator operator, banker, plumber, carpenter, and gas company lineman. Thus, in its first decade, Kensington was established as a solidly middle-class neighborhood.

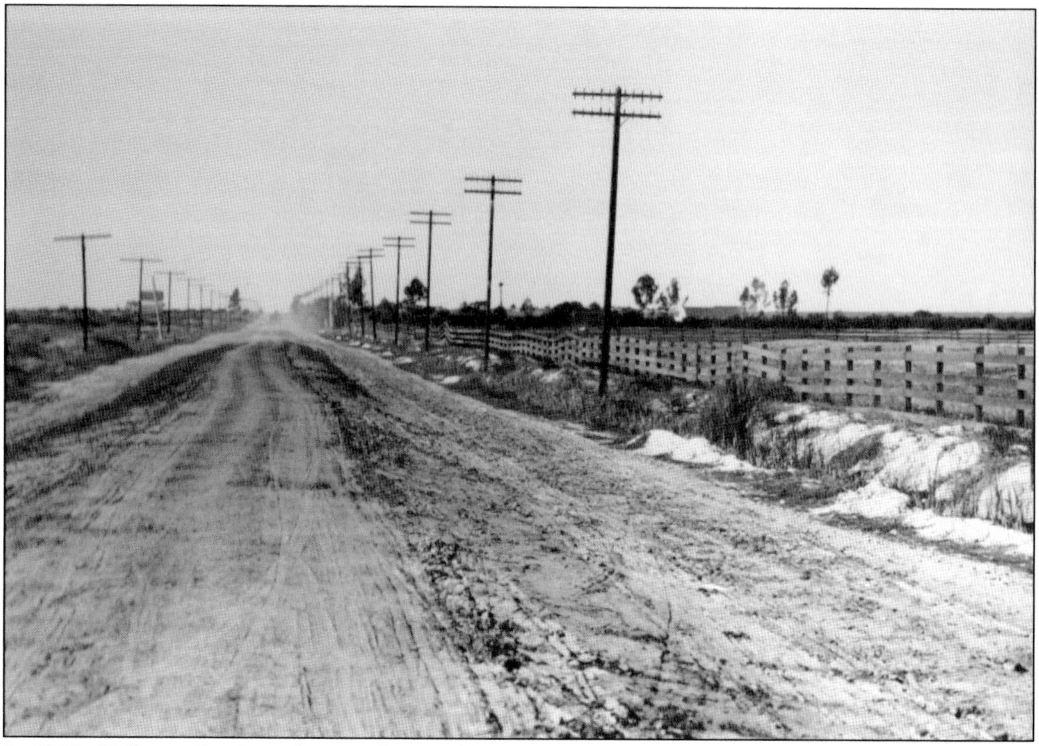

In 1908, El Cajon Boulevard was a dirt road leading through farm land. In this view looking west from the intersection of El Cajon Boulevard and Van Dyke Avenue, the empty land on the right lies between Van Dyke and Copeland Avenues. (Courtesy of Hoover High School.)

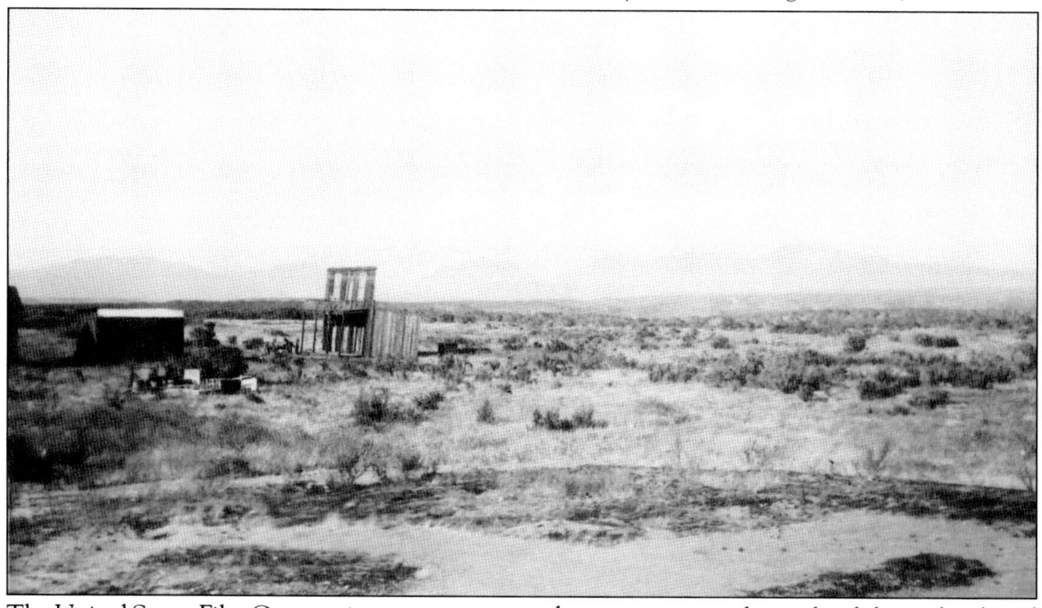

The United States Film Corporation was a movie production company that utilized the undeveloped land in Kensington Park as the location for filming westerns. The remains of a movie set are visible in the vicinity of what would become the 4800 block of Edgeware Road and Forty-Second Street in this early photograph. (Courtesy of San Diego History Center.)

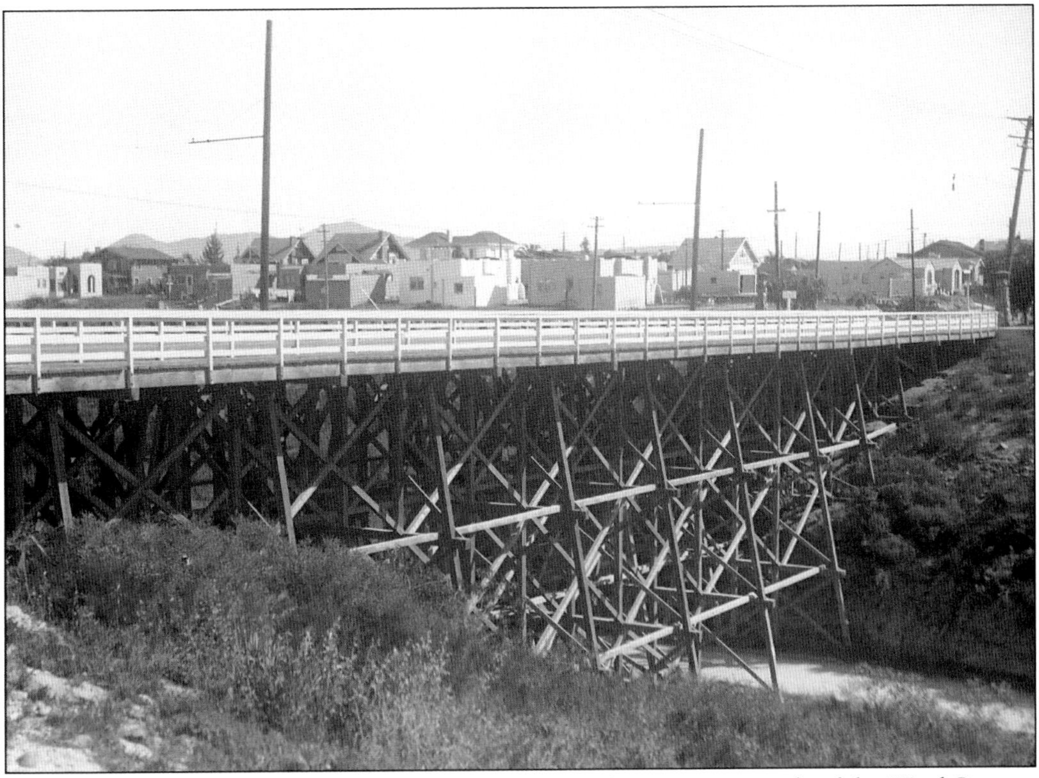

By the early 1920s, numerous houses had been built on the Kensington side of the Ward Canyon trestle bridge. The original bridge was only built for streetcar traffic, with trolley tracks down the middle. In 1913, a second bridge was built adjacent to the first in order to provide automobile access via Adams Avenue. (Courtesy of San Diego History Center.)

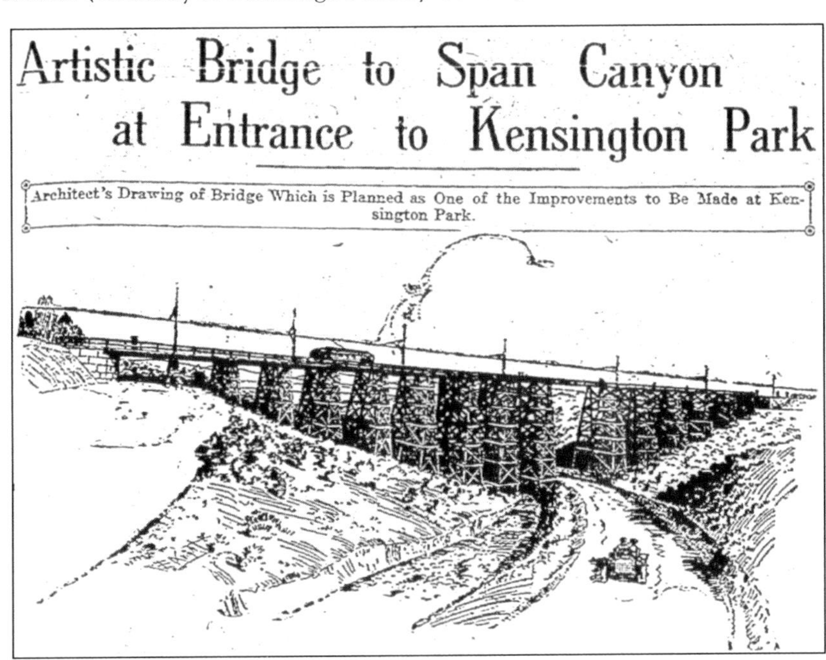

Artistic Bridge to Span Canyon at Entrance to Kensington Park

Architect's Drawing of Bridge Which is Planned as One of the Improvements to Be Made at Kensington Park.

As early as 1909, advertising began for the Kensington Park subdivision. Touting a bridge over Ward Canyon by which to reach Kensington, the tract was in need of streetcar service, as it was a remote suburb of the city of San Diego. (Courtesy of Ron V. May.)

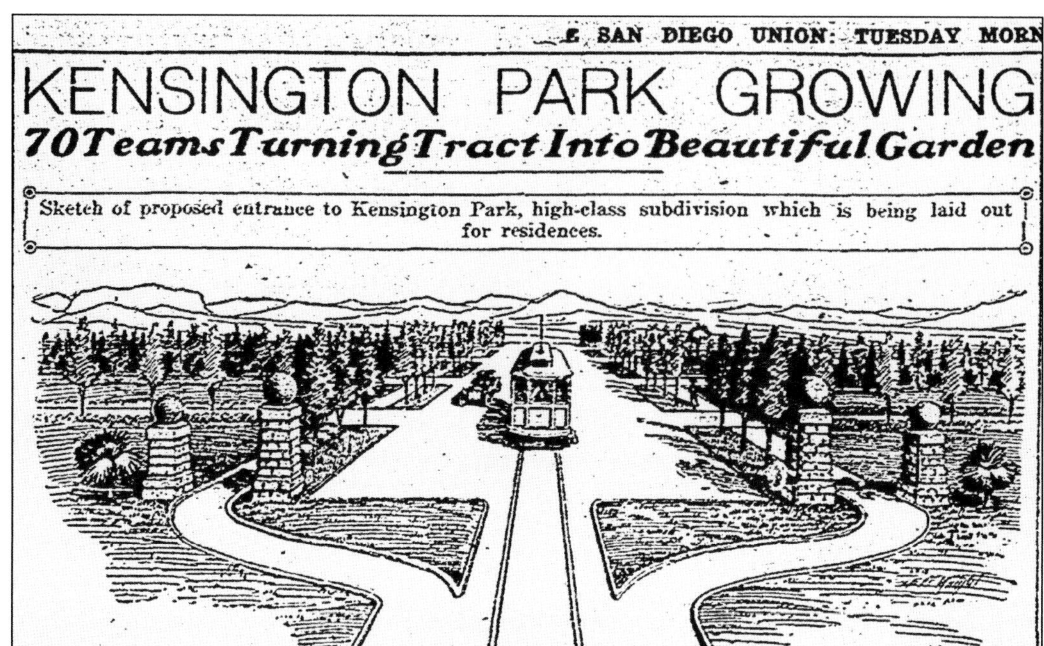

SAN DIEGO UNION: TUESDAY MORN

KENSINGTON PARK GROWING

70 Teams Turning Tract Into Beautiful Garden

Sketch of proposed entrance to Kensington Park, high-class subdivision which is being laid out for residences.

This early rendering of the proposed Kensington Park subdivision depicts the tree-lined streets, cement sidewalks, and cobblestone entrance pillars that were under construction in 1910. As always, the developers emphasized that this would be a "high-class subdivision." (Courtesy of Ron V. May.)

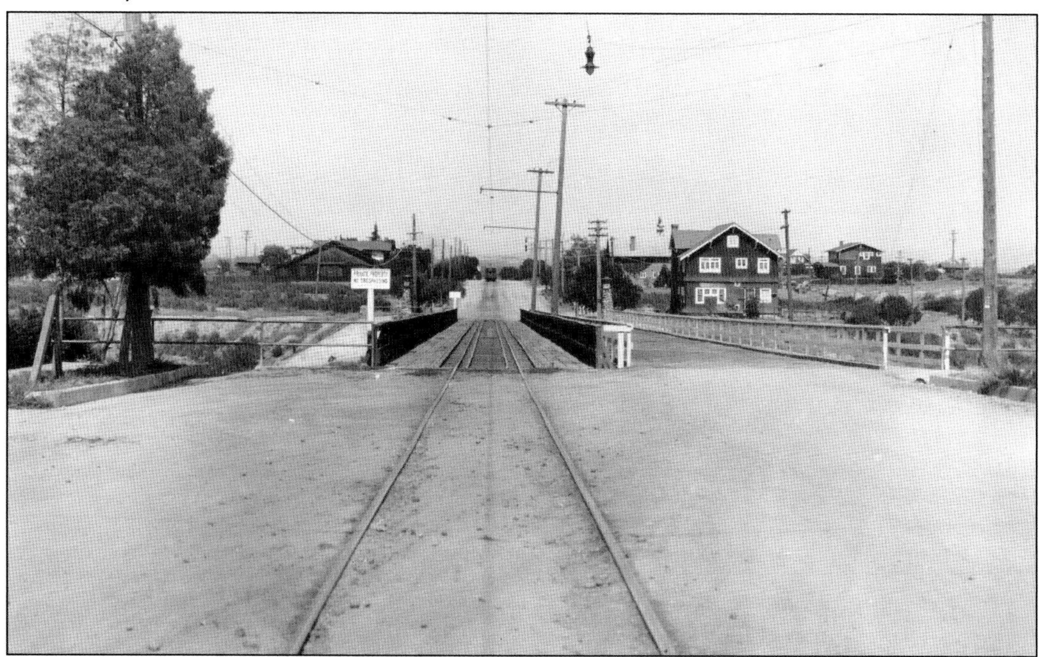

Looking east across the Adams Avenue Bridge over Ward Canyon in 1923, cobblestone entrance pillars and Craftsman homes built between 1910 and 1914 are visible. A San Diego Electric Railway car is seen in the distance near the eastern end of the No. 11 streetcar line. (Courtesy of the Pacific Southwest Railway Museum.)

Kensington Park kids dealt with the warm summers the same way they do today, by cooling off in the sprinklers. Betty Anderson and an unidentified friend pose in their bathing suits in the front yard of the Anderson home in August 1927. (Courtesy of Don Generoli.)

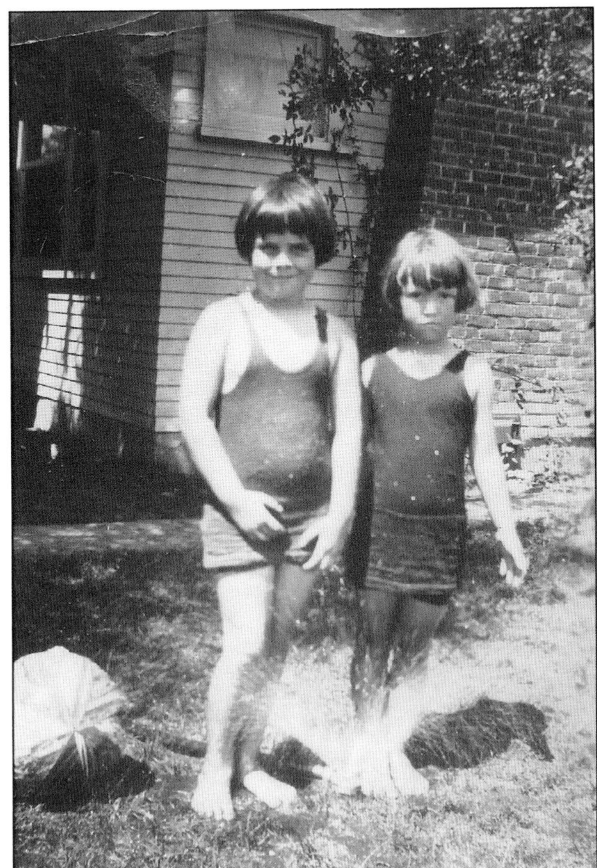

Looking east from 4645 Edgeware Road in 1924 showed nothing but scrubland, where locals liked to hunt for rabbit and quail. Betty Anderson stands in front of a group of unidentified neighbor girls. (Courtesy of Don Generoli.)

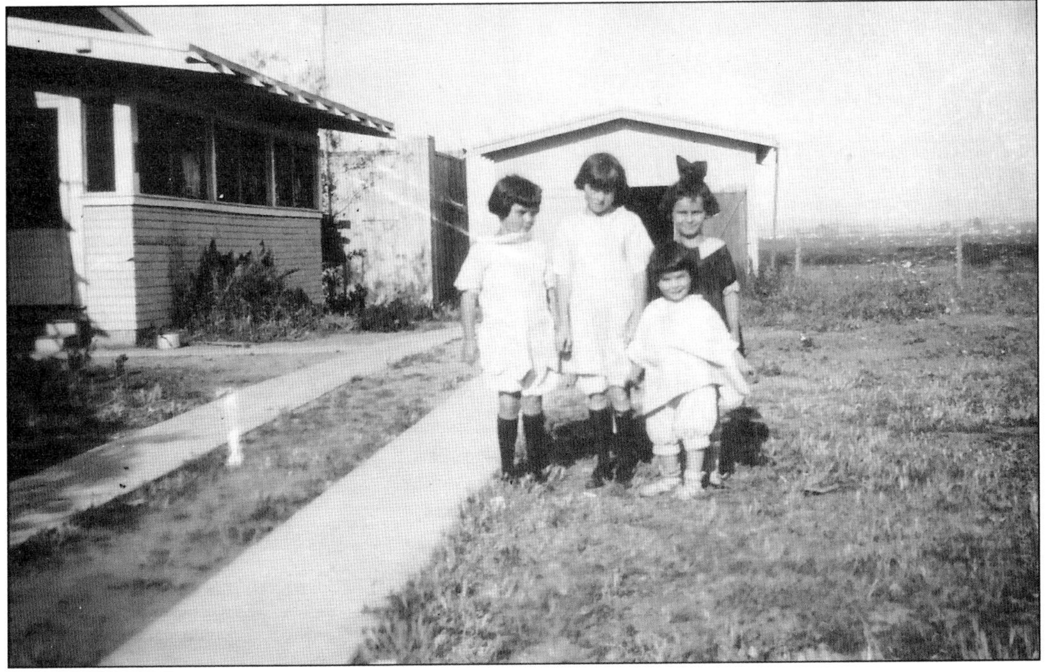

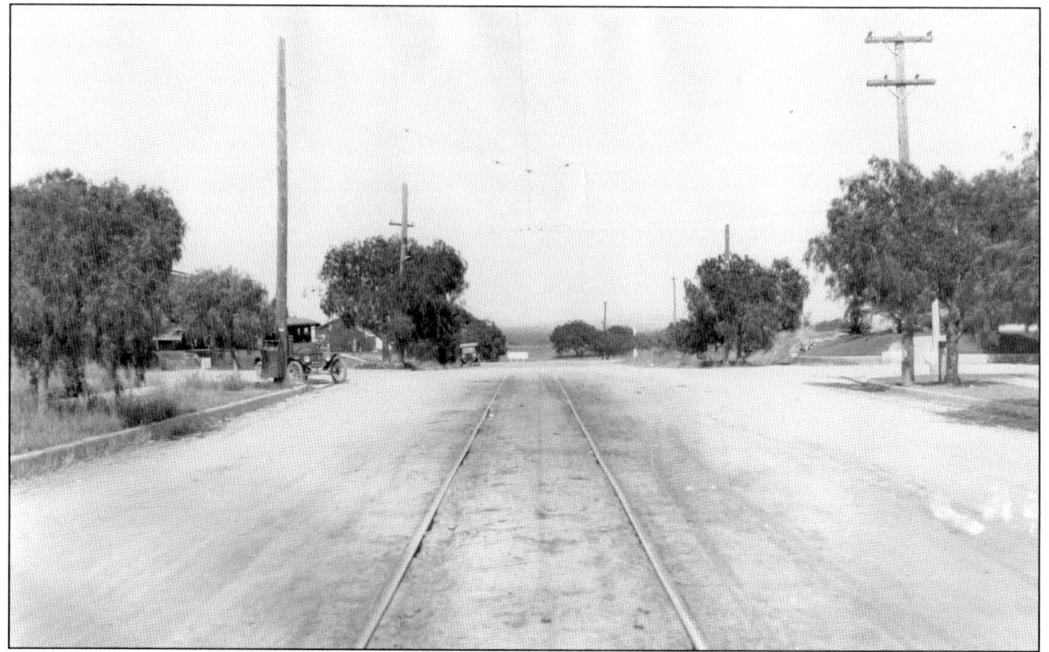

In 1923, the end of the No. 11 route of the San Diego Electric Railway was at the intersection of Adams Avenue and Marlborough Drive. The pepper trees lining the streets were planted in 1910 at the subdivision's inception. (Courtesy of the Pacific Southwest Railway Museum.)

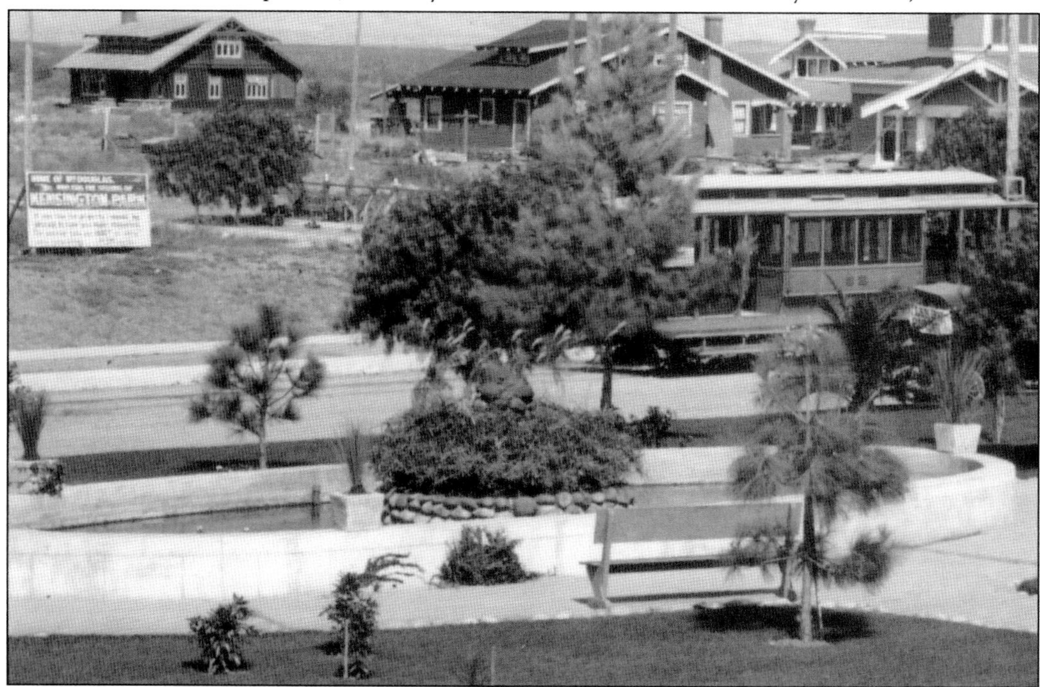

A closer look at the "Pleasure Park" in 1913 shows the original landscaped pond that was demolished around 1935 to make way for the first library building. At this time, the streetcar line terminated directly across from the park where prospective buyers could not miss William Douglas's sales sign. (Courtesy of Robert Sedlock.)

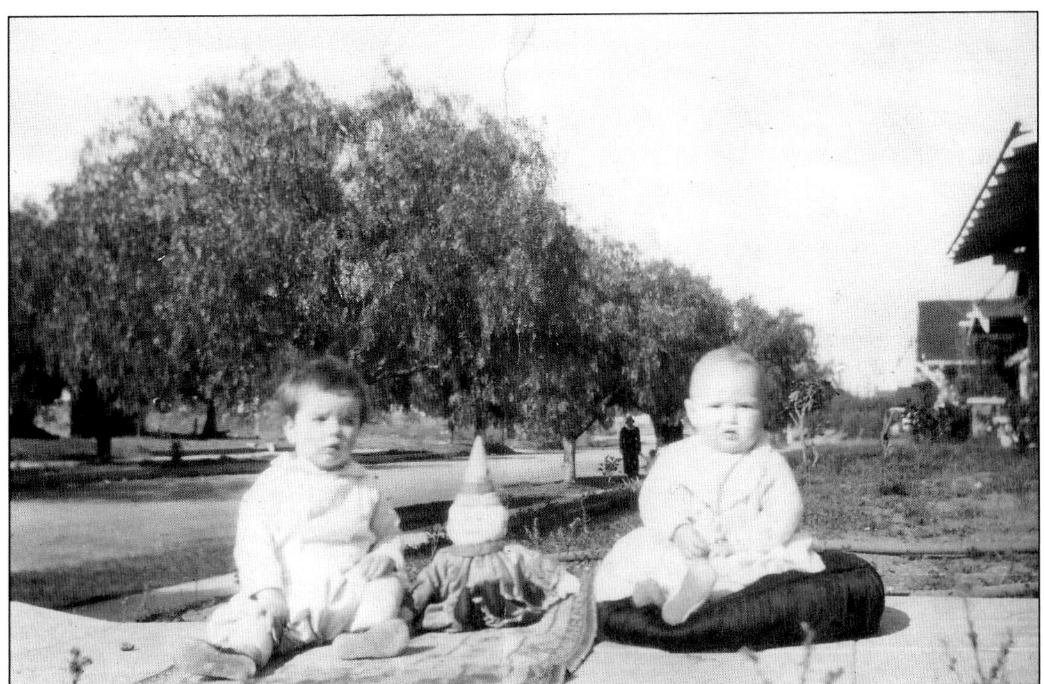

Betty Anderson (left) and Jean Sutton are playing in the sunshine in the front yard of the Anderson family home on Edgeware Road in 1922. Looking north toward Adams Avenue, the original pepper trees that were planted in the parkways of Kensington Park by the developers are already providing shade. (Courtesy of Don Generoli.)

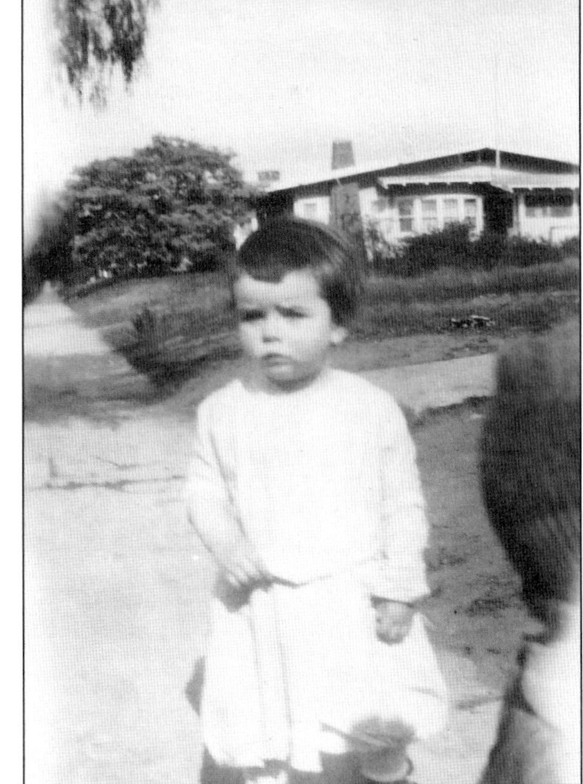

Toddler Betty Rose Anderson, daughter of William and Zilla Anderson, was born at St. Joseph's Hospital in Hillcrest in 1921 while her parents were living on Edgeware Road in the house in the background. The Andersons and their oldest son were born in Pennsylvania, while their youngest son and Betty were both San Diego natives. (Courtesy of Don Generoli.)

"IF DOUGLAS SAYS IT'S SO, IT'S SO."

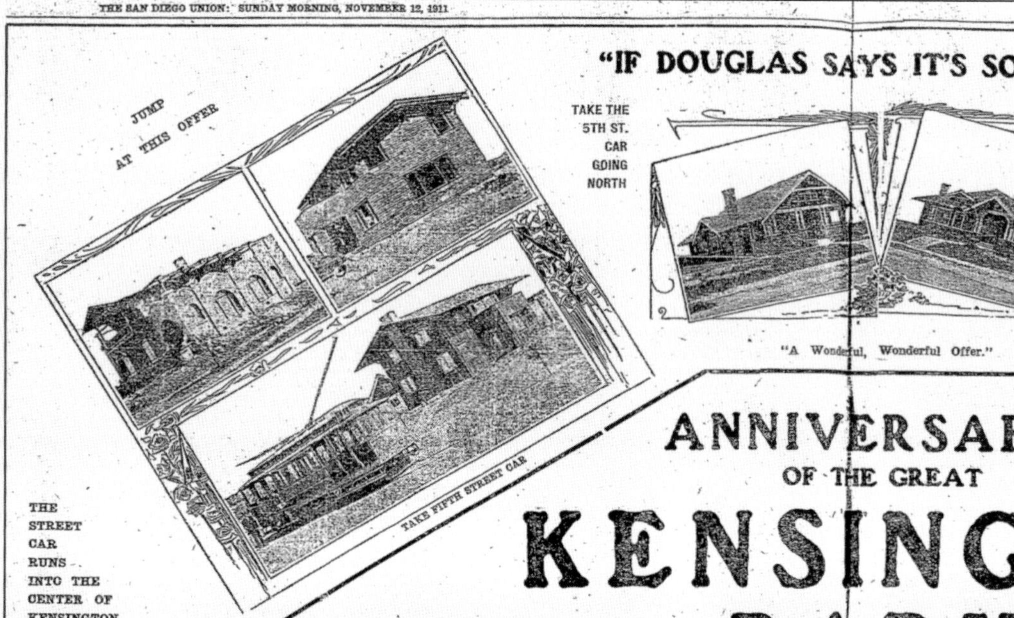

THE STREET CAR RUNS INTO THE CENTER OF KENSINGTON

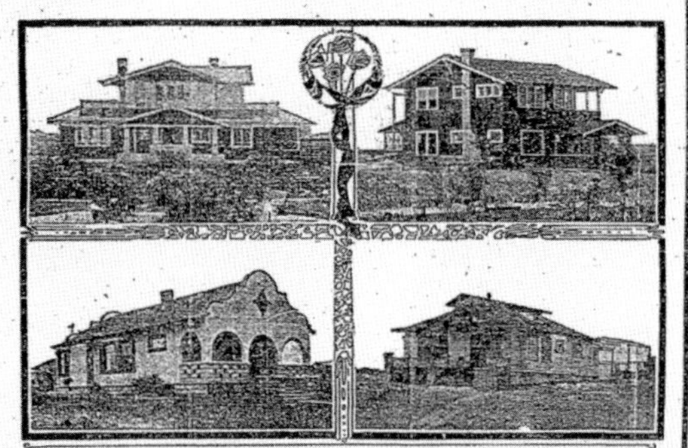

ANNIVERSARY
OF THE GREAT
KENSINGTO
PARK

For One Week Only For One Week On

A 50 FOOT LOT NEXT TO THESE HOME

$25.00 DOWN
AND
$10.00 PER Month

"With Every Improvement a Human Being Could Ask" S

Water—Gas—Electricity—Shade Trees—Corne
A Plaza—With Fountain, Paths and
Wonderful Mountain View and Darn

TAKE ANY CAR GOING UP
5th STREET
AND TAKE IT QUICK;
PLEASE.

Take 5th Street Car Leaving Corner of 5th and D at Ten Minutes to the Hour or 20 Minutes After

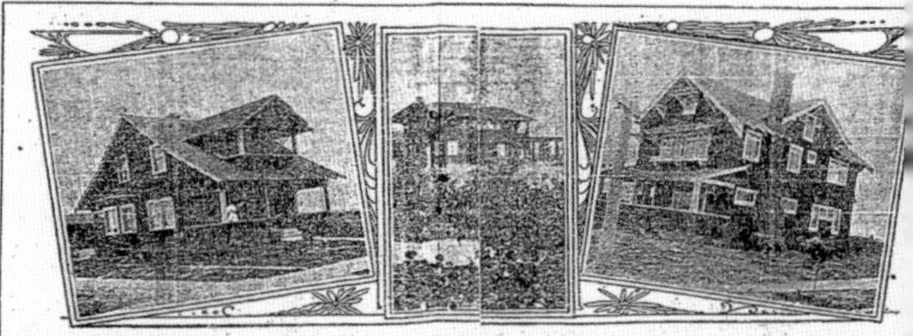

Booklets of Kensington Park Can Be Had at the Company's C

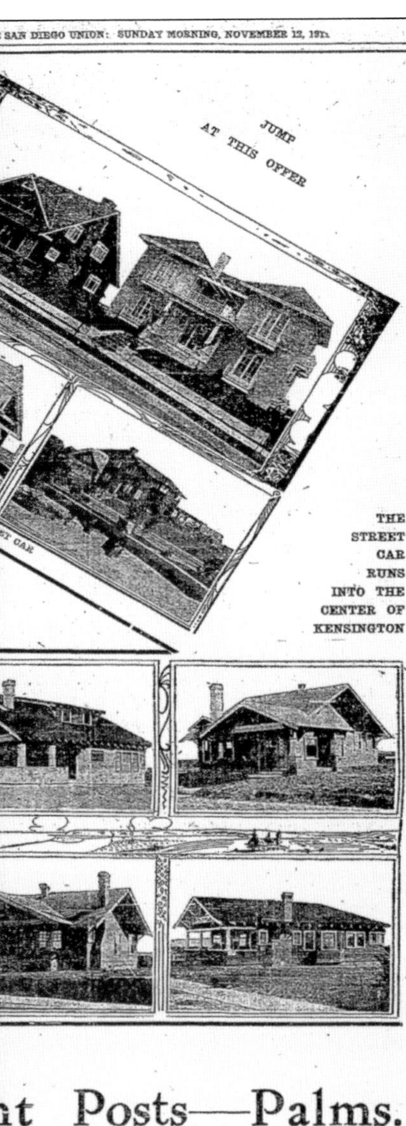

One year after sales of improved lots began in Kensington Park, in this 1911 advertisement, William Douglas urged potential buyers to purchase a lot where every improvement a human being could ask for (with the exception of a sewer system) and a "Wonderful Mountain View and Darn Good Neighbors" could be found. Many of the houses depicted are still in existence. (Courtesy of Ron V. May.)

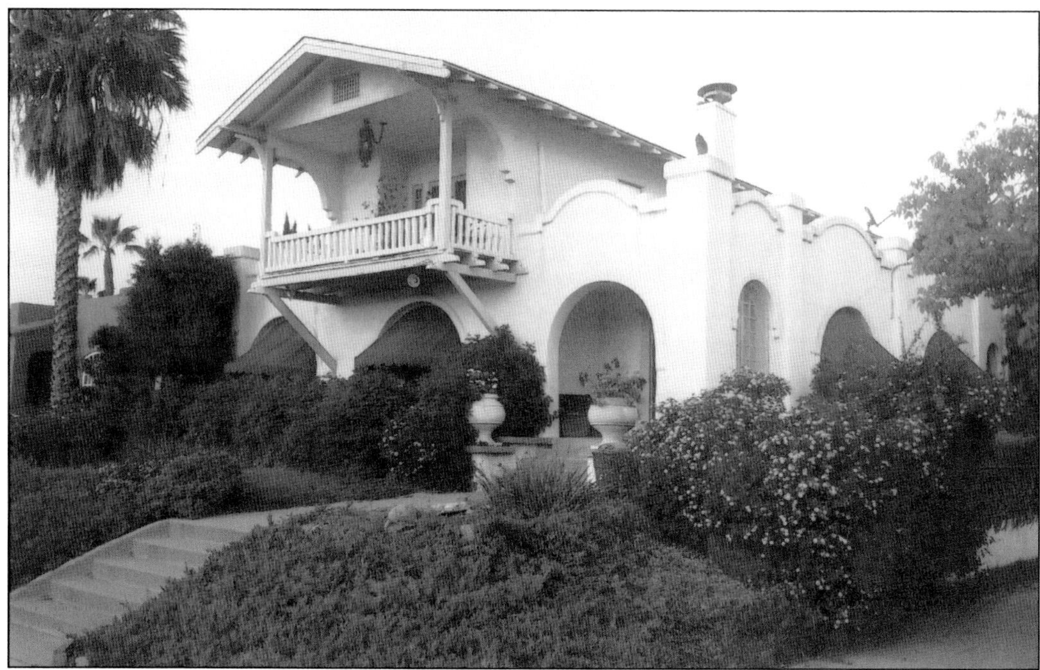

This unique house on the corner of Terrace Drive and Madison Avenue was built in 1912 and features both Craftsman and Mission Revival architectural details. It was one of the houses that agent William Douglas featured in his *San Diego Union* advertisements. In 1930, real estate salesman Bertrand James and his family rented the house for $85 a month. (Courtesy of Kiley Wallace.)

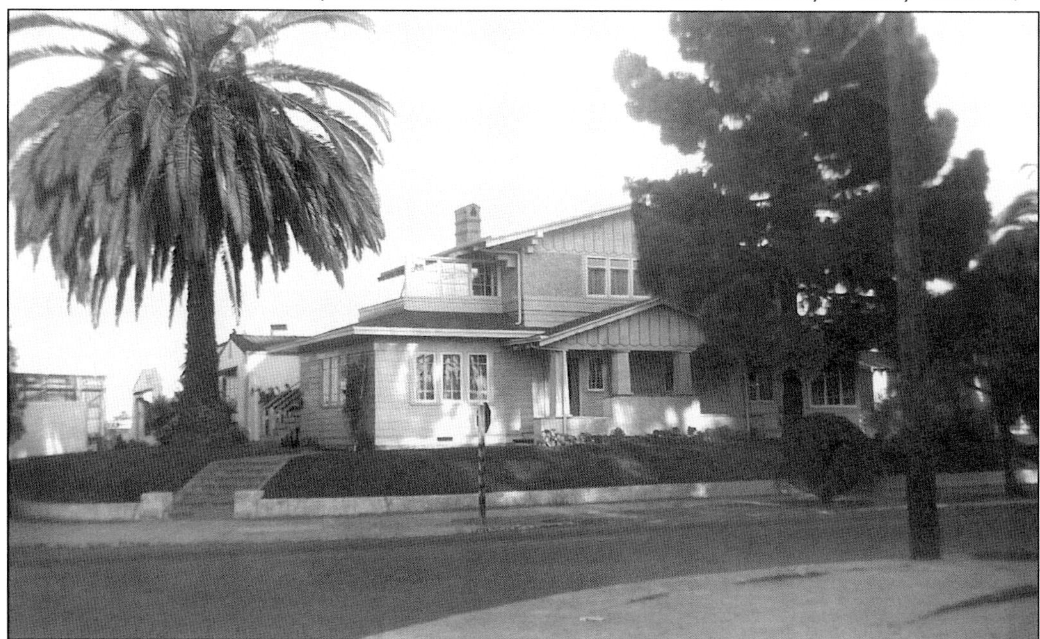

In 1911, R.S. Davis of Los Angeles constructed a large, two-story Craftsman on the southeast corner of Marlborough Drive and Adams Avenue. Dr. Thomas Baumann, a dentist and author of *Kensington-Talmadge, 1910–1985*, bought the house in 1950 and lived here with his family, with his dental office located on the first floor. (Courtesy of Darlene Love.)

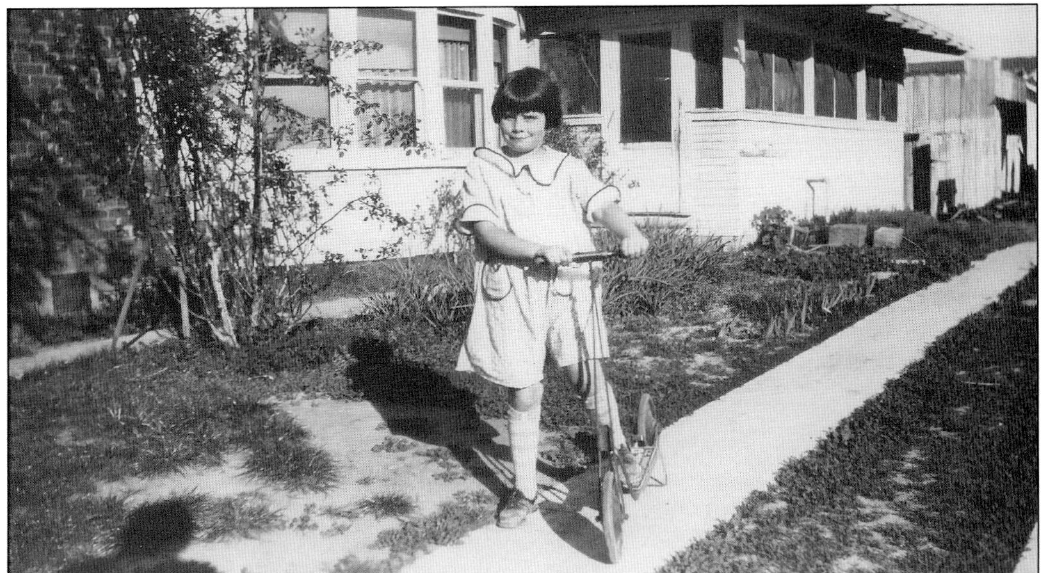

Betty Anderson poses with her scooter outside the family home on Edgeware Road in 1928. Betty's father would later replace the sleeping porch screens with glass windows after an errant shot from a rabbit hunter came through the screens. (Courtesy of Don Generoli.)

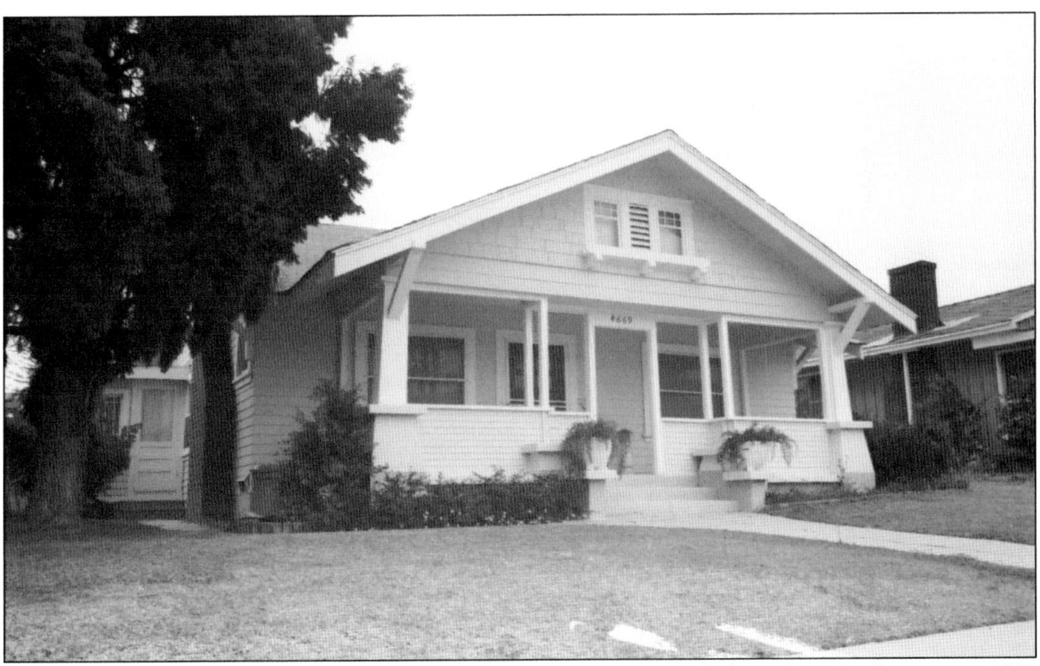

Forty-two houses were constructed in Kensington in 1912, including this Craftsman at 4669 Edgeware Road. Louis and Hulda Duehn, who emigrated from Germany to Pennsylvania in 1864, bought the house in 1914, and lived there with their adult son Leo. Kensington Park houses built at this time had garages at the rear of the property, accessed from the rear alley. There were no driveways cutting across the sidewalk to the street. (Courtesy of San Diego History Center.)

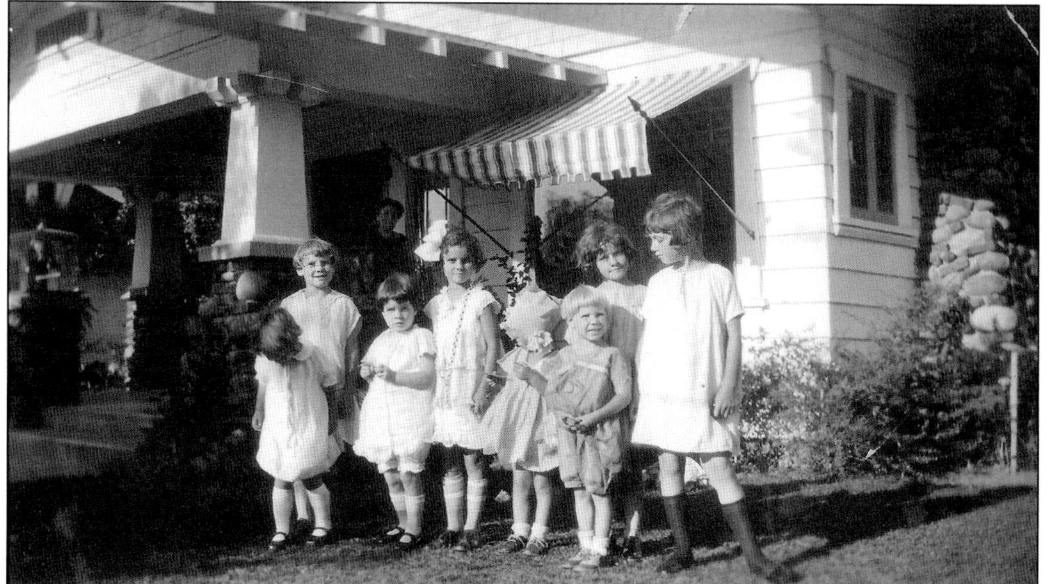

Betty Anderson, third from left, and a gaggle of unidentified neighborhood kids gathered in the front yard of the Anderson's next-door neighbor at 4651 Edgeware Road. This Craftsman house, built in 1912, featured "peanut brickle" chimney and porch column bases, made from clinker brick and cobblestone. (Courtesy of Don Generoli.)

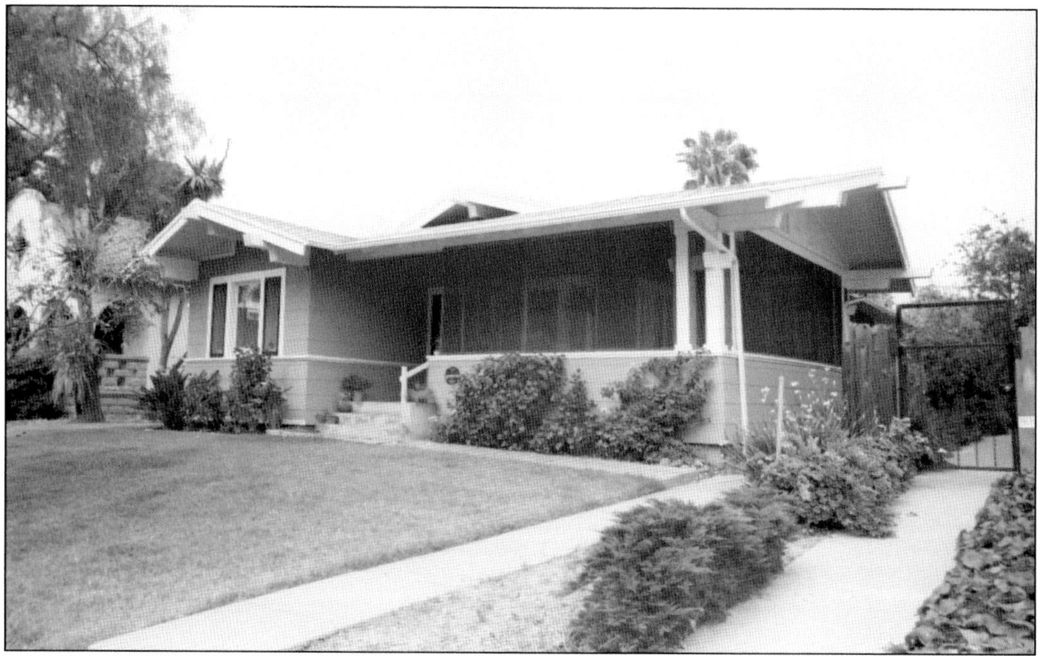

Another Craftsman built in 1912 on Edgeware Road features multiple gabled roofs, exposed beams and rafter tails, deeply overhanging eaves, two-over-two casement windows and a wrap-around porch. This house has a twin built in 1910 at 810 Chester Street in Pasadena, in the Bungalow Heaven National Historic District. Other twins have been identified between San Diego and Pasadena, with one explanation being that the builders reused house plans. (Courtesy of San Diego History Center.)

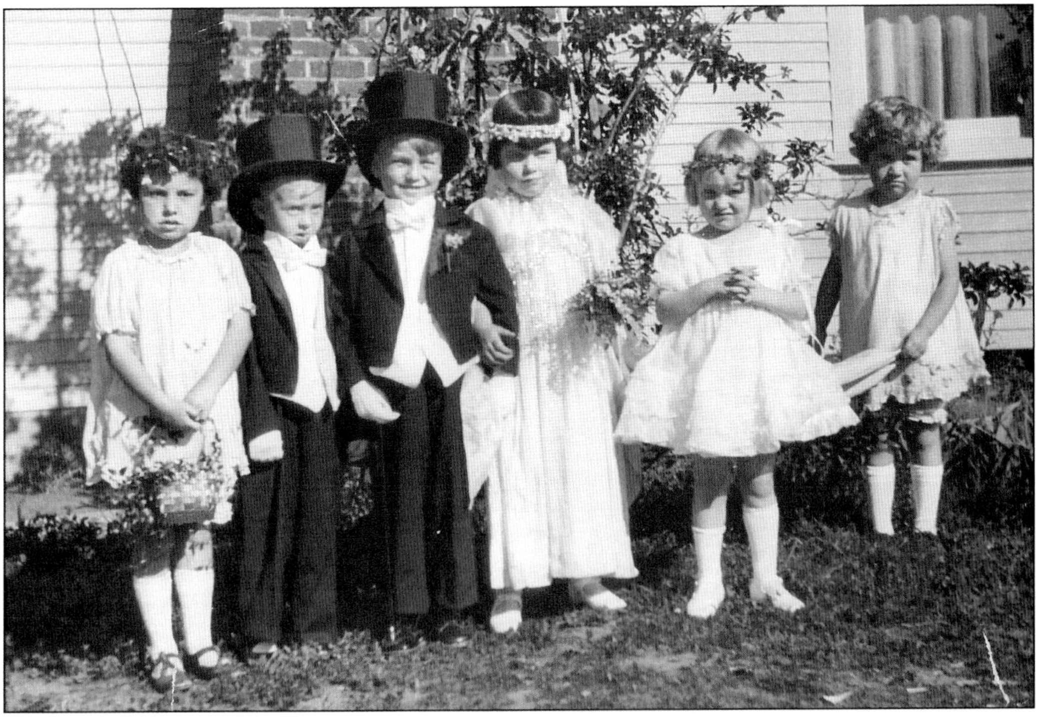

The children of Kensington were pressed into duty to raise money for a building fund for the Oneira Women's Club, a philanthropic club formed by women from Normal Heights, Kensington Park, and Bonnie Brae during World War I. A "Tom Thumb wedding" play was staged at the Carteri Theatre in Normal Heights in January 1926. Four-year-old Betty Rose Anderson played the part of the bride, while James Parks made for a handsome groom. (Courtesy of Don Generoli.)

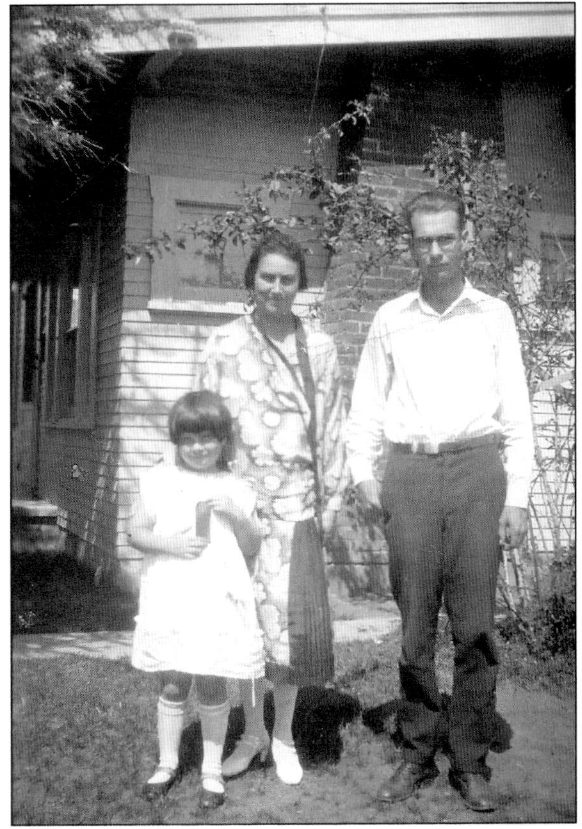

William and Zilla Anderson and their six-year-old daughter Betty pose in the side yard of their home on Edgeware Road in 1927. Anderson was a civil engineer who designed the ferry landings and numerous trestle bridges for the San Diego Electric Railway Company. (Courtesy of Don Generoli.)

Arched Porch Pretty Feature of New Kensington Park Residence

Architect's Drawing of Pretty Mission Style Bungalow, Recently Completed in Kensington Park for H. H. Howe. It Fronts East on Edgeware Road.

Despite its outward appearance of Mission Revival architecture, this house at 4644 Edgeware Road has many Craftsman features. The front and rear facades obscure a front gabled roof, while the interior features built-in cabinetry and ceiling box beams in keeping with the style of 1911. The *San Diego Union* ran an article on February 19, 1911, titled "Arched Porch Pretty Feature of New Kensington Park Residence" and included the architect's drawing of this house that had been built for H.H. Howe. (Above, courtesy of *San Diego Union-Tribune* and NewsBank Inc.; below, courtesy of San Diego History Center.)

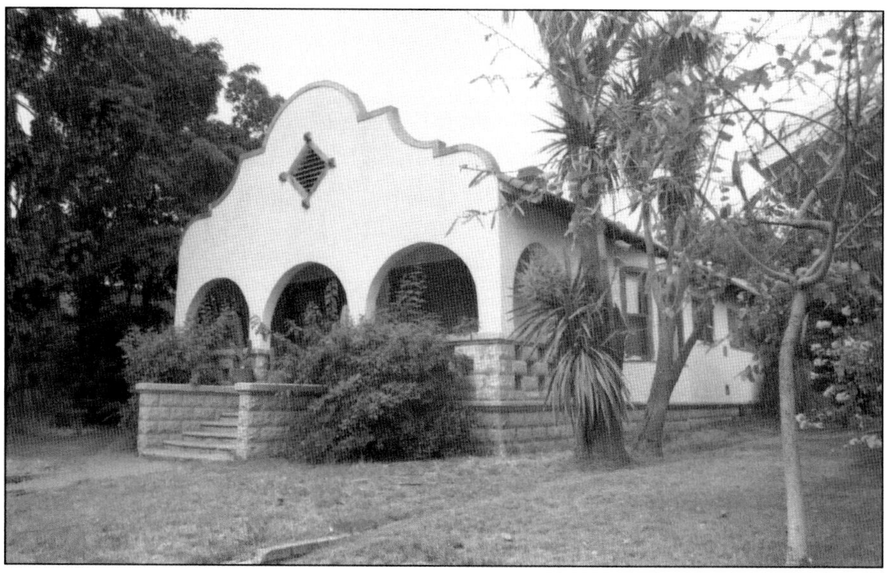

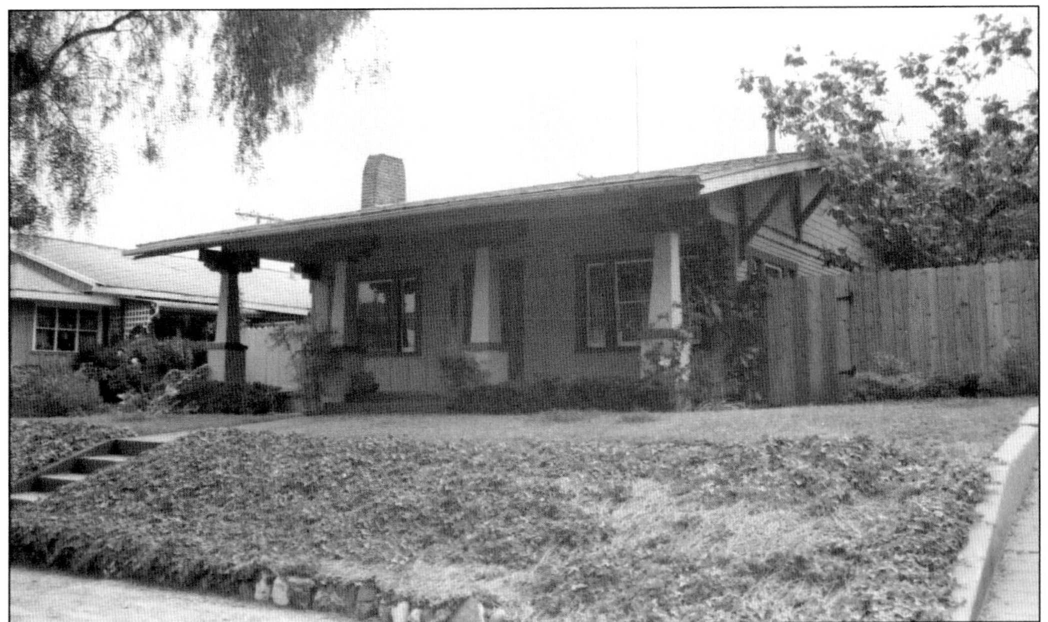

This Craftsman bungalow on Edgeware Road was built in 1912. In 1915, a building contractor from Maine, Bennett Perkins, lived there with his wife, Maria. The wide front porch with tapered columns, exposed rafter tails and roof braces, and shingle over clapboard siding are typical of this style of architecture. (Courtesy of San Diego History Center.)

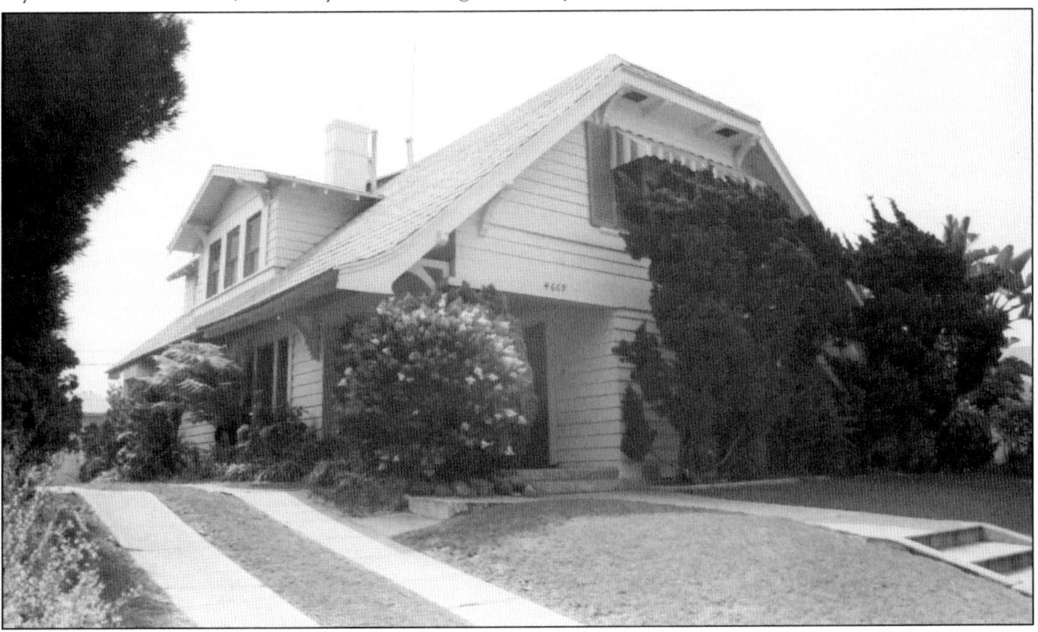

This charming Dutch Colonial Revival house at 4669 Marlborough Drive was built in 1911. The house was altered sometime around World War II when an exterior staircase was added to the back of the house to provide a separate entrance for the upstairs, creating another residence on the top floor. In 1920, Durrell Glidden and his wife, Nancy, lived here. Glidden, a deputy city attorney, was profiled in Samuel T. Black's 1913 book *San Diego County California*. (Courtesy of San Diego History Center.)

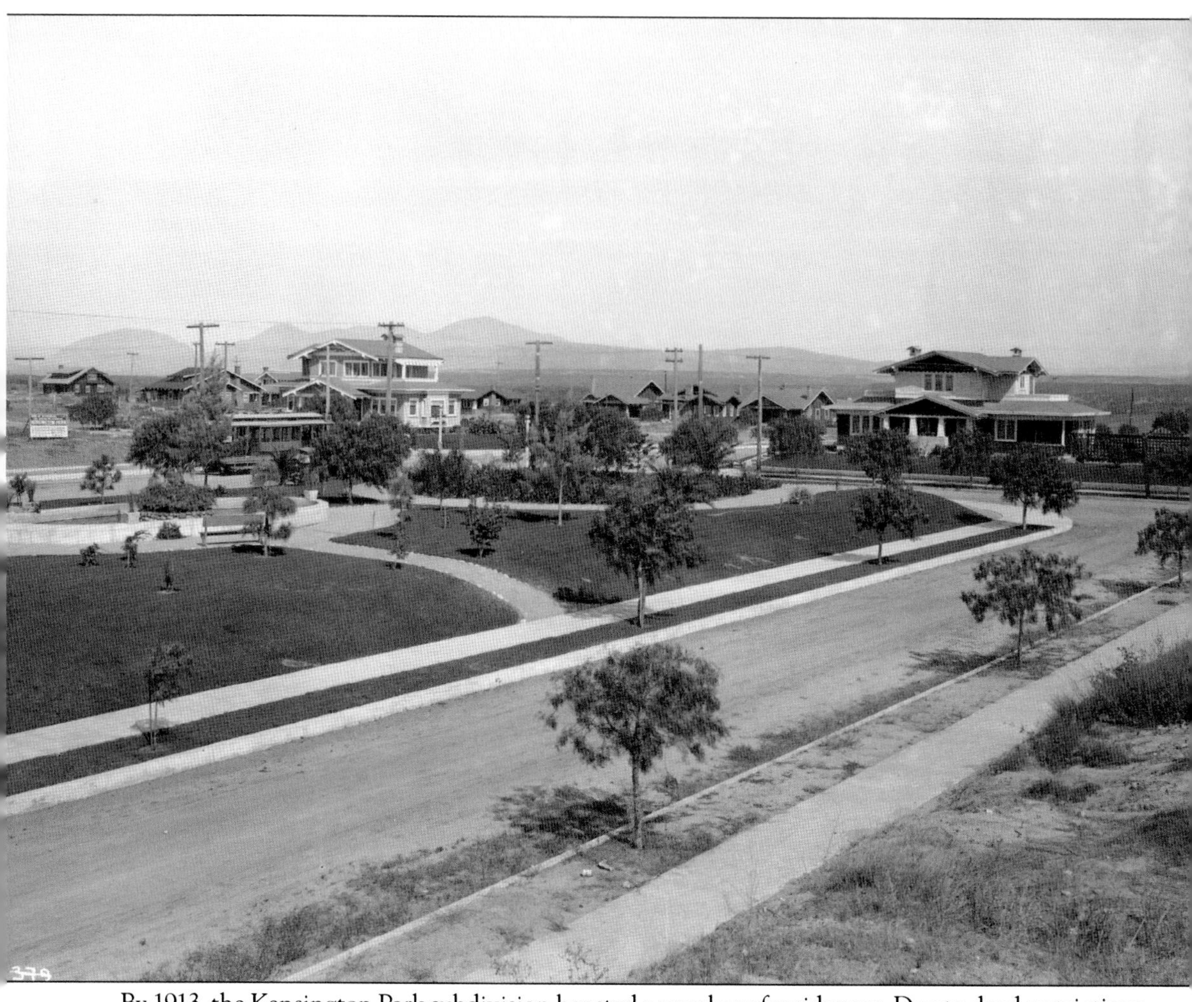

By 1913, the Kensington Park subdivision boasted a number of residences. Due to deed restrictions, only residential buildings were allowed during this time. This view looks to the northeast, across the park that is the current location of the Kensington–Normal Heights Branch Library. The Adams Avenue streetcar can be seen behind the park. The two-story Craftsman-style house on the left, built in 1912, was moved from the northeast corner of Adams Avenue and Marlborough Drive to 4679 Vista Street in 1926, when the deed restrictions expired and commercial buildings were allowed on Adams Avenue. (Courtesy of Robert Sedlock.)

Two

Better Homes in America

America embraced a nationwide campaign of home ownership immediately after World War I, when thousands of European immigrants arrived on our shores. This was the Better Homes Movement, initiated in 1922 in the pages of the Butterick Publishing Company's household magazine, *The Delineator*. The campaign celebrated home ownership as a means of motivating responsible consumer behavior. In cities and towns across the country, annual campaigns, called "better homes demonstration weeks," encouraged citizens to own, build, remodel, and improve their homes, and distributed advice on creating home furnishings and decorations.

To promote the movement, an American Colonial Revival cottage was constructed on the White House lawn. Commerce Secretary Herbert Hoover headed the campaign with the intent of increasing the national home ownership rate.

When postwar building resumed in Kensington, the Colonial Revival style appeared sporadically throughout the neighborhood. Expansion in the first part of the 1920s was to the east of Kensington Park, with Kensington Annex and Talmadge Park Unit No. 1 and Unit No. 2 mapped. The promotion of Talmadge Park was undertaken by Hollywood and Los Angeles businessmen. Developer Roy C. Lichty teamed with investors including Metro-Goldwyn-Mayer executive Louis B. Mayer and theater owner Sid Grauman to promote the "Movie Girl Subdivision," named because of its marketing and investment association with Hollywood silent film stars and sisters Norma, Constance, and Natalie Talmadge. On opening day in 1926, the Talmadge sisters and Natalie's husband, Buster Keaton, were among the dignitaries to cut the ribbon on the new subdivision.

To the immediate north of Kensington Park, the development of Kensington Manor Unit No. 1 commenced in 1925. This time, the dominant architectural style was to be Spanish Colonial Revival, popularized by the architecture of the Panama-California Exposition in Balboa Park. The Kensington Park Land Company teamed with architects and builders from Pasadena to promote and develop Kensington Manor, and the streets were laid out to follow the contours of the surrounding canyons.

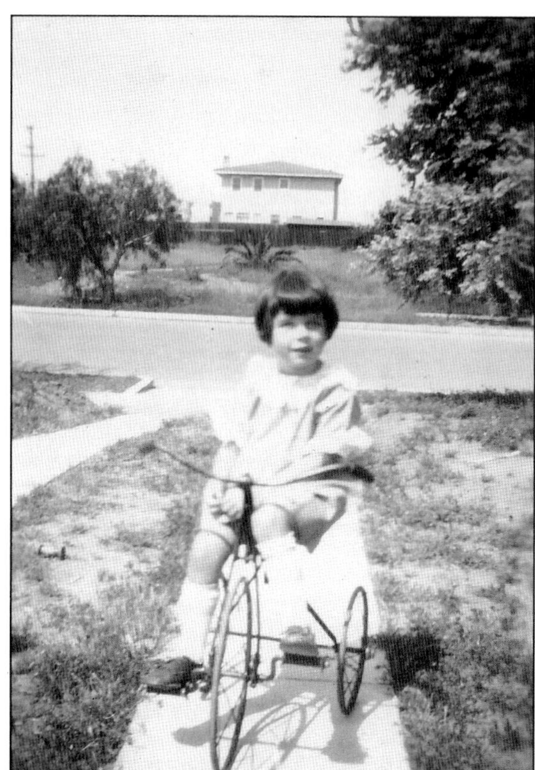

In 1925, the lot across the street from the Anderson family on Edgeware Road was still vacant. The back of the historically designated Dr. James and Leona Parker House, built in 1924 at 4637 Marlborough Drive, is visible behind Betty Anderson. (Courtesy of Don Generoli.)

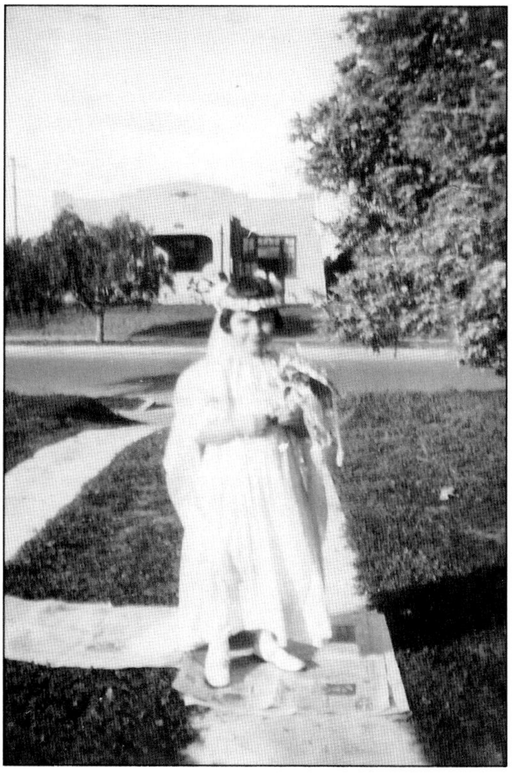

Betty Anderson poses in her front yard in 1926, and in the background can be seen a newly built Mission Revival bungalow at 4638 Edgeware Road. The taste for Craftsman design had passed, and Kensington Park infill followed the changing tastes. (Courtesy of Don Generoli.)

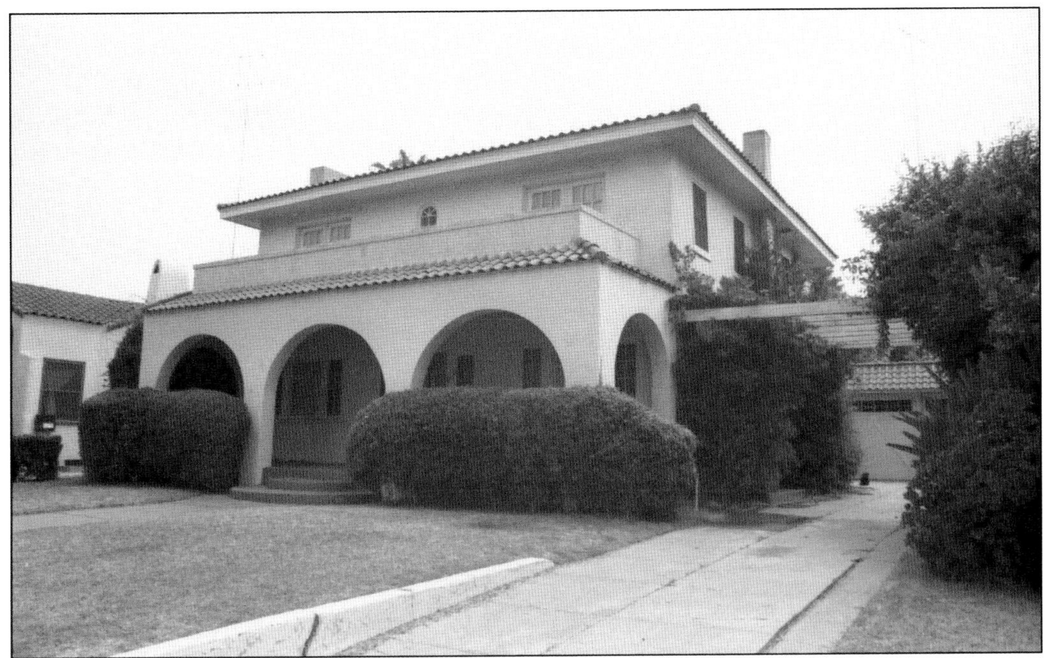

The historically designated Dr. James and Leona Parker House at 4637 Marlborough Drive was built in 1924 by the Great Western Building Company. The house is a unique blend of styles, with a Mission Revival exterior and a Craftsman interior. The Great Western Building Company was incorporated in 1920 and was marketed as the solution to San Diego's housing problem. (Courtesy of San Diego History Center.)

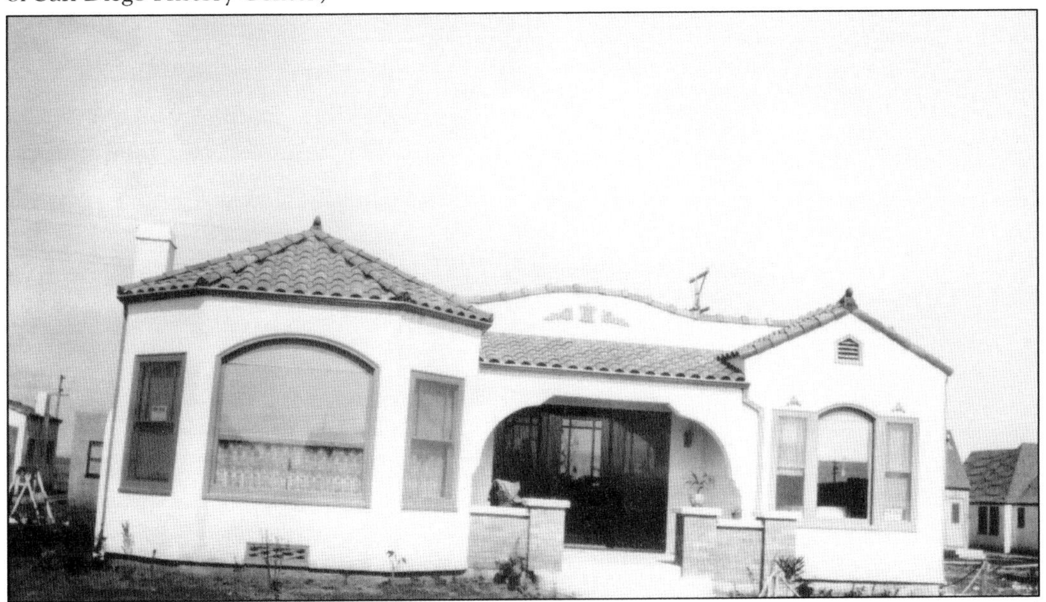

In 1926, the Spanish-style residence at 4641 Vista Street was constructed in the newly opened Kensington Park Annex subdivision. Charles and Anna Stark, the original owners, emigrated from Sweden in the early 1900s, settling in Chicago until their San Diego home was completed. Charles and his sons Carl and Theodore were carpenters. The home remained in the family for nearly 80 years. (Courtesy of Sonya Sparks.)

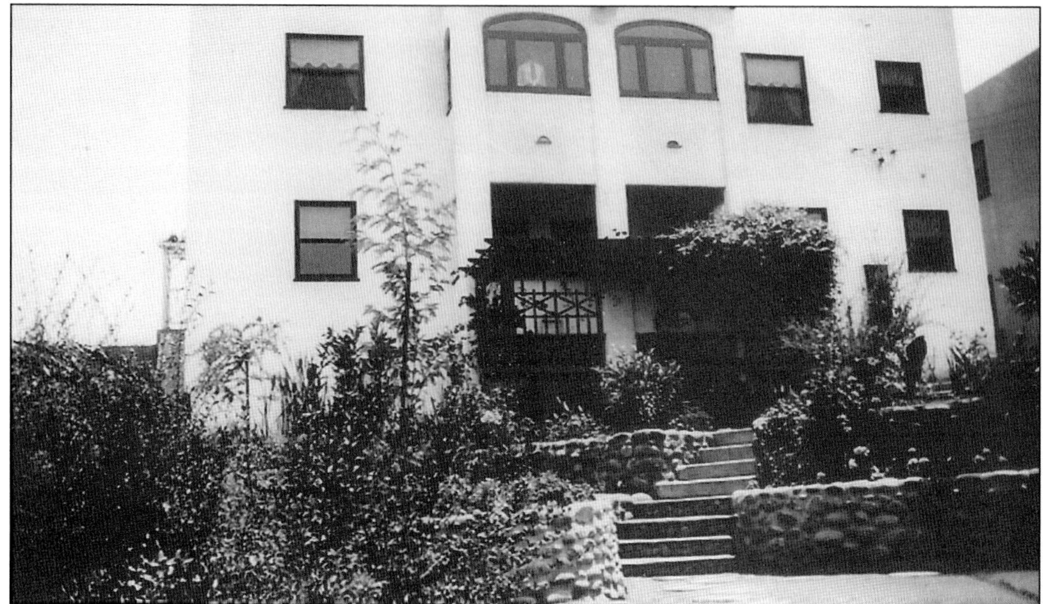

John Wilkinson gazes out a window overlooking the canyon behind his home at 4174 East Canterbury Drive. Wilkinson was a successful building contractor in Chicago, having built many fine homes in the Chicago suburb of Beverly Heights. Wilkinson built the R.W. Evans House on South Longwood Drive in Chicago, designed by Frank Lloyd Wright. In 1922, Wilkinson moved his family to Kensington and built this home for his family on East Canterbury Drive in 1927. (Courtesy of the Croff family.)

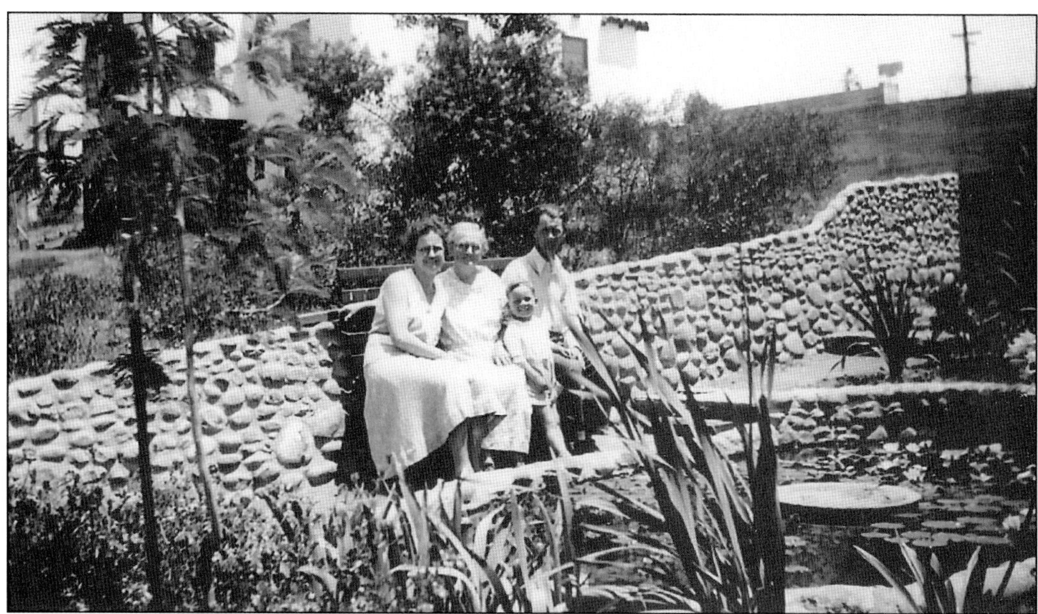

Maude Wilkinson, center, poses in the family's backyard on East Canterbury, along with her daughter Rae and son George, and grandson Warren. Maude's husband, John Wilkinson, not only built the family home but also the cobblestone walls in the backyard, hauling the stones from the canyon in a wheelbarrow. (Courtesy of the Croff family.)

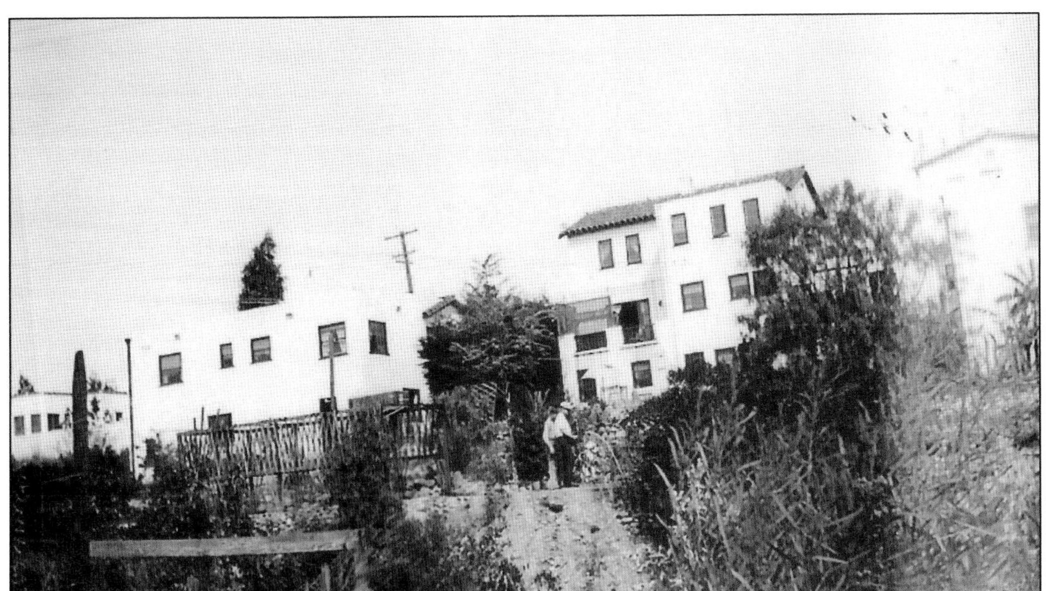

Looking north across the canyon from the Wilkinson house on East Canterbury, the rear of two historically designated houses on Lymer Drive can be seen. On the left is the George and Mary Williams House, and on the right is the T.D. Biller House, both built in 1929. (Courtesy of the Croff family.)

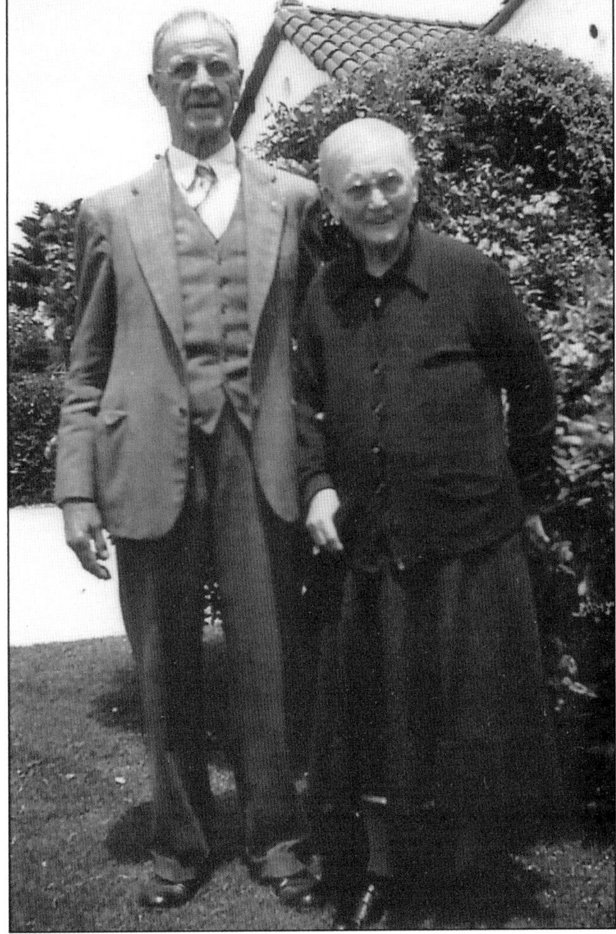

John Wilkinson was about 76 years old when this photograph of him and his wife, Maude, was taken in their front yard on Canterbury Drive in 1940. John worked up until his death of a coronary occlusion in 1941, and Maude developed Alzheimer's disease and perished a day after falling down the stairs and breaking her hip in 1940. (Courtesy of the Croff family.)

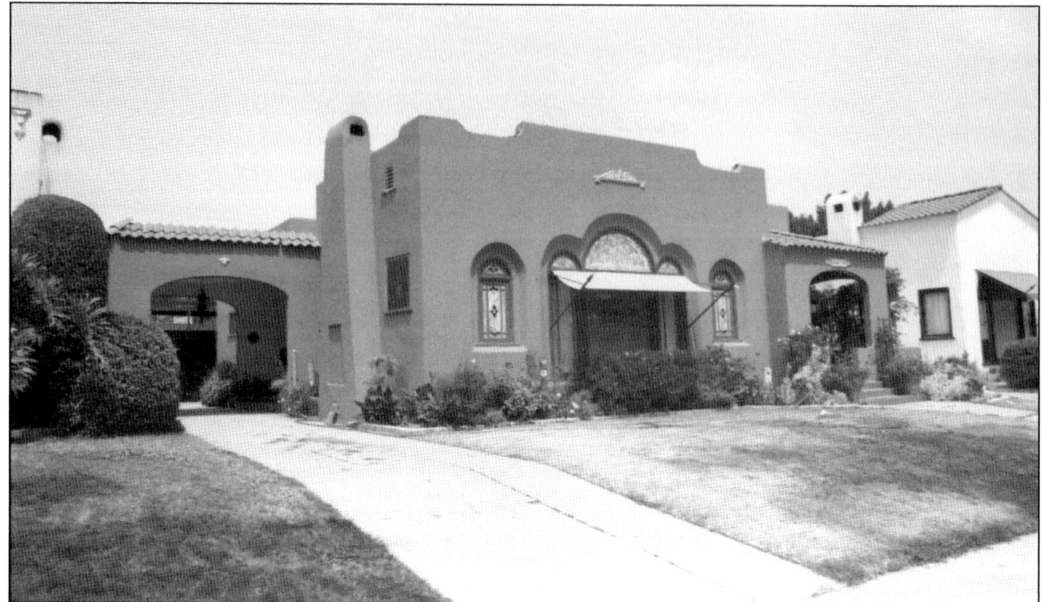

This Spanish Eclectic–style house on Kensington Drive, built in 1924, features arched windows with colored glass panes, a porte cochere, and a towering chimney. The houses in Kensington Park built in the 1920s still had the garage located at the rear of the property, but access was via the driveway from the street instead of from the alley. (Courtesy of San Diego History Center.)

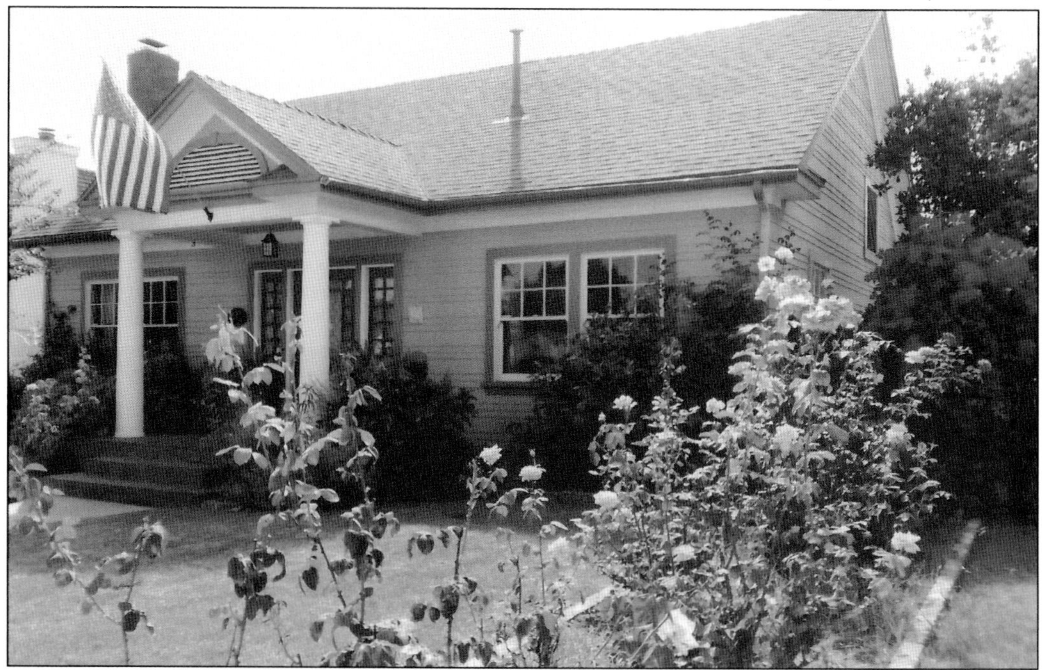

The Maxwell H. and Frances G. Manning House at 4640 Biona Drive is an excellent example of the American Colonial Revival style, built in response to the Better Homes in America movement. Located in the Kensington Park Annex subdivision, it is the first known house to be built by Maxwell Manning, who was only 21 years old when he and his wife, Frances, bought the property. (Courtesy of Margaret McCann.)

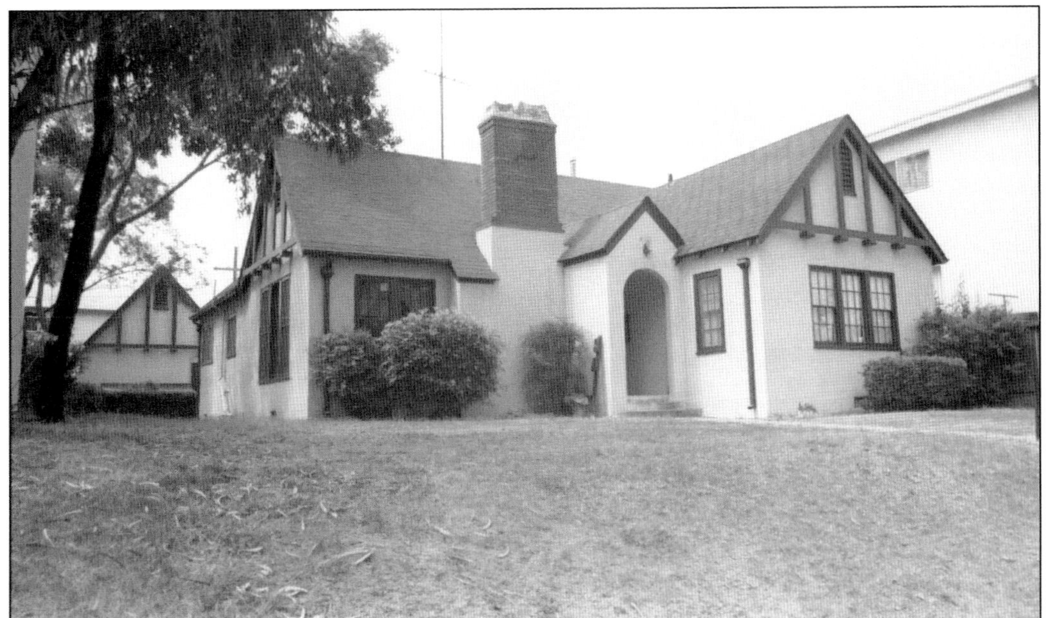

Olaf Jensen Norsven, a carpenter from Norway, designed and built this house in 1926 on Park Place, behind the library park. An advertisement in the *San Diego Union* from June 13, 1926, states that Norsven "has had years of experience in federal buildings and finest eastern residences." (Courtesy of San Diego History Center.)

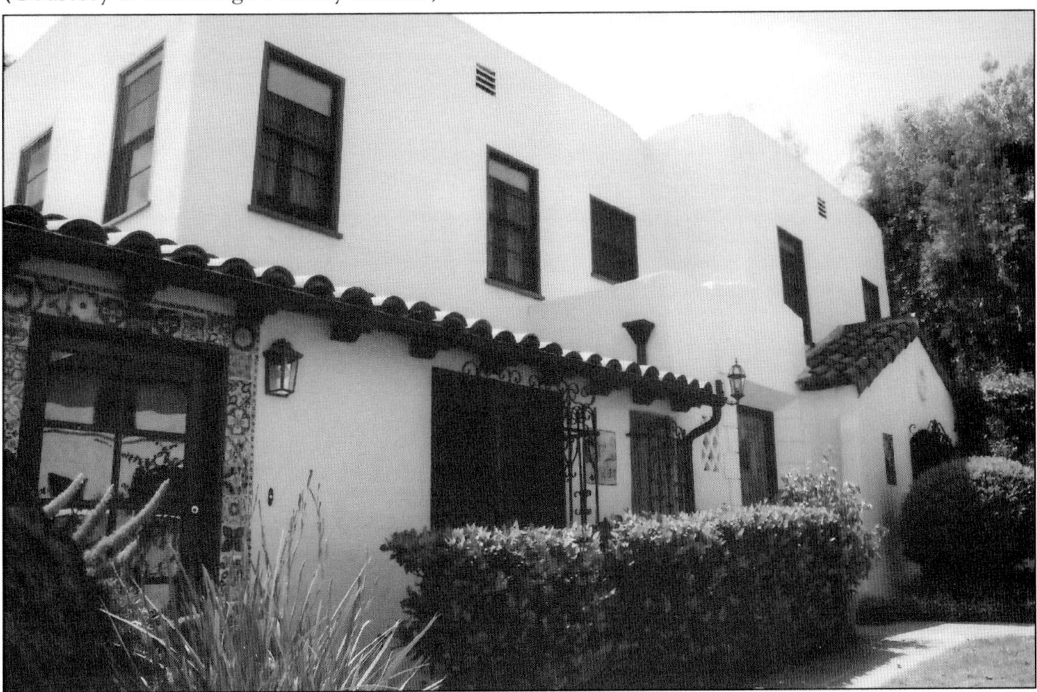

This house is the former home of Gen. Pasqual Ortiz Rubio, the 33rd president of Mexico. A Spanish Mission Revival built in 1928 in the Talmadge Park Unit No. 2 subdivision, it was occupied by General Rubio in the mid-1930s after he resigned the Mexican presidency, the start of which was marked by his attempted assassination on inauguration day. (Courtesy of Margaret McCann.)

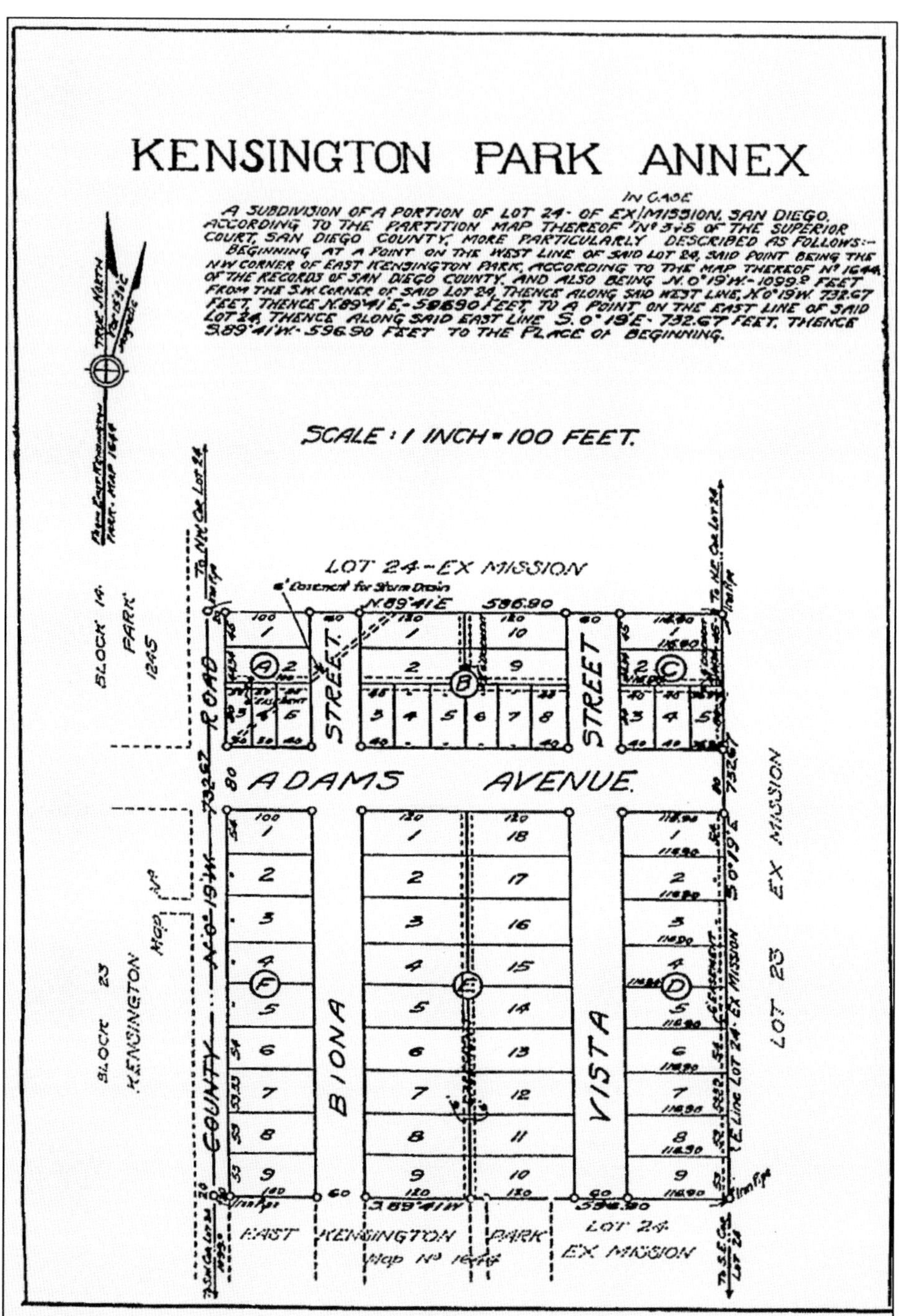

Gager C. and Emily Tyler Davis recorded the Kensington Park Annex subdivision on February 13, 1924. It was a narrow tract of land, with Forty-Second Street (then called County Road) forming the western boundary. The subdivision was within the city of San Diego, while Kensington Park to the west was part of San Diego County. People familiar with the 4600 block of Vista Street south of Adams Avenue will note that the street curves and the parkways disappear when heading south. This change coincides with the boundary between the Kensington Park Annex and Kensington Park East subdivisions. (Courtesy of Ron V. May.)

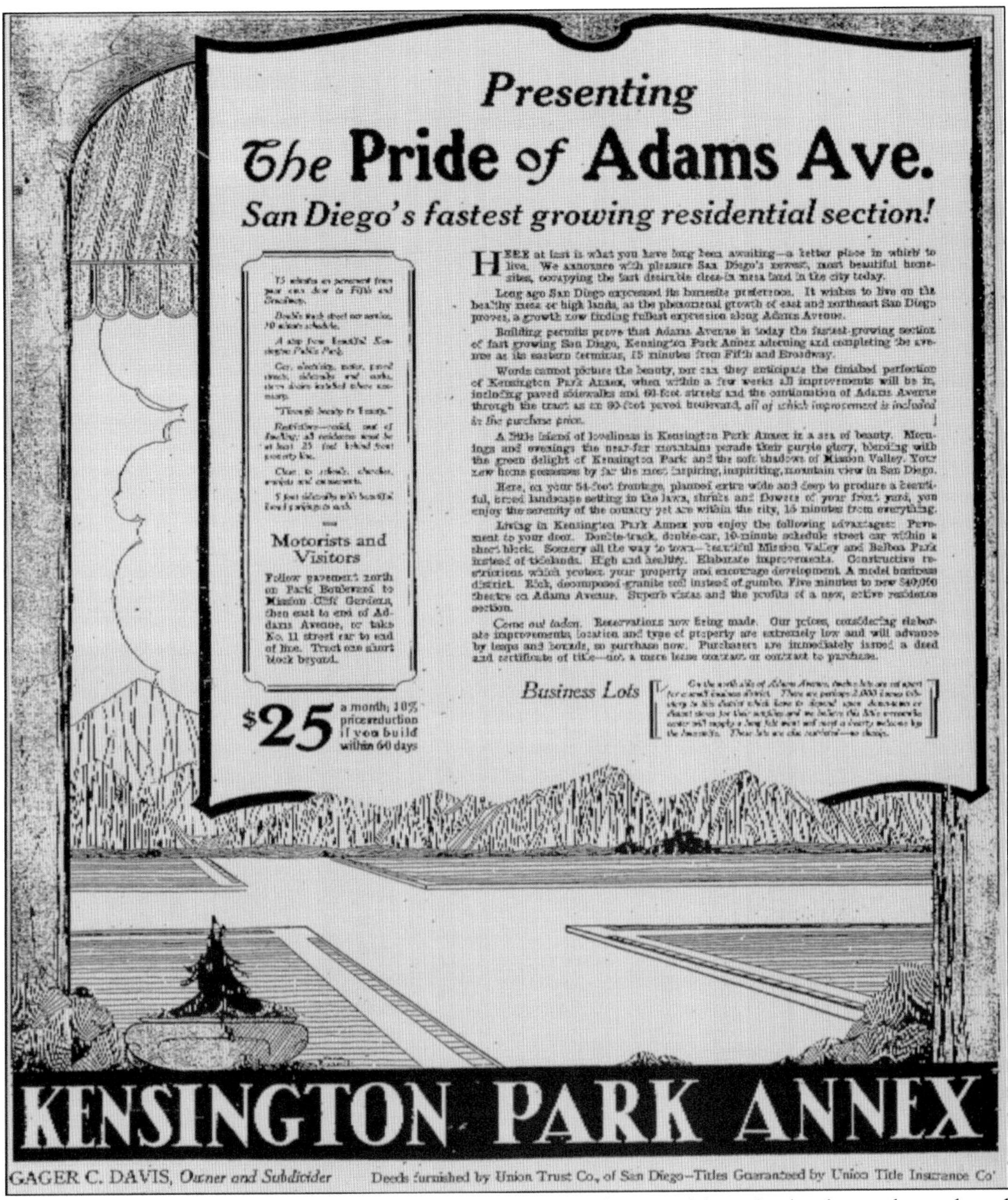

Gager C. Davis, owner of Kensington Park Annex, advertised lots for both residential and commercial buildings. Twelve lots on the north side of Adams Avenue were set apart for a small business district, "no shacks" allowed. The deed restrictions in Kensington Park had not yet expired, hence the desire of this developer to provide commercial building opportunities. (Courtesy of Ron V. May.)

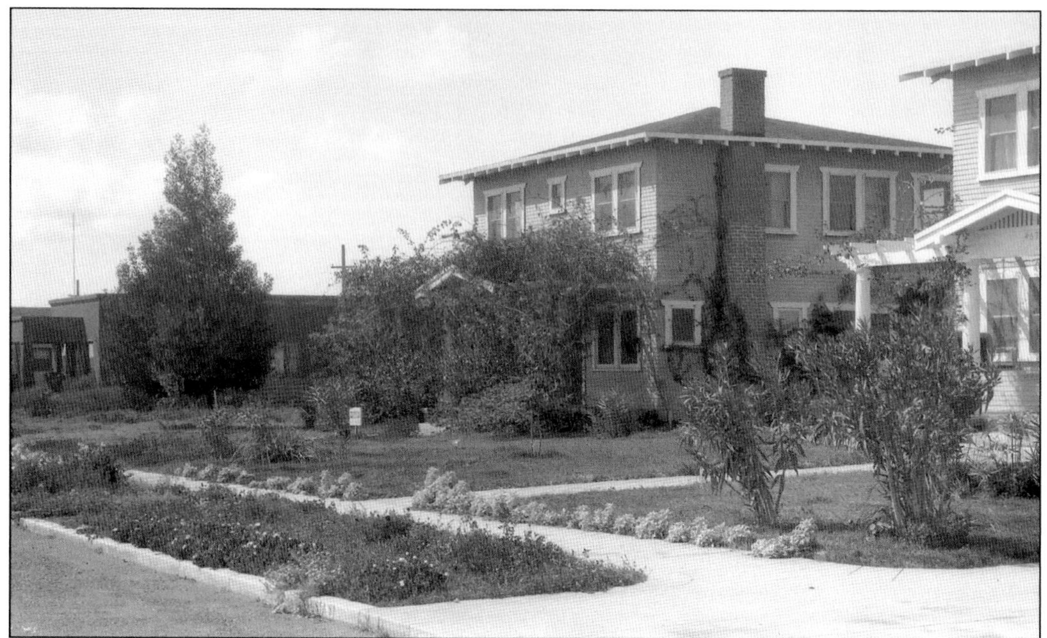

A pair of two-story Craftsman houses were built in the Kensington Park Annex on Vista Street. Likely built in 1924, they seem to reflect a tie to the Kensington Park subdivision to the west. No other Craftsman-style houses were built in this tract. (Courtesy of San Diego History Center.)

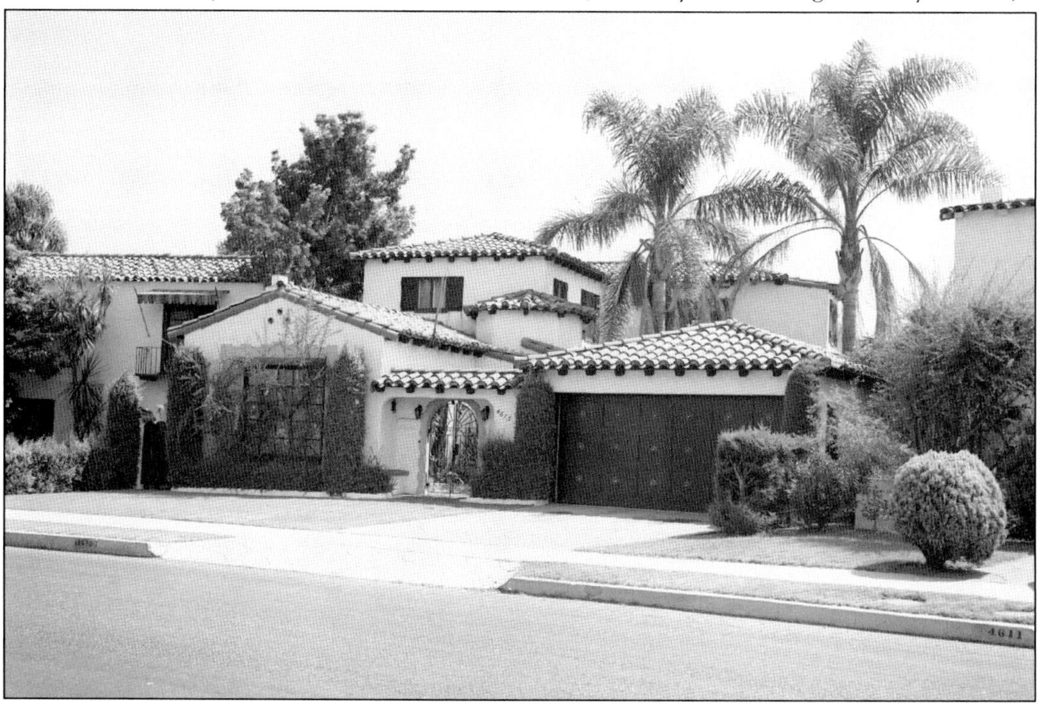

Domenico DeLuca and his wife, Rita, moved into 4615 East Talmadge Drive in the 1930s. Domenico passed away in 1960, and Rita remained in the home until 1994. A native of Italy, she was fascinated by house design. According to her obituary, this home was one of several of her designs that were constructed. (Courtesy of San Diego History Center.)

By the 1940s, the first unit of the Talmadge Park subdivision had been largely built up. Although residences in the Spanish Colonial style were most popular, others such as Tudor and French Eclectic are seen. (Courtesy of San Diego History Center.)

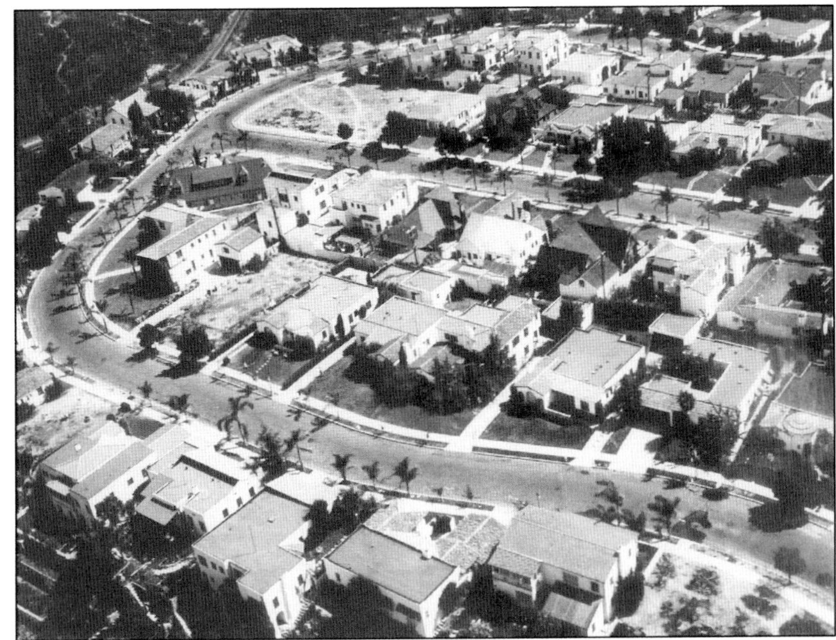

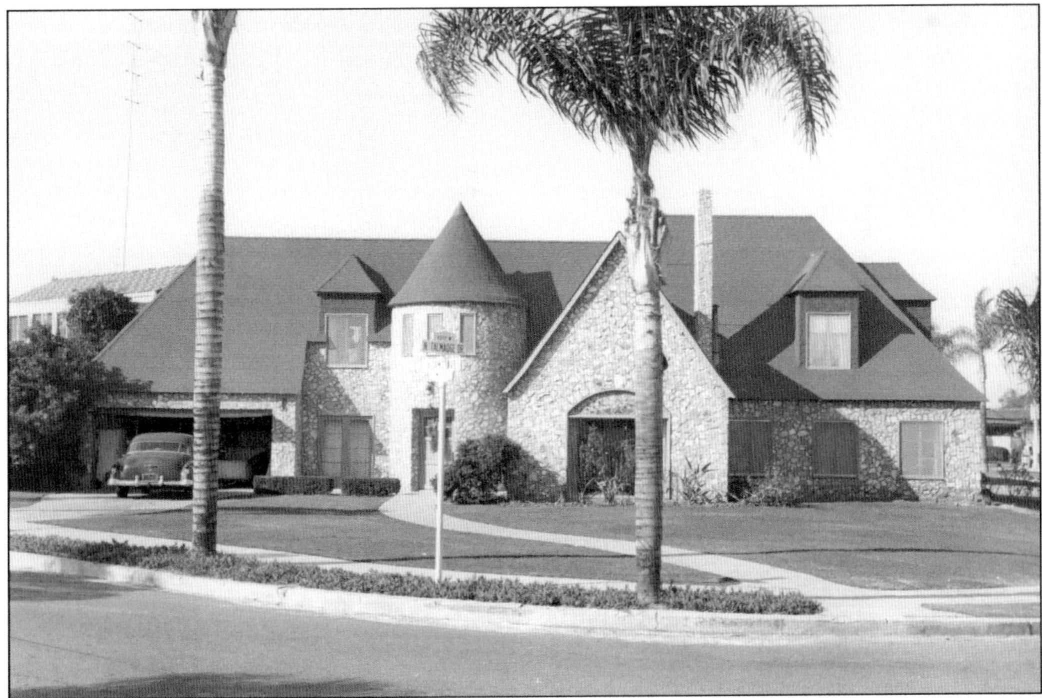

The Wonder House of Stone, designed by Ralph E. Hurlburt and built in the style of a French chateau in 1926, was the architectural focal point of the Talmadge Park development. The house was utilized by Roy C. Lichty as a sales office for the subdivision from 1926 to 1929. Never the home of the Talmadge sisters, as rumored, it was not used as a residence until 1937, when it was rented to a chauffeur for the Yellow Cab Company. (Courtesy of Robert Sedlock.)

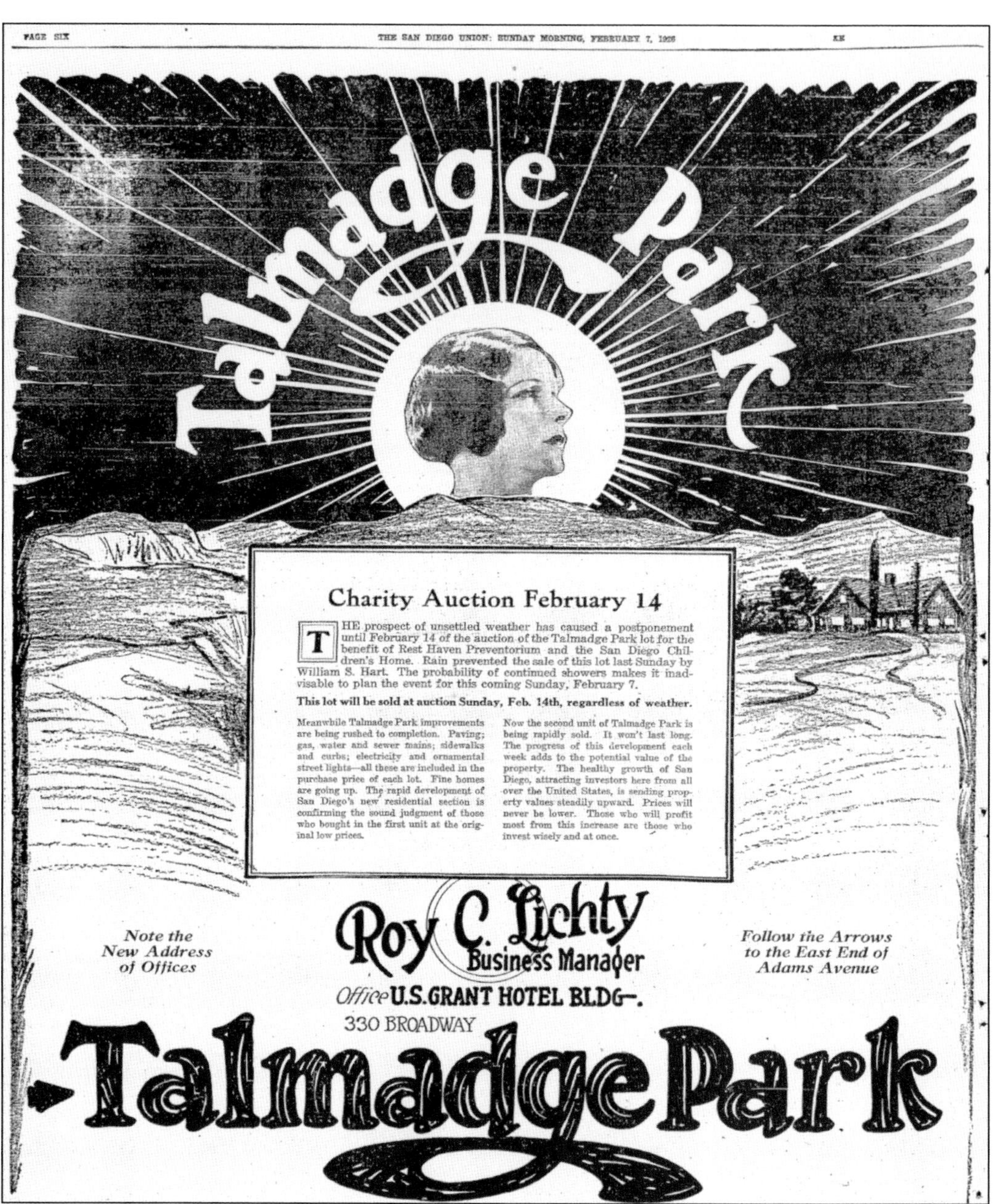

PAGE SIX THE SAN DIEGO UNION: SUNDAY MORNING, FEBRUARY 7, 1926 KE

Charity Auction February 14

THE prospect of unsettled weather has caused a postponement until February 14 of the auction of the Talmadge Park lot for the benefit of Rest Haven Preventorium and the San Diego Children's Home. Rain prevented the sale of this lot last Sunday by William S. Hart. The probability of continued showers makes it inadvisable to plan the event for this coming Sunday, February 7.

This lot will be sold at auction Sunday, Feb. 14th, regardless of weather.

Meanwhile Talmadge Park improvements are being rushed to completion. Paving; gas, water and sewer mains; sidewalks and curbs; electricity and ornamental street lights—all these are included in the purchase price of each lot. Fine homes are going up. The rapid development of San Diego's new residential section is confirming the sound judgment of those who bought in the first unit at the original low prices.

Now the second unit of Talmadge Park is being rapidly sold. It won't last long. The progress of this development each week adds to the potential value of the property. The healthy growth of San Diego, attracting investors here from all over the United States, is sending property values steadily upward. Prices will never be lower. Those who will profit most from this increase are those who invest wisely and at once.

Note the New Address of Offices

Roy C. Lichty
Business Manager
Office U.S. GRANT HOTEL BLDG.
330 BROADWAY

Follow the Arrows to the East End of Adams Avenue

Talmadge Park

Talmadge Park Unit No. 1 development began in 1926. With great fanfare, the image of Hollywood actress Norma Talmadge was used in this advertisement in the *San Diego Union* on February 27, 1926. Norma's husband, movie mogul Joseph M. Schenck, was an investor in the development, along with developer Roy C. Lichty and other Hollywood titans. (Courtesy of Ron V. May.)

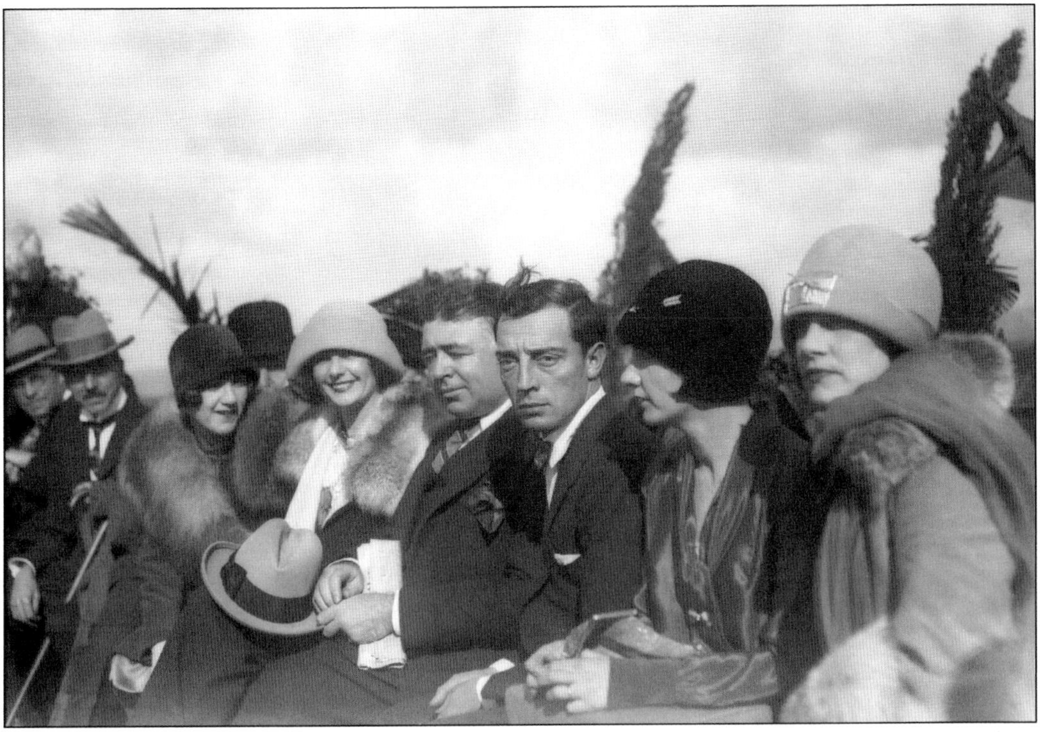

From left to right, Constance Talmadge, her sister Norma, film director Clarence Brown, silent film star Buster Keaton, Natalie Talmadge (Keaton's wife), and an unidentified woman attend the January 3, 1926, dedication ceremony for the Talmadge Park subdivision. The *San Diego Union* described the throng of attendees as "estimated to be the largest that ever has attended a real estate tract opening." (Courtesy of San Diego History Center.)

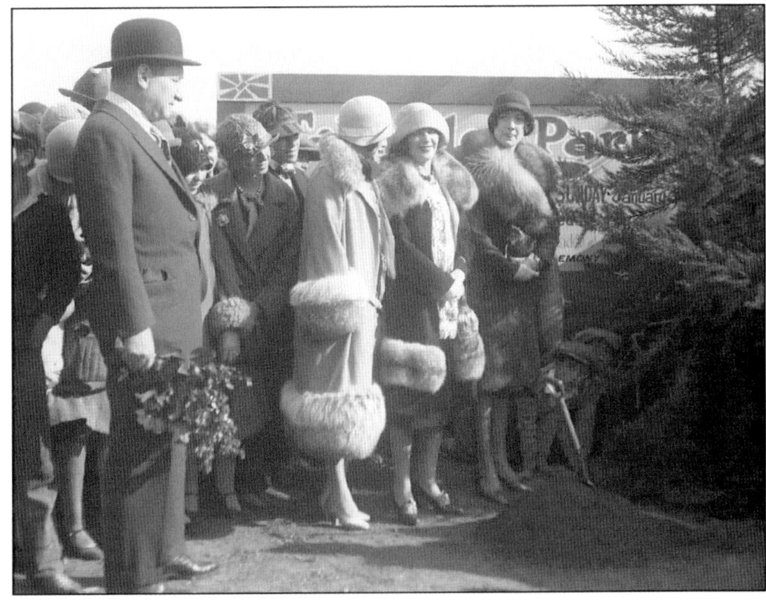

The Talmadge sisters plant a Monterey pine tree on a lot overlooking a canyon during the 1926 dedication ceremony of the Talmadge Park subdivision. Located at the intersection of Adams Avenue and East Talmadge Drive, the lot was auctioned off for $2,500 the following month, and the proceeds given to two children's charities. (Courtesy of San Diego History Center.)

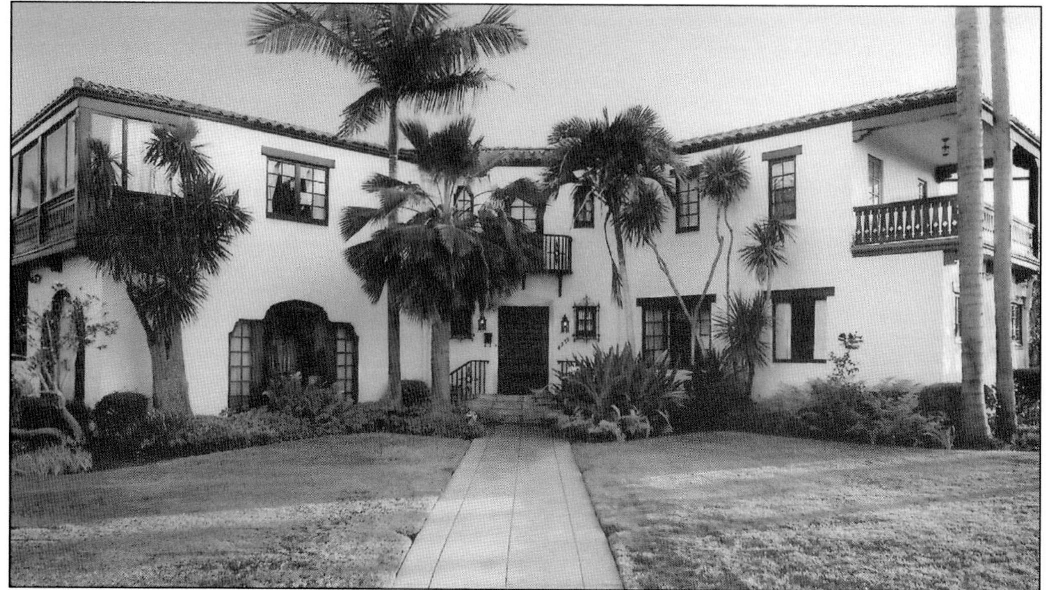

In 1926, architect Louis Gill, nephew of famed architect Irving Gill, designed this grand Spanish Colonial–style home on North Talmadge Drive for his friend, local developer Bertram Carteri. Forced by financial hardship to sell the home before occupying it, Carteri sold it to Gen. Abelardo Rodriguez and his wife, Aida, in 1926. General Rodriguez served as Mexico's president from 1932 to 1934 after the resignation of Pres. Pascual Ortiz Rubio, and was governor of the Mexican states of Sonora and Northern Baja California. This residence was not the first project that Louis Gill and Carteri collaborated on. Several commercial buildings along Adams Avenue in the Normal Heights neighborhood were constructed by Carteri with Gill's designs. (Above, courtesy of Daniel Soderberg; below, courtesy of *San Diego Union-Tribune* and NewsBank Inc.)

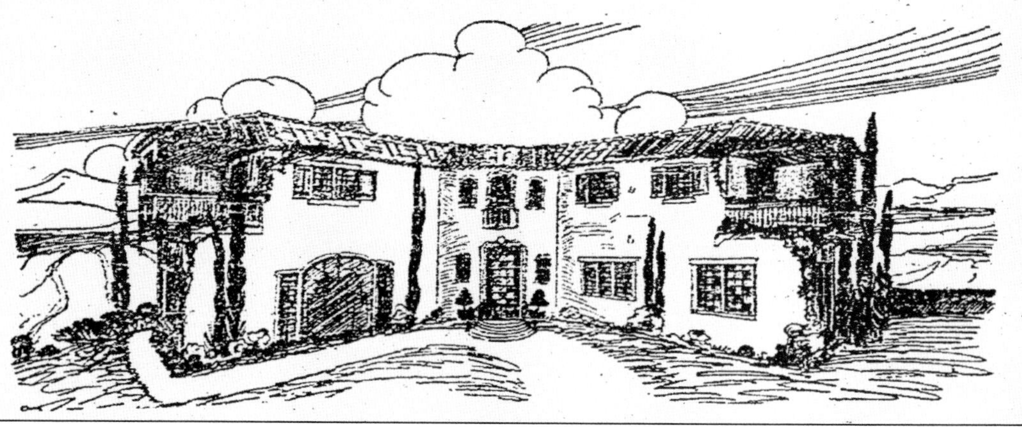

$30,000 Talmadge Park Residence Impetus to Record Tract Activity

Artist's sketch of $30,000 Southern California type home now being built for himself by B. J. Carteri, local realtor and developer, in Talmadge Park, the subdivision recently opened at the east end of Adams avenue.

Three

Creating a Neighborhood Identity

The 1930s saw further expansion of the neighborhood, with the opening of the Kensington Heights subdivision from Hilldale Road north to the rim of the mesa overlooking Mission Valley. The developers of Kensington Heights, George Forbes, and the Davis-Baker Company of Pasadena decided that a commercial center was needed at the intersection of Hilldale Road and Marlborough Drive. At the same time, the deed restrictions in Kensington Park expired in 1926, making way for the first commercial properties along Adams Avenue.

It was during this period that master architect Richard Requa made his mark on Kensington. Requa designed three model homes in Kensington Heights, and through his "architectural committee" scrutinized the drawings of other architects and required changes that would be in keeping with his idea of "Southern California Architecture," as Requa called it. Requa had strong opinions about what constituted a proper house, and through his *San Diego Union* column, railed against "claptrap atrocities" and encouraged simplicity of design, harmony of house and garden, and Spanish features such as arches, colonnades, and window grills festooned with flowering potted plants. Many other noted architects and builders were at work in Kensington at the same time, but it was Requa's association with George Forbes and the Davis-Baker Company that created the distinct Spanish Colonial Revival character of Kensington Heights.

The Kensington Community Church was formed and began building its first church structure on Marlborough Drive in 1929. That same year, the first building was constructed for Benjamin Franklin Elementary school on the corner of Monroe Avenue and Copeland Avenue. Along Adams Avenue, several Craftsman houses were either moved or repurposed to make way for shops and gas stations. The Pleasure Park was deeded to the County of San Diego, and a small branch library was built where the pond once was.

Kensington was reaching toward an era of self-sufficiency in which everything a family needed, from hairdresser to groceries to library books, could be found within walking distance. However, the onset of the Great Depression left a checkerboard of unbuilt lots throughout the neighborhood.

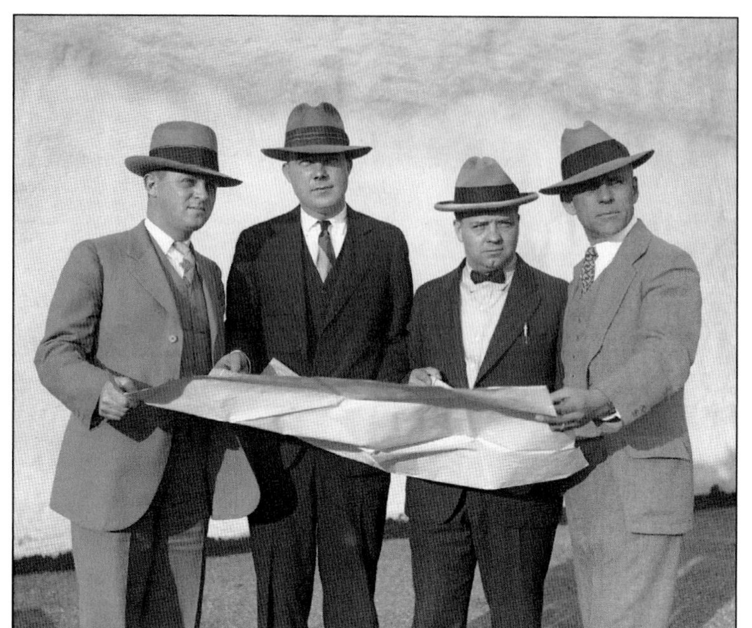

The key players in the development of Kensington Heights study a map in 1926. From left to right, they are Harrison Baker and Richard Davis of Pasadena's Davis-Baker Company, real estate agent and developer George Forbes, and sales manager Alfred Merrick. Forbes, who owned much of the land on which Kensington Heights was developed, hired the Davis-Baker Company to subdivide, develop, and promote his property. (Courtesy of San Diego History Center.)

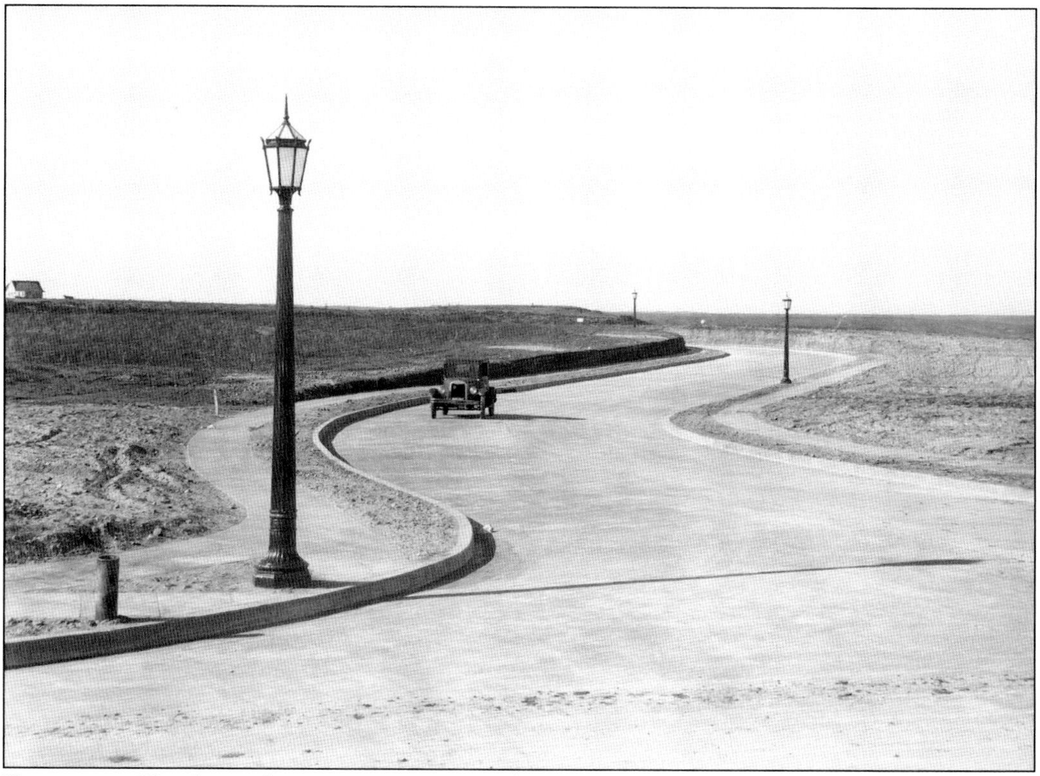

Kensington Heights utilizes a curving street design in contrast to the grid patterned streets seen in nearby subdivisions such as North Park. Early automobile suburbs often utilized curving streets guided by the contours of the hills. This neighborhood design style is attributed to the influential landscape architect Frederick Law Olmsted (1822–1903). (Courtesy of San Diego History Center.)

Pictured in 1926, the first Kensington Heights sales office, located at the intersection of Marlborough Drive and Hilldale Road, was a simple wooden structure. It was replaced by a permanent building at that intersection in the late 1920s. The "Prize Spanish Home" is visible in the background. An Electrolier street lamp, many of which are still visible throughout Kensington Heights, stands in the foreground. (Courtesy of Robert Sedlock.)

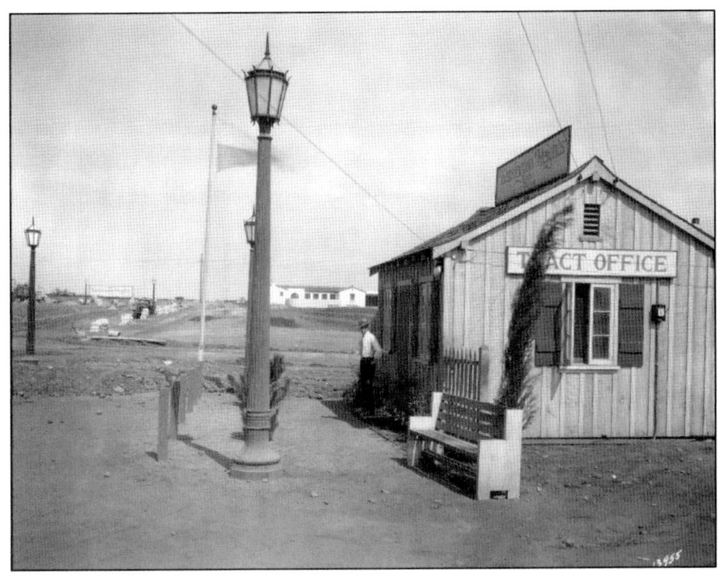

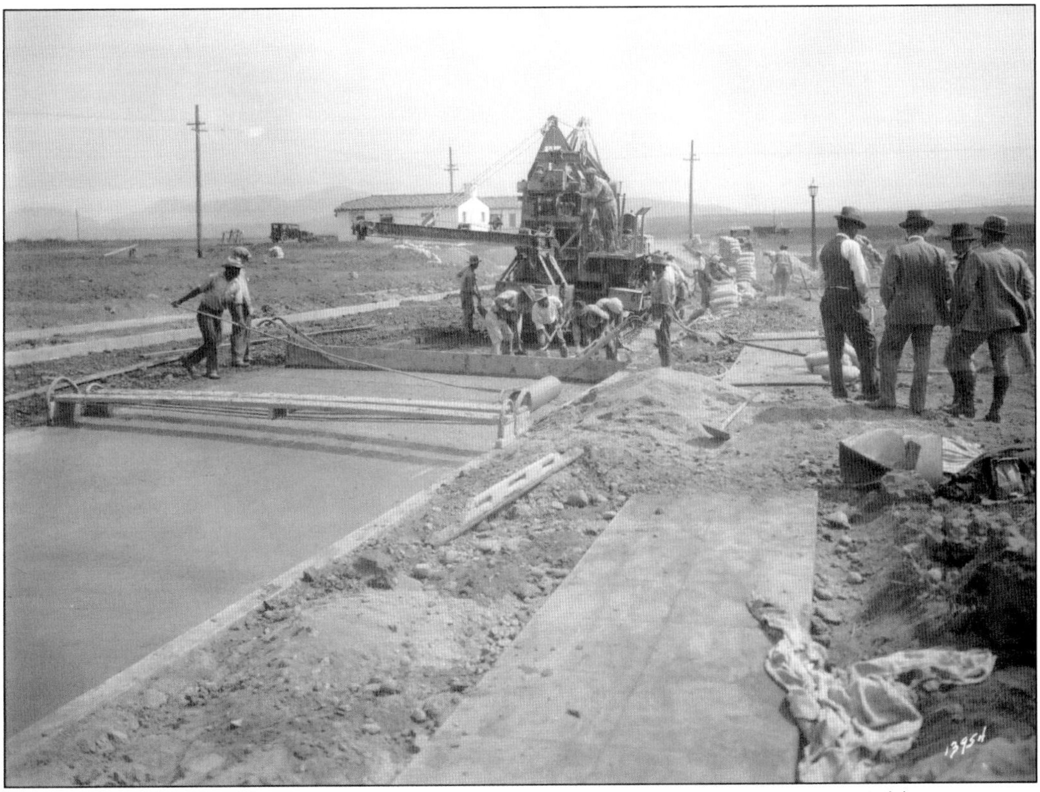

A crew lays concrete along Middlesex Drive west of Marlborough Drive in 1926. Unlike many new housing developments where homeowners sometimes endured dirt roads for years, the Davis-Baker Company installed amenities such as paved roads, curbs, sidewalks, and uniform street lighting before Kensington Heights was opened to the public for sale. The Prize Spanish Home model residence designed by Richard Requa is seen in the background. (Courtesy of Robert Sedlock.)

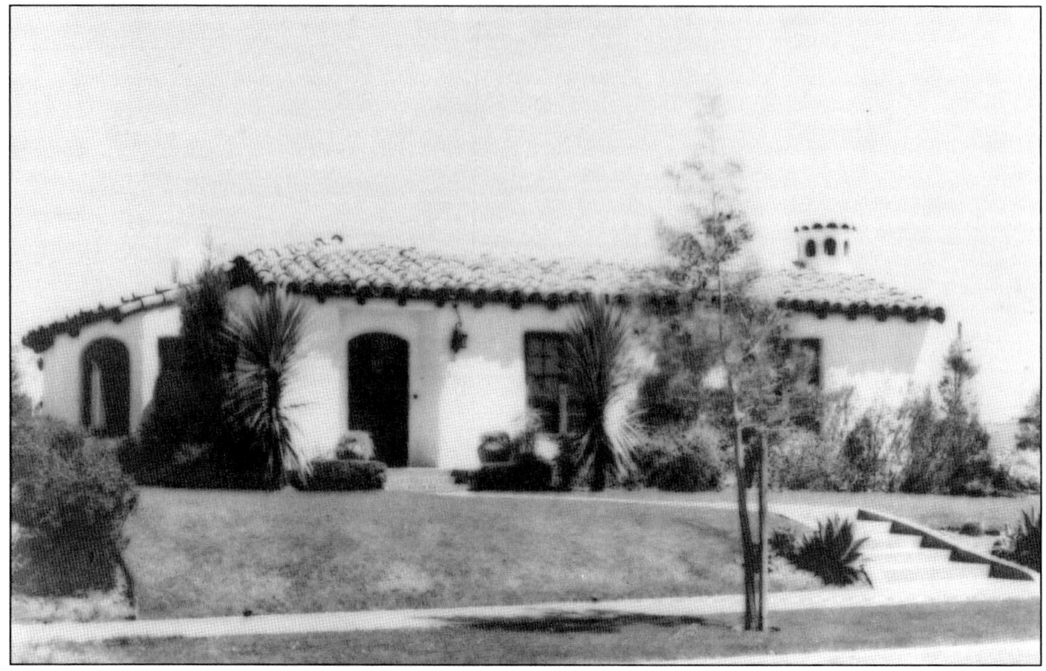

Built at the northeast corner of Marlborough Drive and Middlesex Drive in 1926, Kensington Heights' first model home was architect Richard Requa's concept of ideal Southern California Architecture. It was purchased in 1927 by George H. Prudden, an aviation pioneer and founder of Prudden-San Diego Airplane Company, a precursor to Solar-Turbines International Inc. (Courtesy of Kensington–Normal Heights Branch Library.)

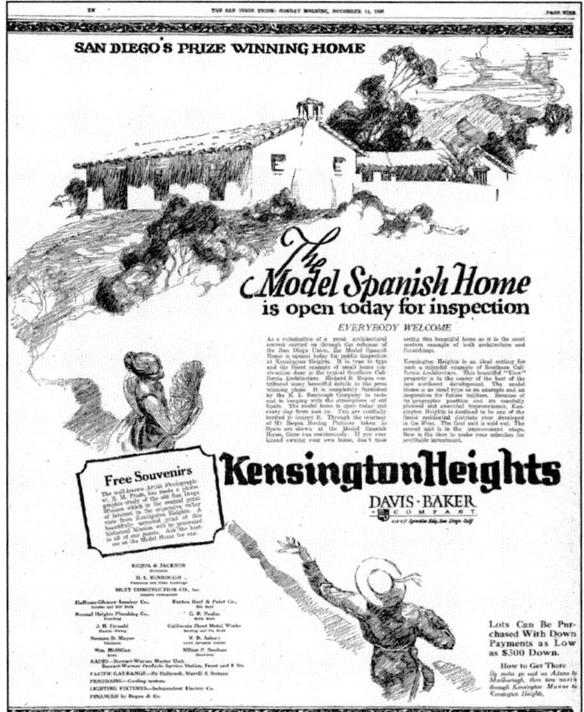

To generate interest in the Kensington Heights subdivision, a local newspaper advertising campaign solicited model home design plans from the public and offered a $100 cash prize for the best one. A "winner" was selected from nearly 400 entries, but the plans were actually drawn by architect Richard Requa. Thousands attended the home's premiere on November 14, 1926. (Courtesy of *San Diego Union-Tribune* and NewsBank Inc.)

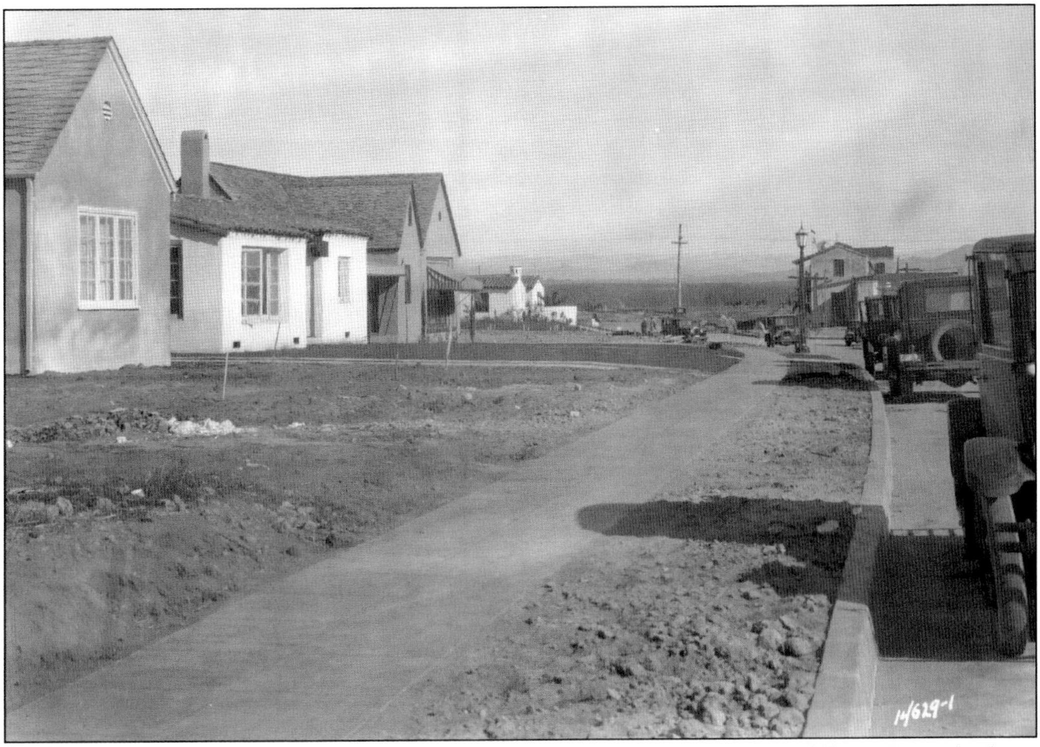

Contractor William F. Riley constructed all five homes in this view of Middlesex Drive looking east. Completed in 1926, they were the earliest in Kensington Heights. Riley moved from Valdez, Alaska, to San Diego around 1910 and established himself as a builder of homes and bridges. With the help of his son Al, he constructed the original portion of the Kensington Community Church in 1929. (Courtesy of Robert Sedlock.)

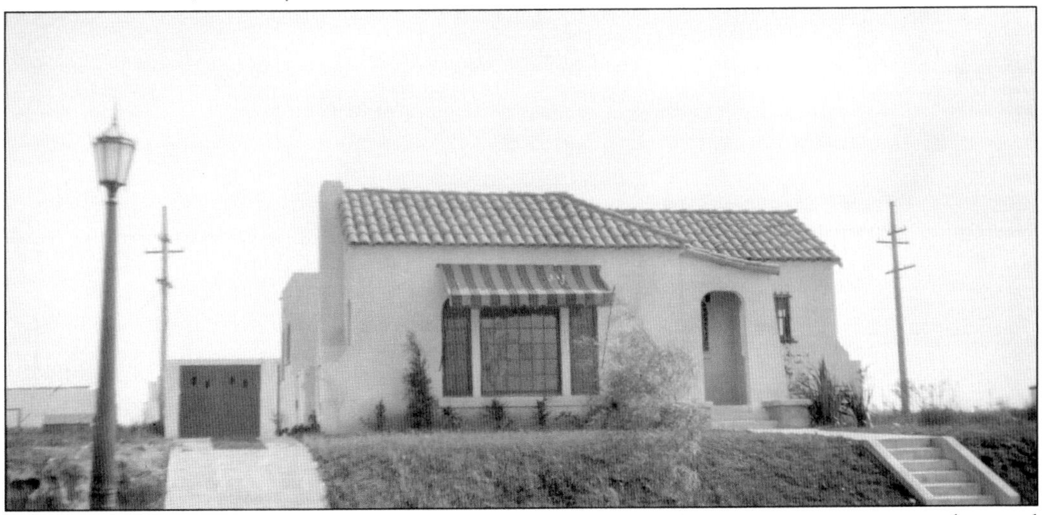

To appeal to homebuyers of more modest means, the Davis-Baker Company constructed several smaller, less elaborate Spanish Colonial residences, including this one on Middlesex Drive. Originally used as a model home in 1928, local newspapers advertised it as "La Chiquita," (Spanish for "The Little One") and as a "triumph of good taste over purse." (Courtesy of Kensington–Normal Heights Branch Library.)

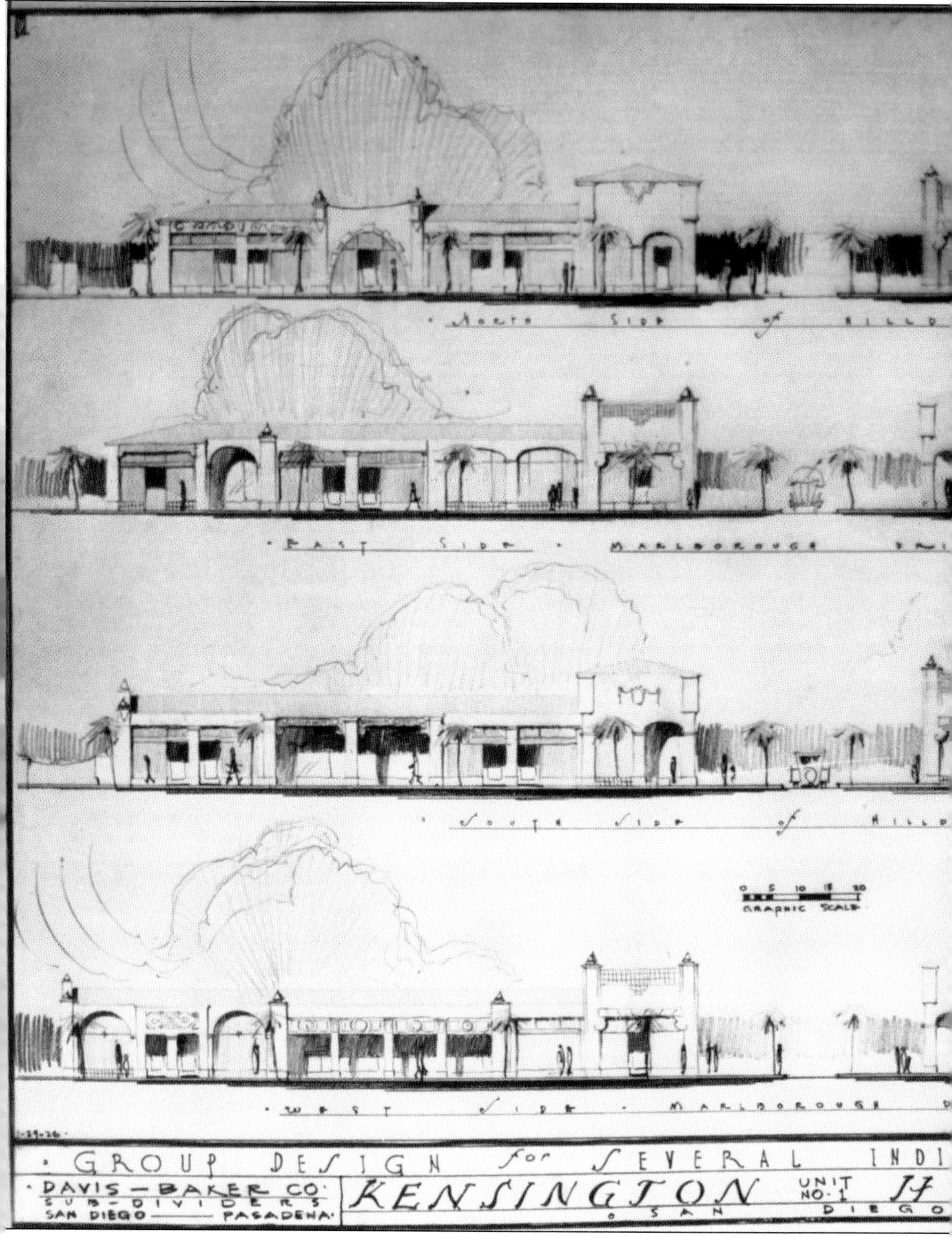
NORTH SIDE of HILLD
EAST SIDE · MARLBOROUGH DRI
SOUTH SIDE of HILLD
0 5 10 15 20
GRAPHIC SCALE
WEST SIDE · MARLBOROUGH D
1-29-26
GROUP DESIGN for SEVERAL INDI
DAVIS—BAKER CO.
SUB-DIVIDERS
SAN DIEGO —— PASADENA
KENSINGTON
UNIT NO-1
SAN DIEGO

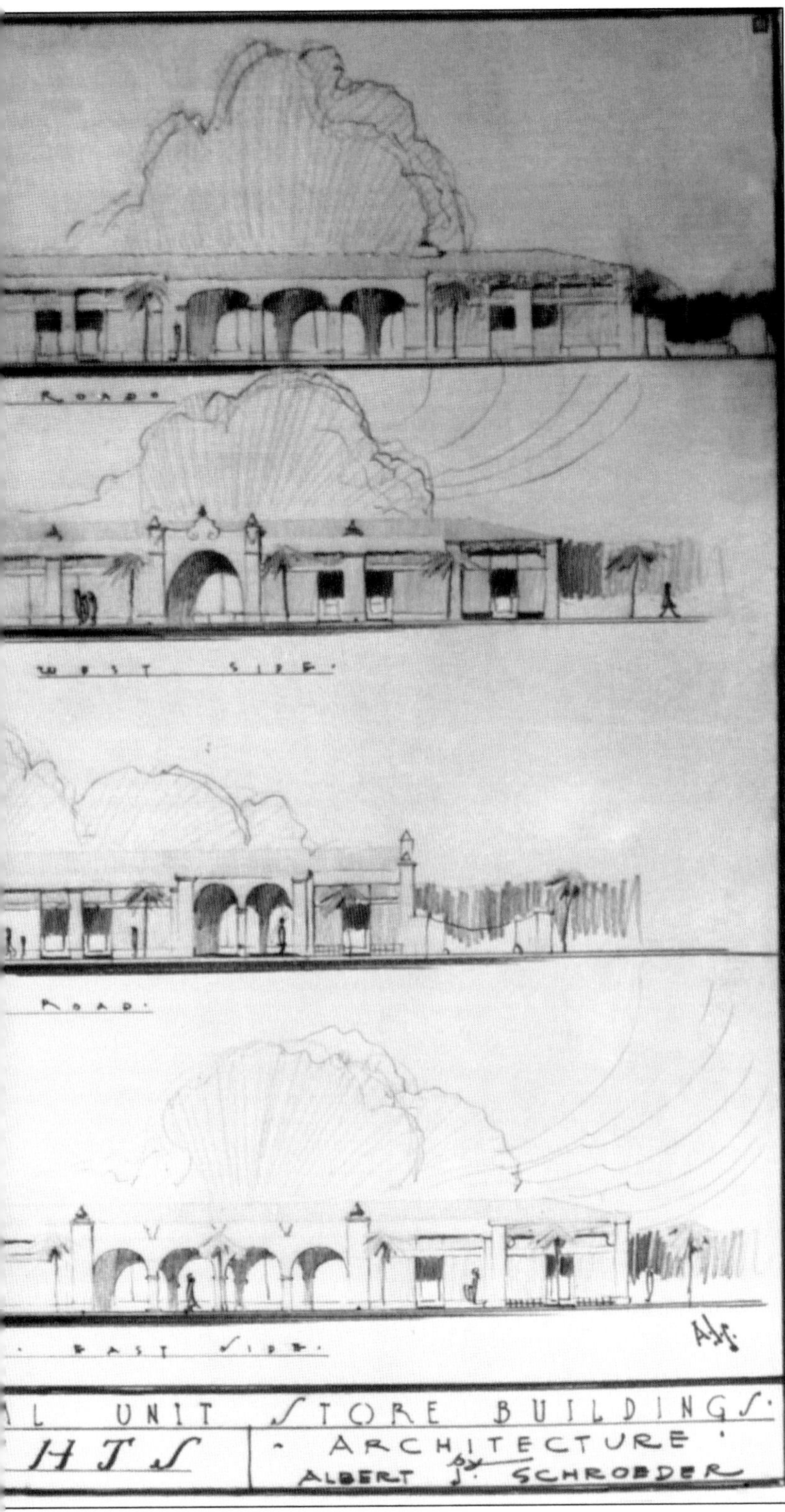

The small commercial center constructed at the northwest corner of Marlborough Drive and Hilldale Road was originally intended to occupy all four corners of that intersection. Pasadena-based architect Albert J. Schroeder completed this rendering of the proposed center in 1926. His plan was scaled down because by the late 1920s, the business district along Adams Avenue had begun to develop. (Courtesy of San Diego History Center.)

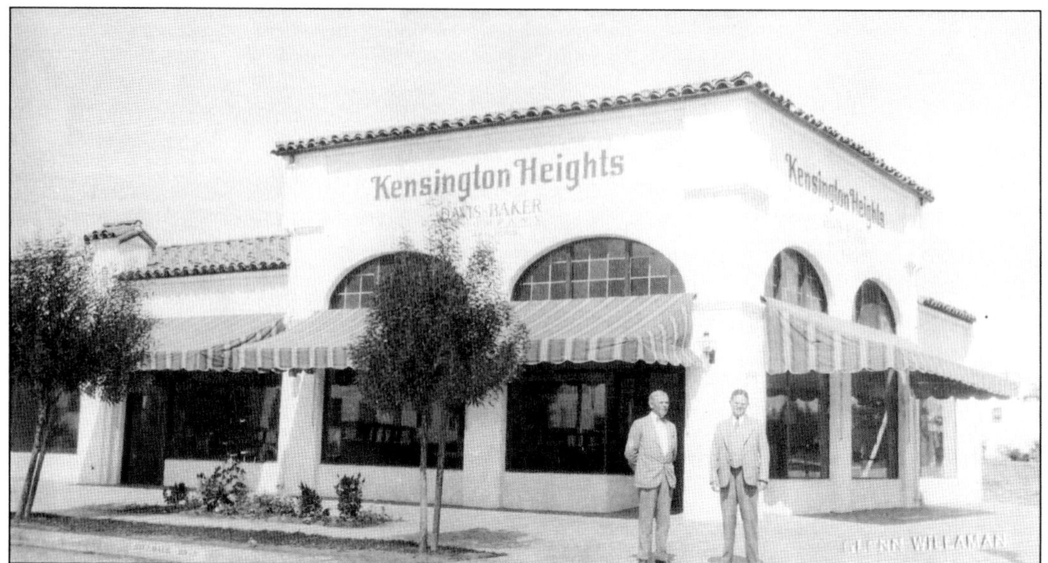

Developer and real estate agent George T. Forbes (right) and an unidentified man stand outside the Kensington Heights Company realty office around 1930. Forbes was instrumental in the development and promotion of Kensington Heights and later played a similar role in the San Diego subdivisions of Allied Gardens, Del Cerro, and San Carlos. His office was located in this building until he retired in the 1960s. (Courtesy of Robert Sedlock.)

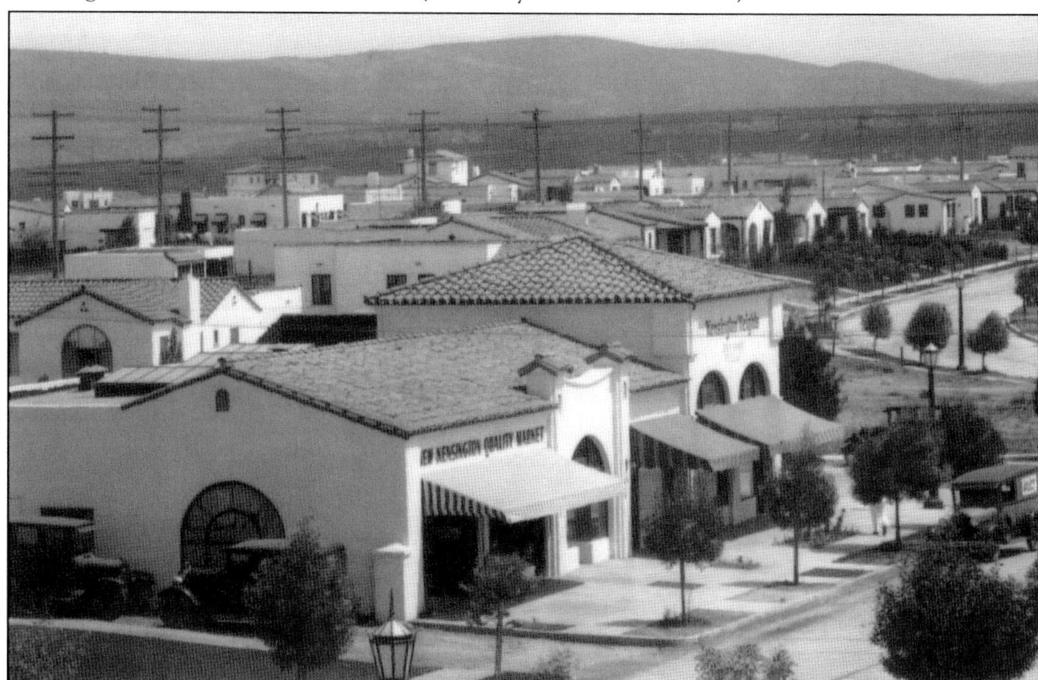

Pictured in the late 1920s, the small commercial hub at the northwest corner of Marlborough Drive and Hilldale Road originally housed the Kensington Heights real estate sales office and a small grocery called the New Kensington Quality Market. A small cafe was added later. Though altered, the building is now known as Marl-Dale and houses private offices. (Courtesy of Robert Sedlock.)

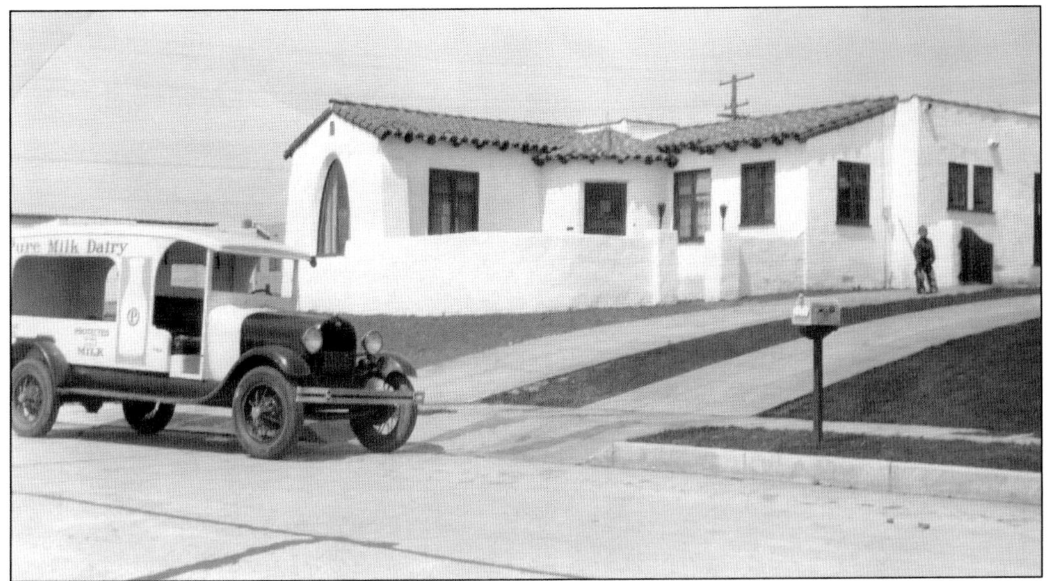

The Pure Milk Dairy makes a delivery to a home on Hilldale Road in the 1920s. Many of the new and stylish Spanish homes of Kensington originally had a small milk delivery door that allowed delivery men to drop off fresh milk and other dairy products and pick up empty glass bottles while the residents were away. (Courtesy of Kensington–Normal Heights Branch Library.)

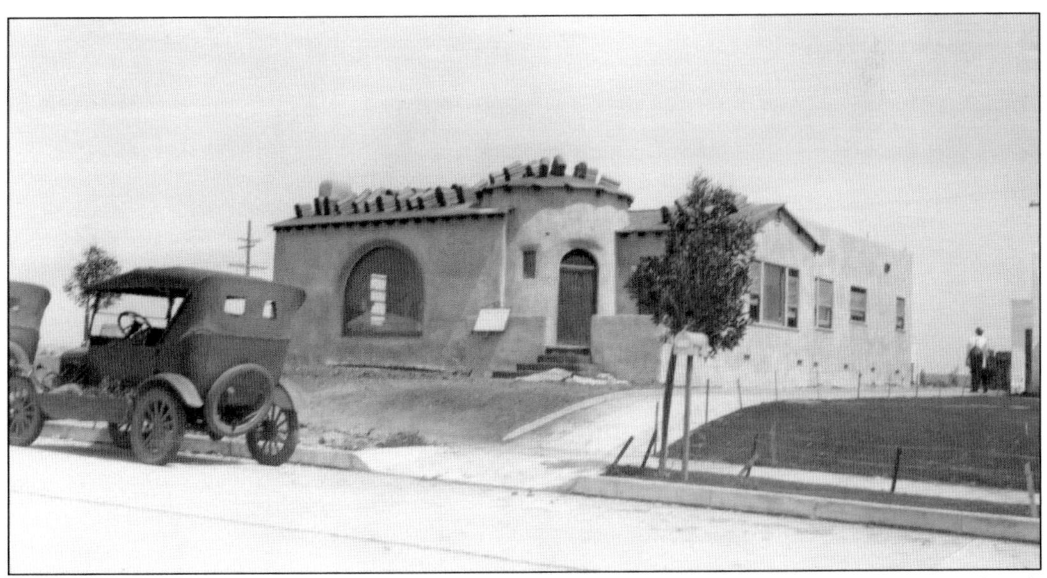

Nearing completion in the late 1920s, 4024 South Hempstead Circle is soon to be roofed with half-round mission clay tiles. Despite their claim of being hand-formed over a "maiden's thigh," by the 1920s the vast majority of these tiles were produced in Southern California factories. (Courtesy of Kensington–Normal Heights Branch Library.)

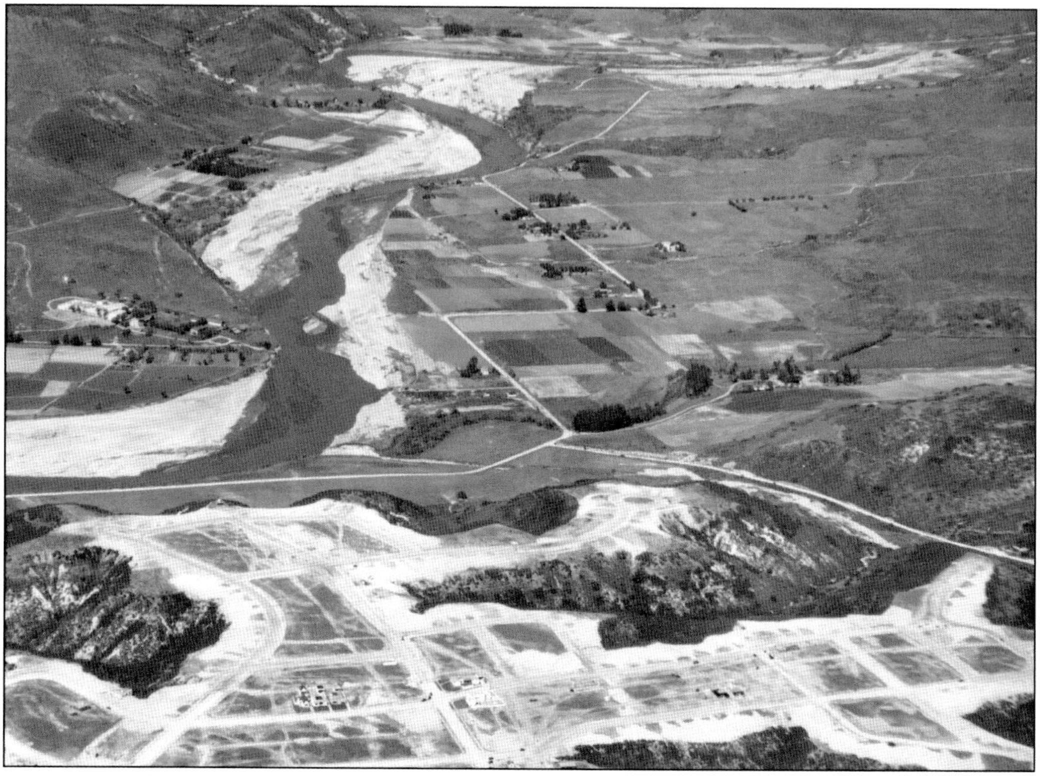

Kensington Heights, in the foreground, was developed on a mesa overlooking Mission Valley to the north as shown in this 1927 aerial view. Although only a few miles from downtown San Diego, the area was considered rural at the time, and Mission Valley was largely agricultural. The Mission San Diego de Alcala, built in 1769, is visible at center left. (Courtesy of Robert Sedlock.)

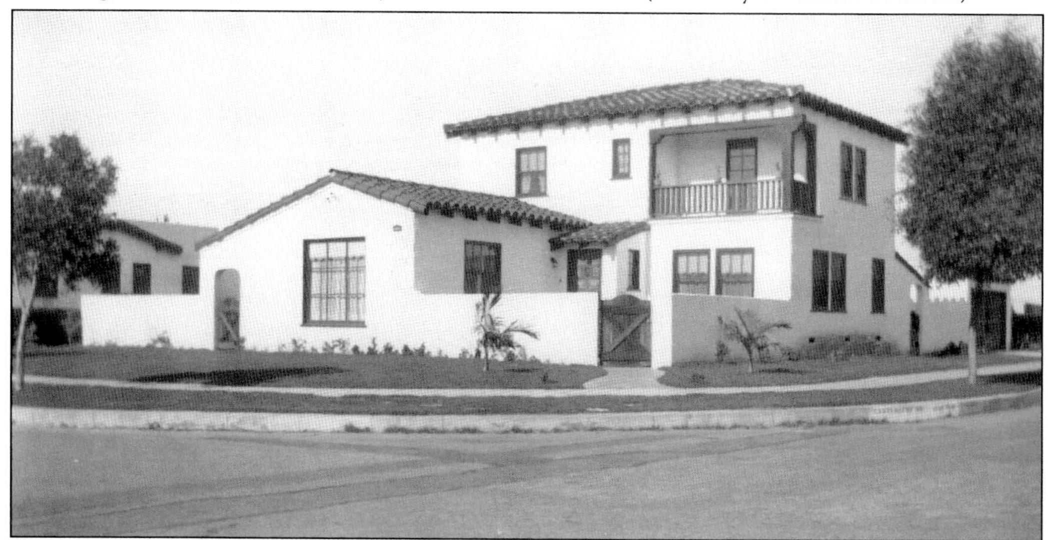

This two-story house at 4901 Kensington Drive exhibits many of the details of a Monterey-style Spanish Revival, with a shallow, pitched hipped roof covered with clay tiles, a second story covered balcony, carved balcony porch posts, and tall, narrow, multi-light double-hung windows grouped in pairs. (Courtesy of Dave Ussell and Gayle Hicks.)

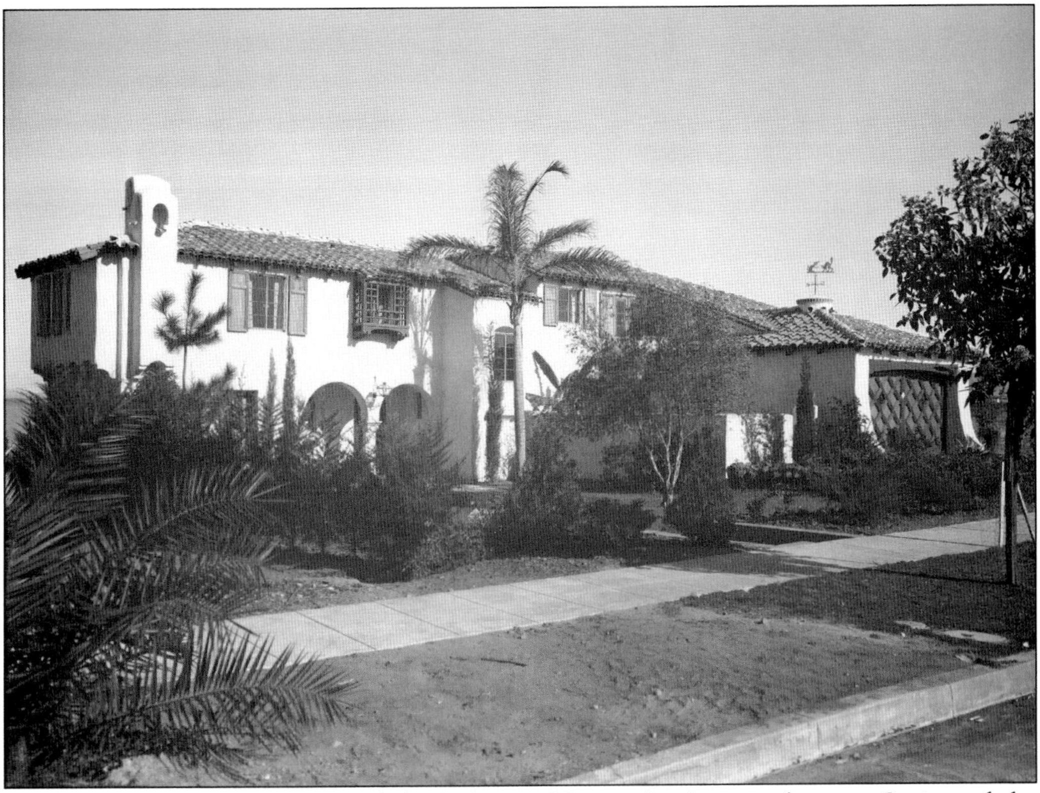

Architect Richard Requa designed the Ridgeway House after his expedition to Spain and the Mediterranean, which was sponsored by the Portland Cement Company. Constructed as a luxurious model home in 1929, it was part of the Davis-Baker Company's marketing strategy to attract wealthy buyers, investors, and builders of opulent custom homes to the Valley Rim section of Kensington Heights Unit No. 3. (Courtesy of Robert Sedlock.)

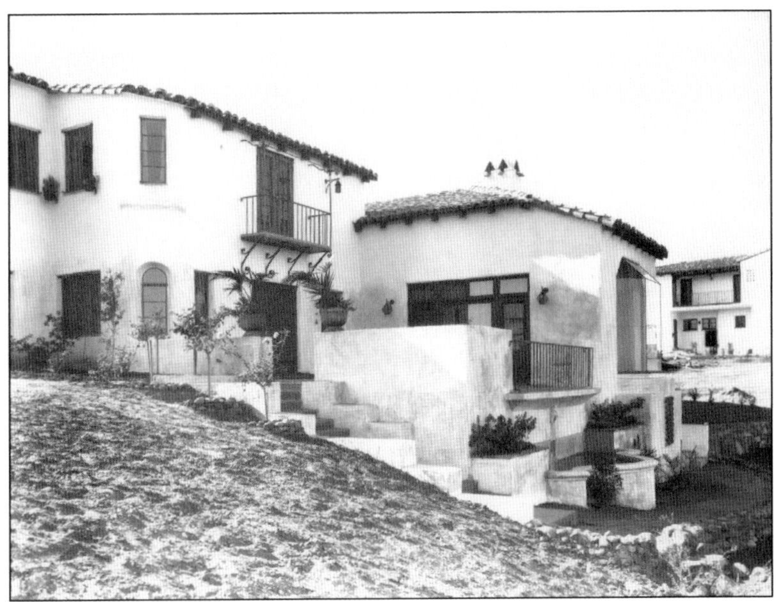

Architect Richard Requa chose this site to construct the Ridgeway House because of its location at the head of a canyon, which provided the rear of the home with a view of Mission Valley and the Mission de Alcala. This 1929 photograph shows the innovative large bay window that served to frame a view of these locations, much like a living picture. (Courtesy of Robert Sedlock.)

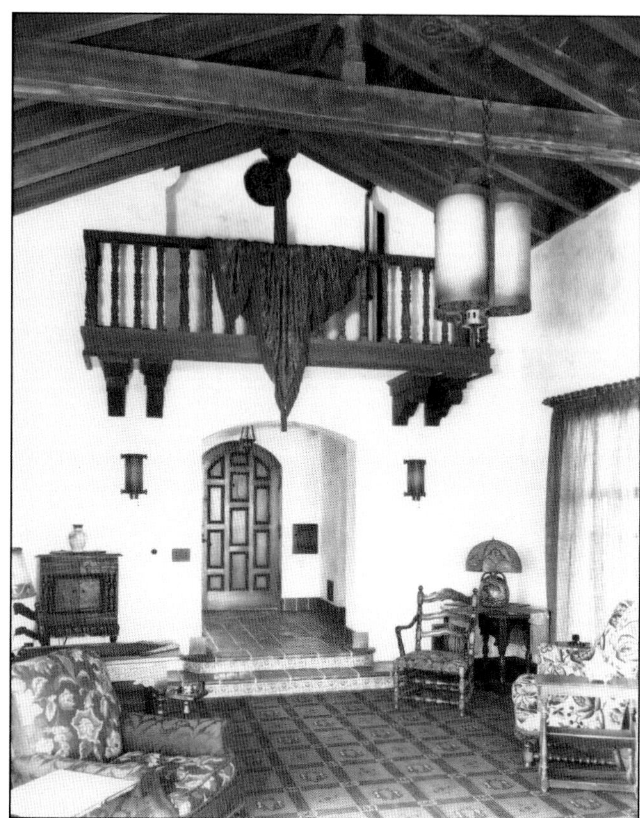

In this 1929 photograph, the rustic wood ceiling and balcony, arched doorways, and medieval-style door of the Ridgeway House evoke the feel of a Spanish residence from a bygone era. The H.L. Benbough Furniture Company, San Diego's leading home furnishings store during the 1920s, provided the pieces used to stage the residence during its time as a model home. (Courtesy of Robert Sedlock.)

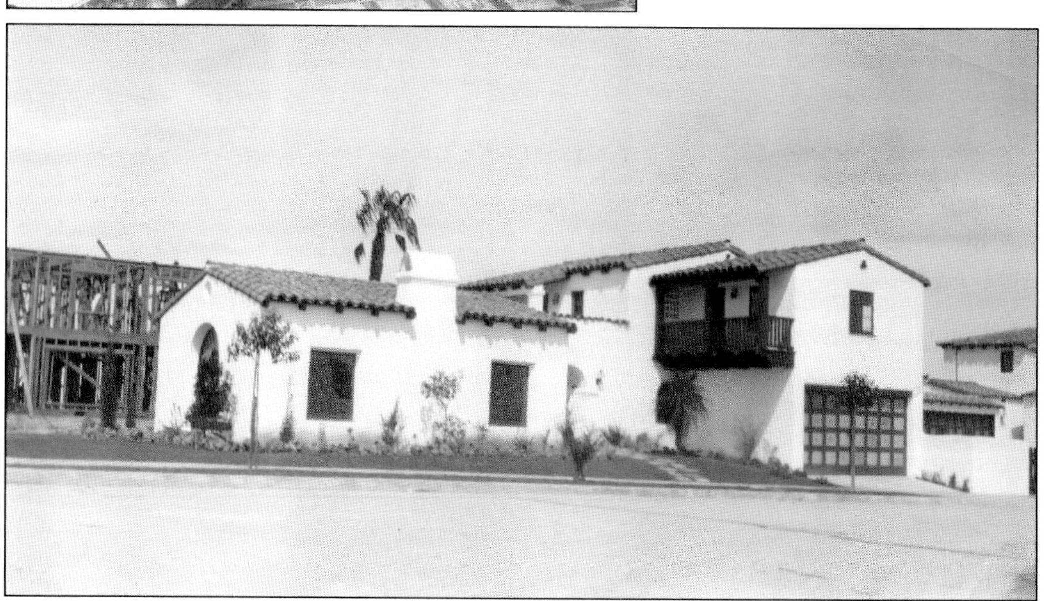

Headed by Herbert R. Bathrick, the Bathrick Brothers Construction Company of Pasadena built several Kensington homes, including this one at 5301 Marlborough Drive. Specializing in large two-story Spanish Colonial–style residences, the company also left its mark on San Diego's Loma Portal neighborhood, as well as Pasadena and Altadena near Los Angeles. (Courtesy of Kensington–Normal Heights Branch Library.)

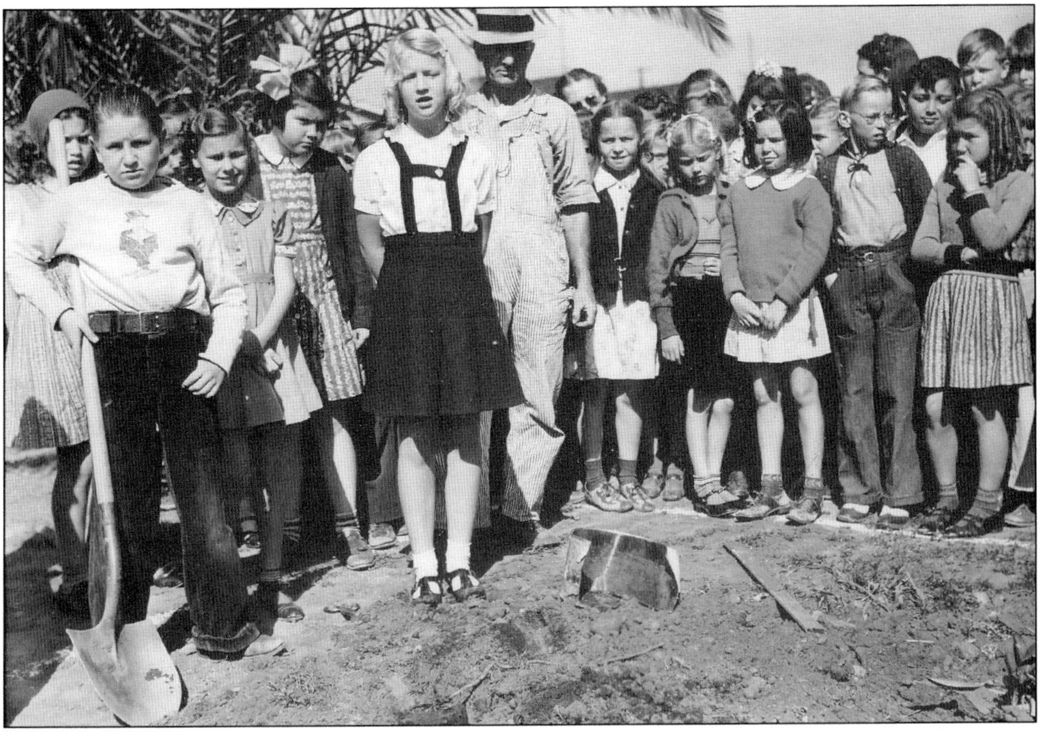

Conservation Week was celebrated at Benjamin Franklin School around Arbor Day each year. In 1939, the festivities included the planting of a tree by the students, and the recitation of a poem while the custodian looked on. (Courtesy of Franklin Elementary School.)

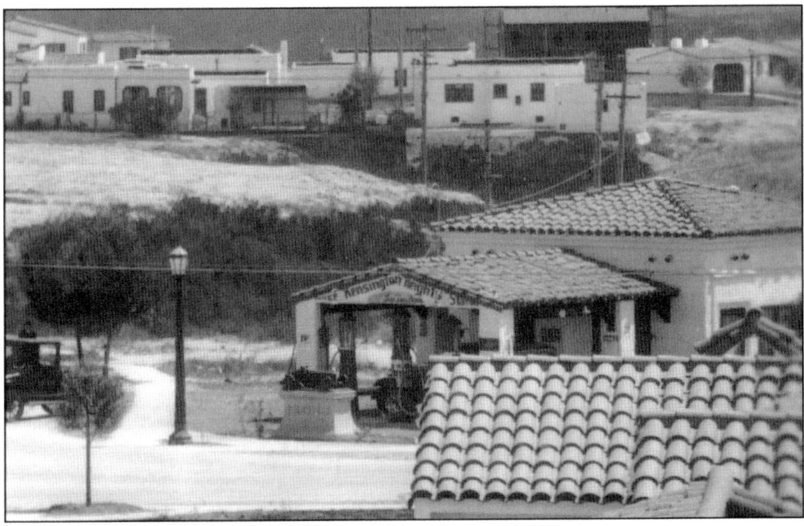

George Forbes conceived of a commercial center at the intersection of Marlborough Drive and Hilldale Road. A gas station, the Kensington Heights Station, was built on the southeast corner as seen in this view looking east. (Courtesy of Robert Sedlock.)

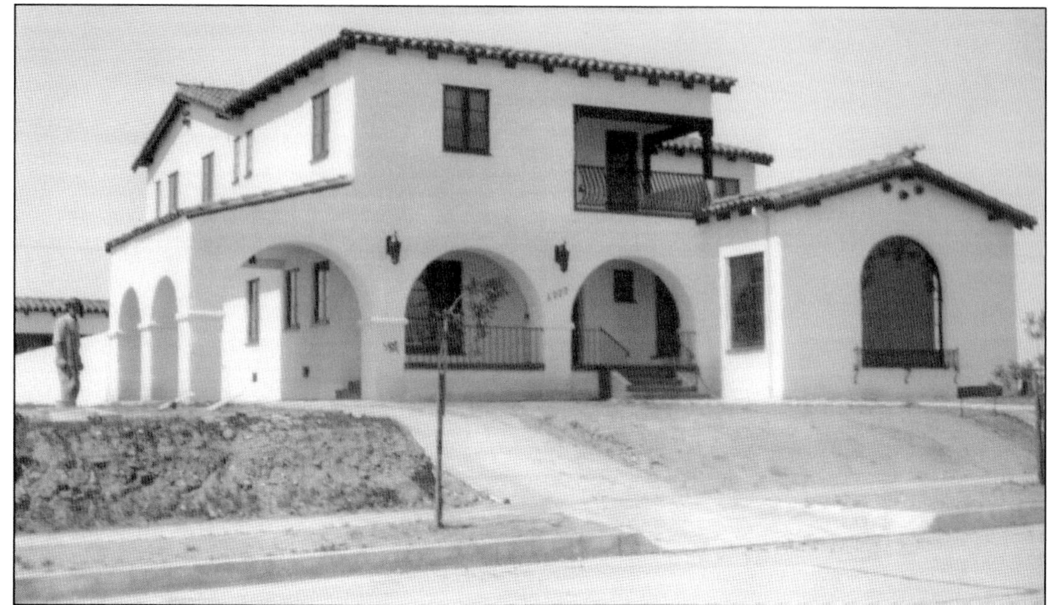

Carl B. Hays constructed this Spanish Colonial–style home at 5232 Marlborough Drive in 1929 for Enrique and Esperanza Aldrete, who lived there with their children for 10 years. Enrique, a former mayor of Tijuana, Mexico, was a prominent businessman there, and also served as vice mayor of Mexico's coastal town of Ensenada. The home originally sat on a triple lot and featured a tennis court on its southern side. (Courtesy of Devin and DeLayne Harmon.)

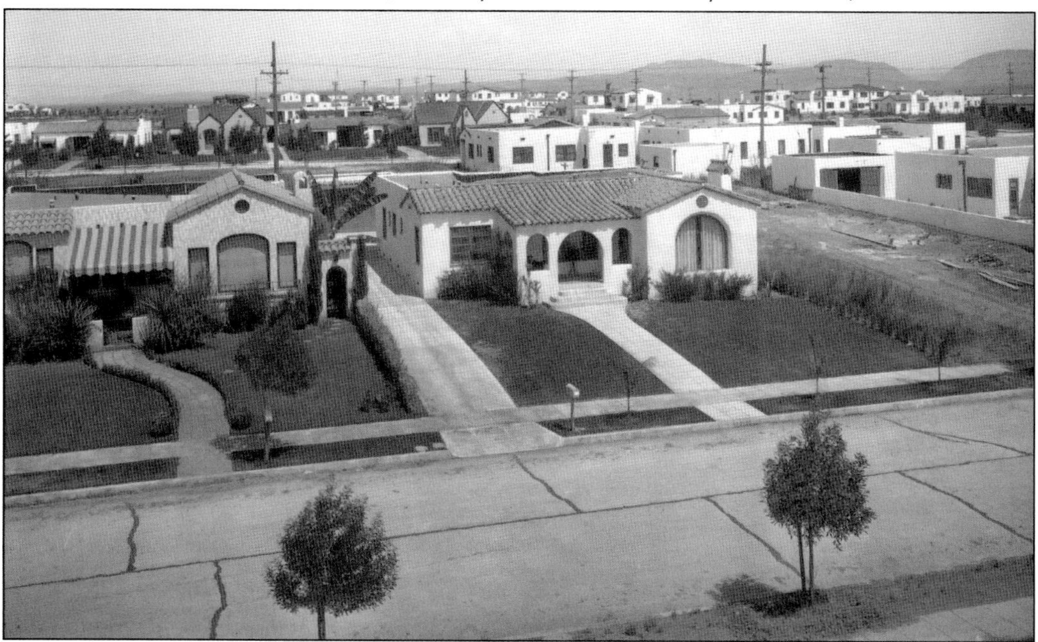

By the late 1920s, the result of the Kensington Heights deed restrictions on architectural styles was apparent. Implemented for a harmonious appearance of Spanish Colonial homes, the cohesive use of stucco and red clay tile roofs gave the neighborhood the feel of a Spanish village. The two Tudor homes in the background were constructed before the restrictions on architectural styles were enacted by the Davis-Baker Company. (Courtesy of Robert Sedlock.)

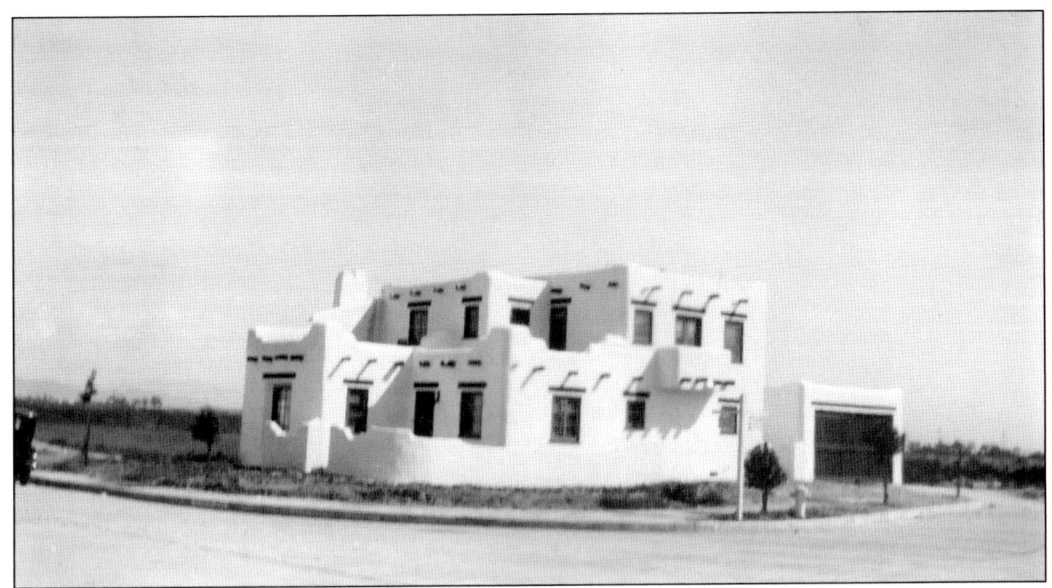

One of the less common architectural styles seen in Kensington is Pueblo Revival, although at least three such homes were constructed on Braeburn Road. The style was modeled after the Native American pueblos of the southwestern United States. Shown as it appeared in the late 1920s, the home at 4401 Braeburn Road has since been altered to a Spanish Colonial appearance. (Courtesy of Kensington–Normal Heights Branch Library.)

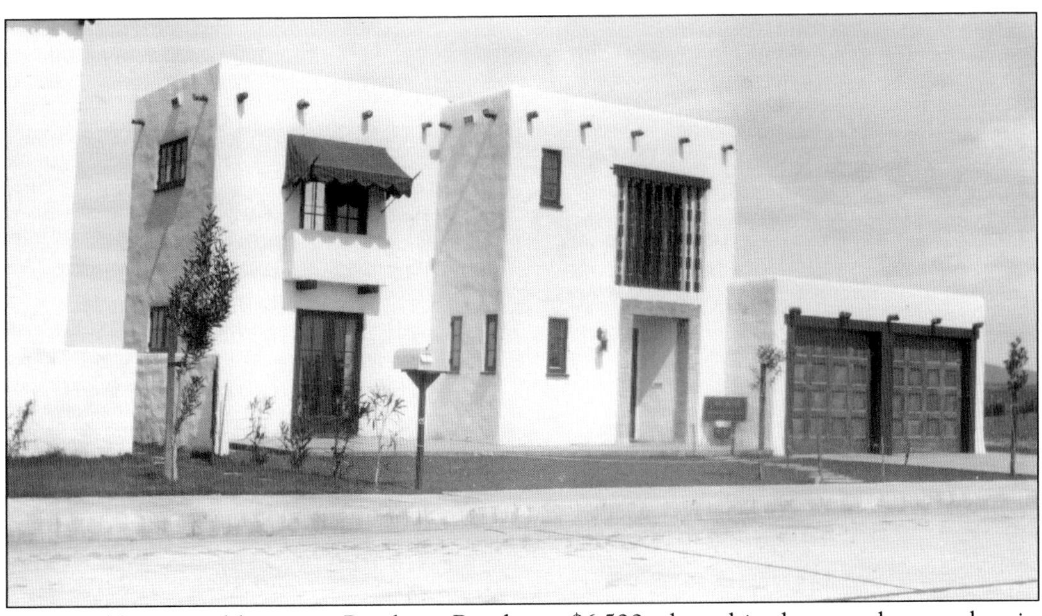

This Pueblo Revival home on Braeburn Road cost $6,500 when this photograph was taken in 1928. The home shows a mixture of Pueblo and Spanish architectural styles. The round wooden roof *vigas*, or beams, flat roofs, and irregular stucco surfacing are modeled after the indigenous architecture of the Pueblo Indians of the Southwest. A large, full scale pueblo village was built in Balboa Park as part of San Diego's 1915 Exposition and likely influenced the style locally. (Courtesy of Sarah Risso and Peter Risso.)

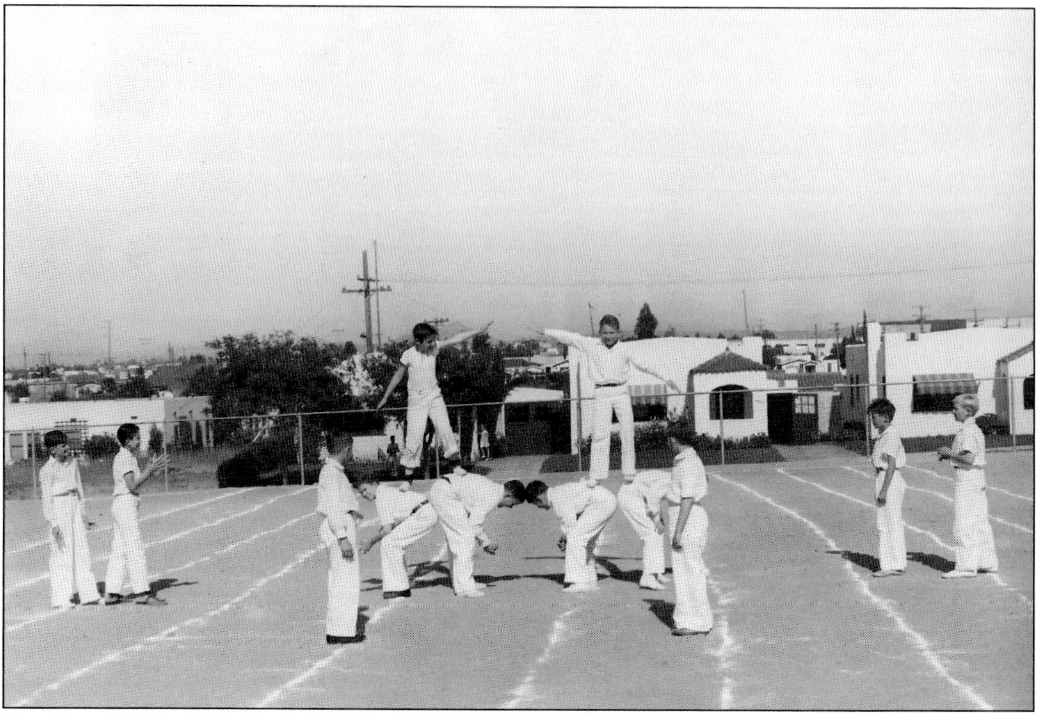

Franklin students are enjoying Play Day on the grounds of Benjamin Franklin School in 1935. Parents would accompany their children on Play Day and join in games such as mother-daughter newspaper races, and the boys, led by teacher Norman Knoles, would demonstrate their gymnastic skills by building a human pyramid. (Courtesy of Franklin Elementary School.)

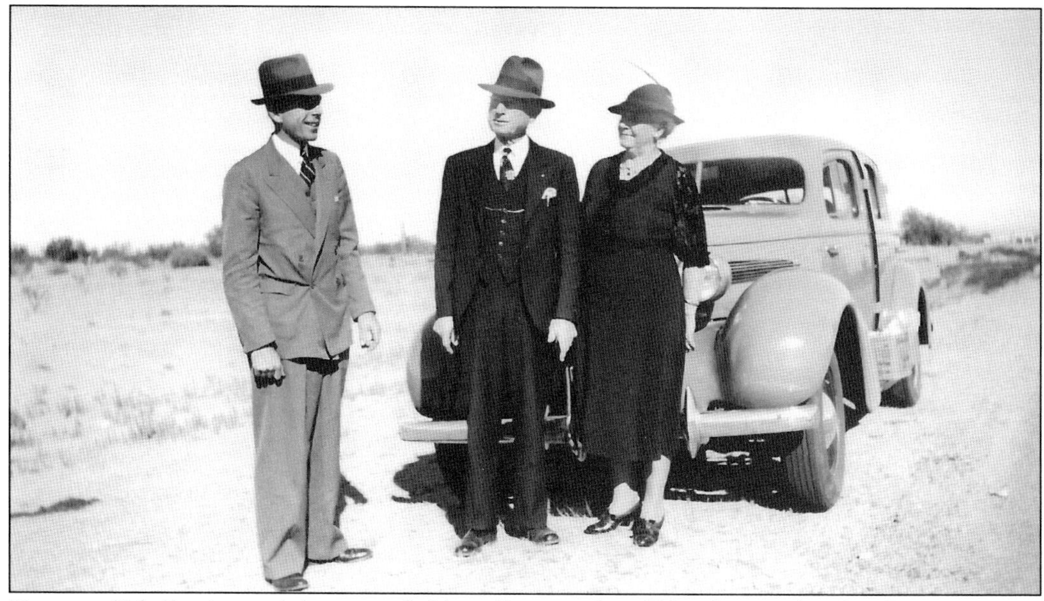

Harry and Ida Perrigo and their two children, Raymond and Hazel, moved to San Diego in 1928. Harry and son Ray launched a house building career, and built their first house in Kensington at 4150 Lymer Drive in 1929. In this photograph from 1939, Ray (left) and his parents are scouting for another empty lot on which to build the next house. (Courtesy of Joyce Gilchrist.)

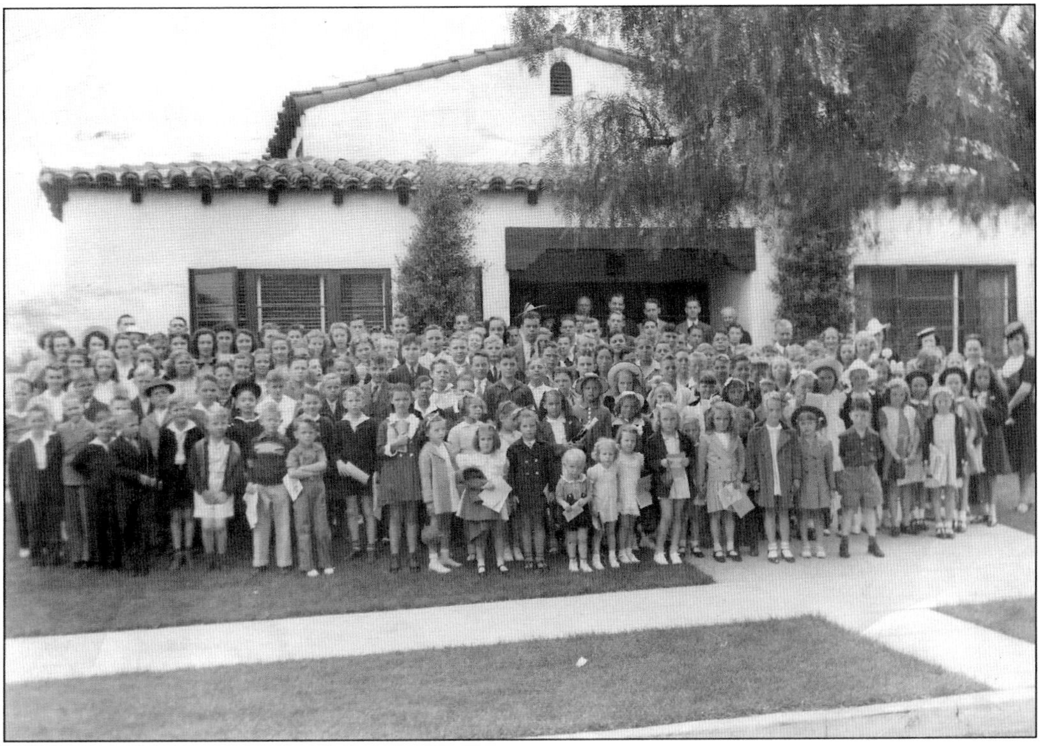

The Kensington Community Church Sunday School class fills the front lawn of the church in this image from 1941. Under the leadership of Dale Van Harten, assisted by Mrs. Stanley Mackie, attendance reached 200 by the end of 1939. (Courtesy of Joyce Gilchrist.)

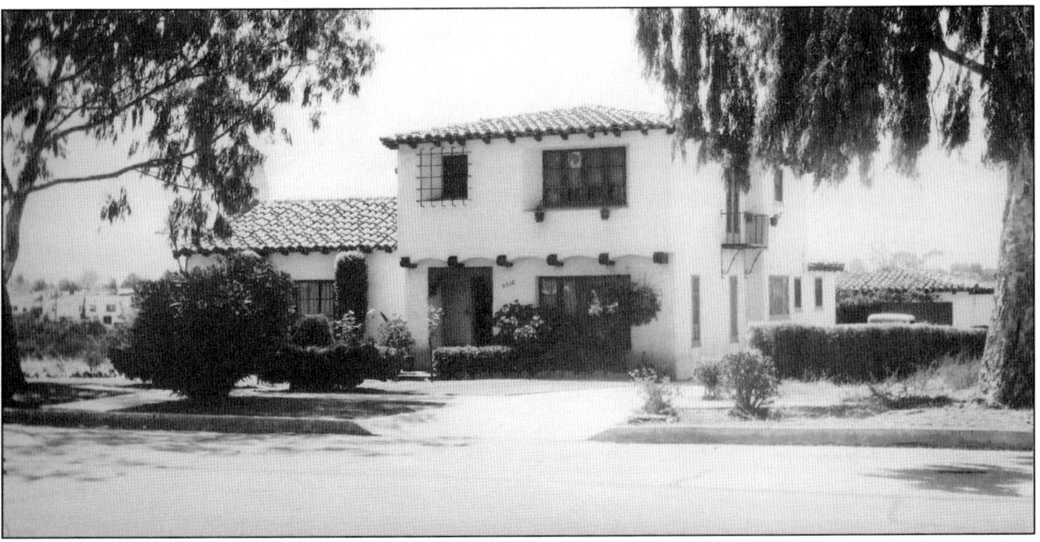

Developer George T. Forbes commissioned master architect Richard S. Requa to design this Spanish Mediterranean–style home at 5318 Canterbury Drive. Constructed by master builder Pear Pearson in 1931, this was one of five model homes used by Forbes to show the potential for building a home in the Kensington Heights Unit No. 3 subdivision. The house was the home of Judge Clarence and Sarah Fitzpatrick Harden and family from 1933 to 2002. The house has been designated as the Forbes-Requa Model House. (Courtesy of Timothy Blood.)

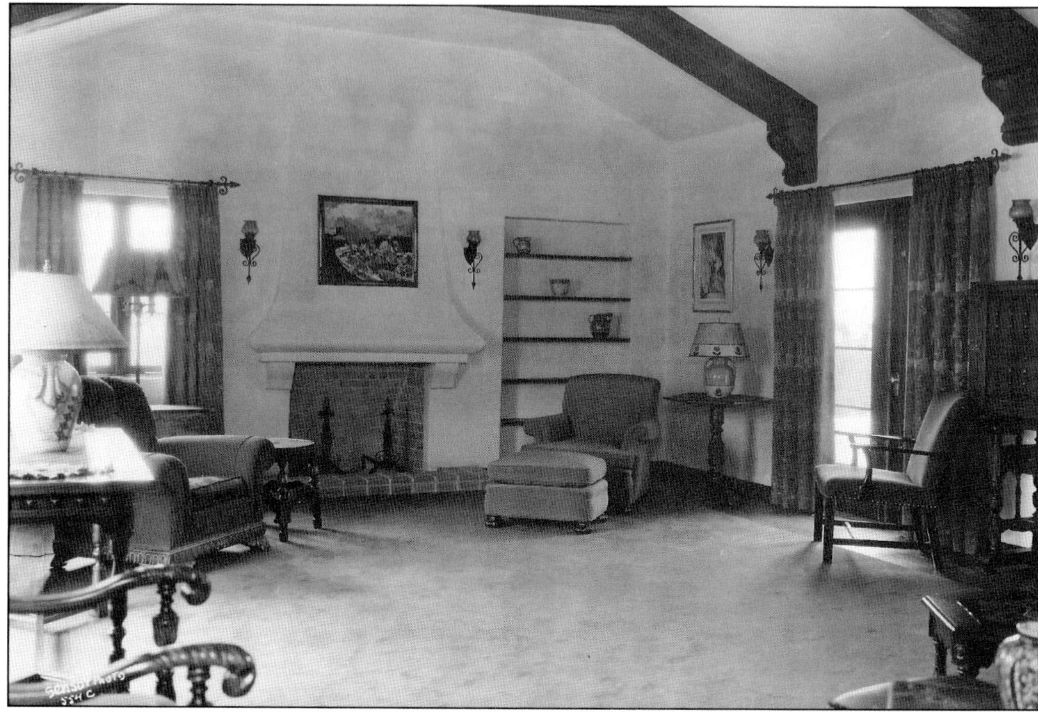

George T. Forbes furnished the model home at 5318 Canterbury Drive and had professional photographs taken for real estate marketing of the Kensington Heights subdivision. In this photograph from 1932, the model home furnishings in the living room complement the original design details, such as the stenciled wooden beams on the ceiling, plastered fireplace mantel, inset bookshelf, and wrought iron curtain rods and lighting sconces. (Courtesy of Timothy Blood.)

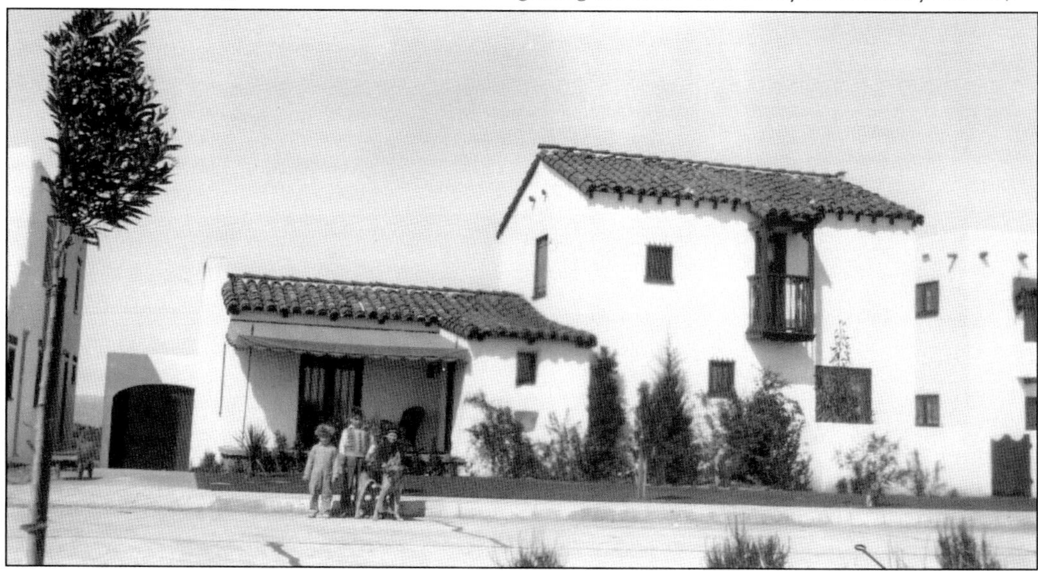

Children stand guard with their German shepherd outside this Spanish Colonial home on Braeburn Road in the late 1920s. The narrow width of the wooden balcony is unusual, as the balconies typically span farther across the front of the home or are offset to one side and wrap around a corner. (Courtesy of Kensington–Normal Heights Branch Library.)

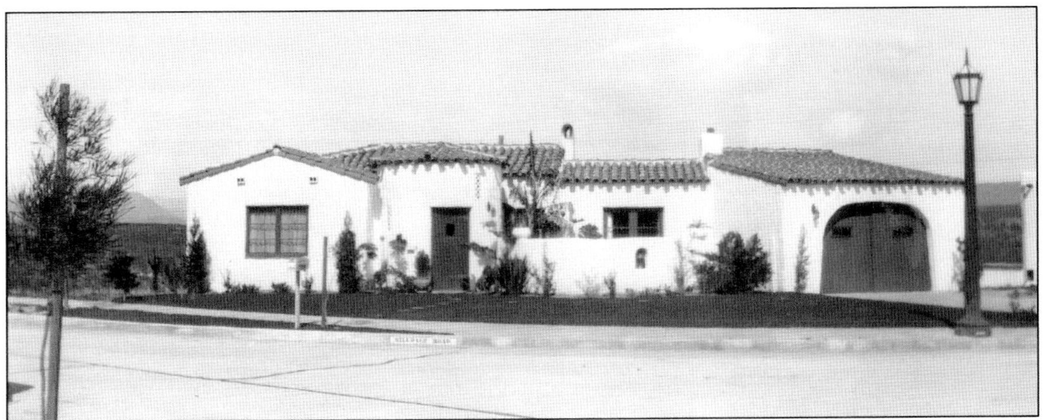

This Spanish Colonial–style home on Hilldale Road, pictured in the late 1920s, has the stucco walls, red tile roof, walled front patio, and turret entryway familiar to Kensington residents; however, its attached front facing garage is slightly unusual for the era. In the 1920s, automobiles were viewed as oily, smelly, and somewhat dangerous; hence, the detached rear garages and side driveways more typically seen in Kensington. (Courtesy of the Kensington–Normal Heights Branch Library.)

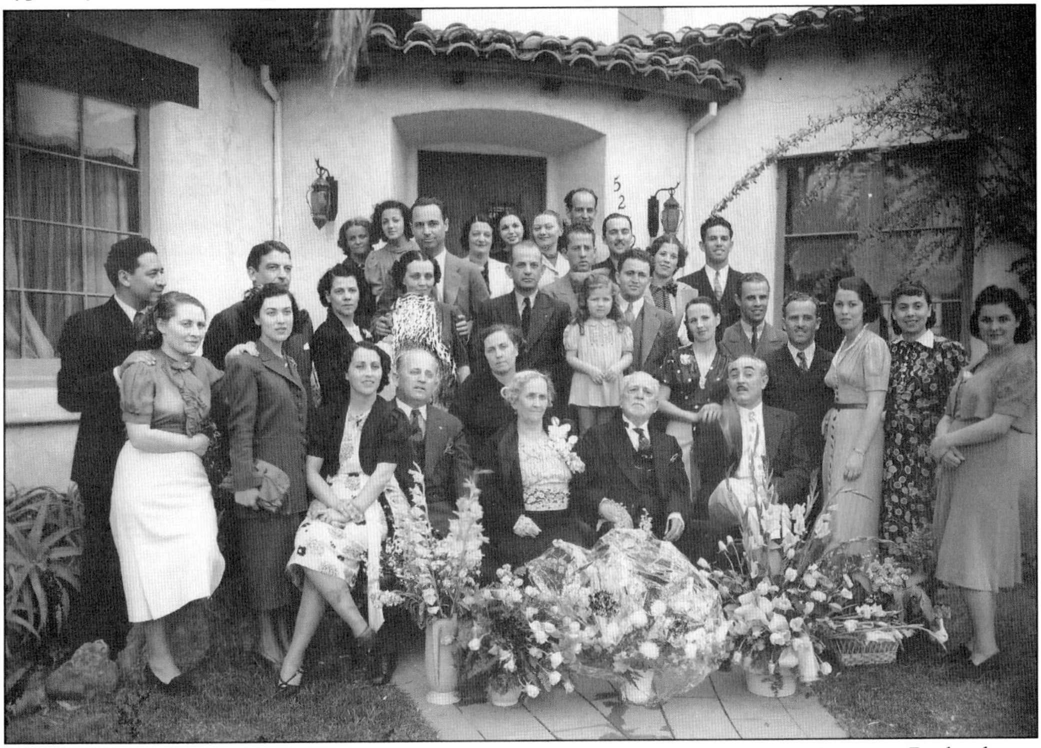

The 50th wedding anniversary of Manuel A. Barbachano and Maria Lucia Ramirez Barbachano in 1939 provided an occasion for the whole family to gather at their home at 5289 Canterbury Drive. The small girl is Gloria Herrera Barbachano (de Amezcua). Her parents, Carlos Daniel Herrera and Maria Lucia Guillermina Barbachano-Ramirez de Herrera, are on the far left, while the honorees are seated front and center. Seated next to Manuel Sr. is their son Manuel Jr. The younger Manuel was president of the Border Electric and Telephone Company, built the Tijuana-Ensenada paved highway, constructed a large radio station at Rosarito Beach, and built the Rosarito Beach Hotel in 1929. (Courtesy of Cammi Drevo-Amezcua.)

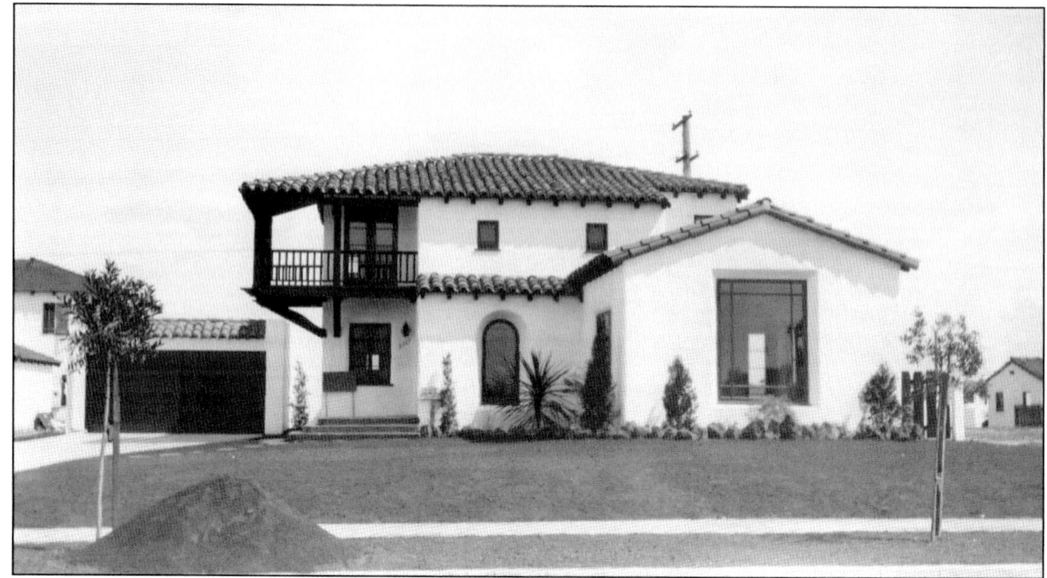

Originally a model home named "Casa Descanso," Spanish for "The House of Repose," the Monterey-style wooden corner balcony of this Marlborough Drive residence is cantilevered, an uncommon variation. The ground-level arched window and focal window at right are inset into the stucco walls to mimic the look of the thick adobe walls seen on California's missions and other early buildings. (Courtesy of San Diego History Center.)

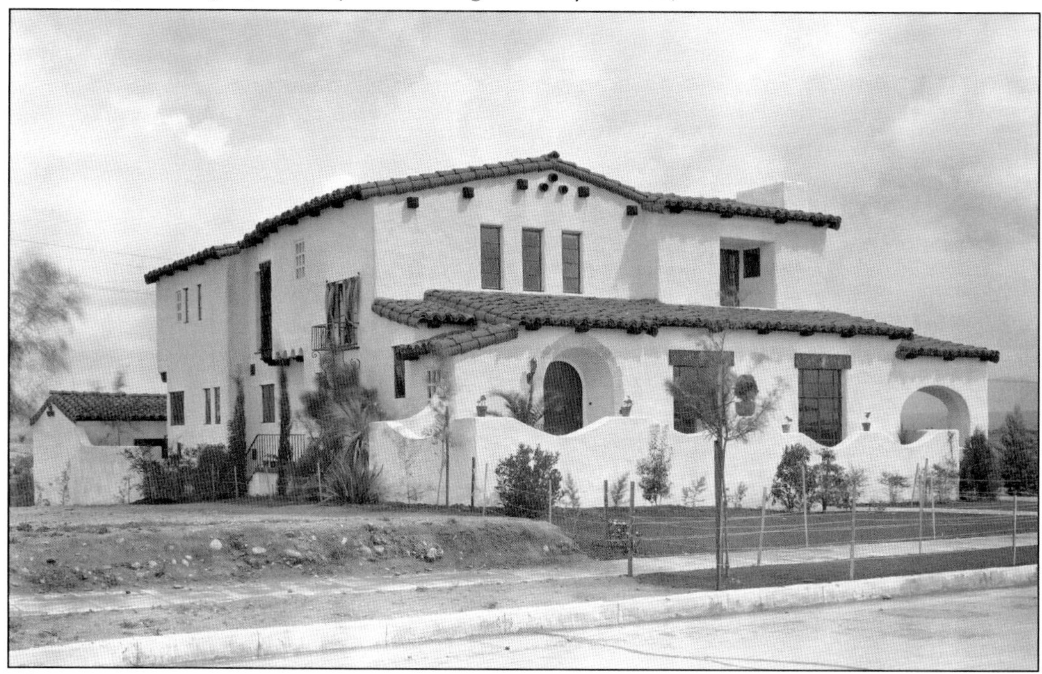

This grand residence features all the hallmarks of the Spanish Colonial style, including the clay tile roof, stucco walls, and a deep inset arched door opening. The front patio is surrounded with an unusual undulating stucco wall. As in Spain, outdoor living space was incorporated into many San Diego Spanish-style homes because of its Mediterranean climate. (Courtesy of San Diego History Center.)

Originally from Iowa, Augustus and Laura Rehkopf were early settlers of El Centro, California, where they owned hundreds of acres. After retiring from ranching, their Kensington home at 4302 Adams Avenue was built by Pear Pearson in 1931. The couple frequently traveled to El Centro to manage the Rehkopf Building, a commercial property they owned. It still stands in El Centro's downtown area. (Courtesy of Kate Miller.)

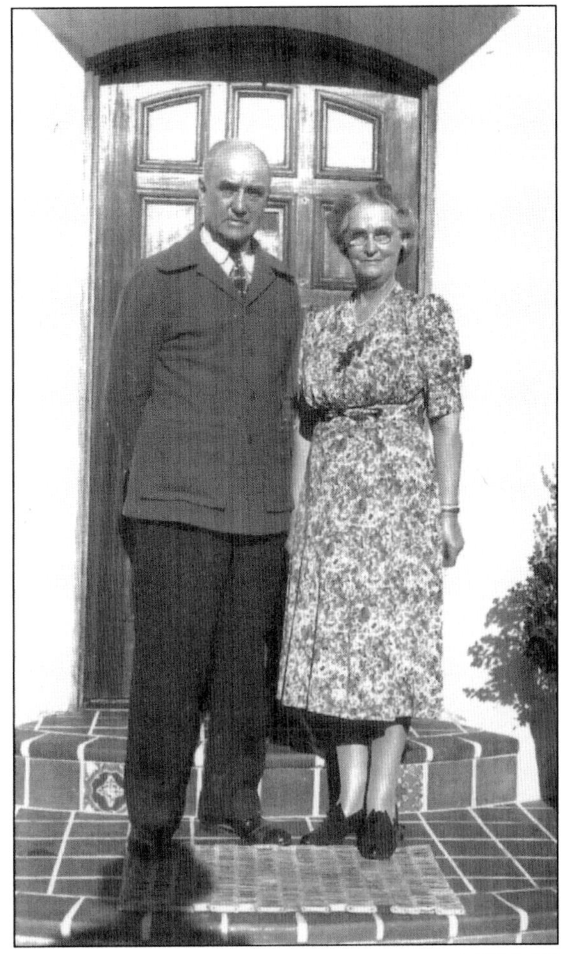

Pictured shortly after completion in 1928, the home at 5150 East Bedford Drive was originally utilized as a model home named "Casa Grande" (Spanish for "Big House") before being occupied by Fred and Louise Annable in 1929 and 1930. During that time, Fred served as president of the San Diego and Arizona Railway, which was founded by local entrepreneur John D. Spreckels in 1906. (Courtesy of Kensington–Normal Heights Branch Library.)

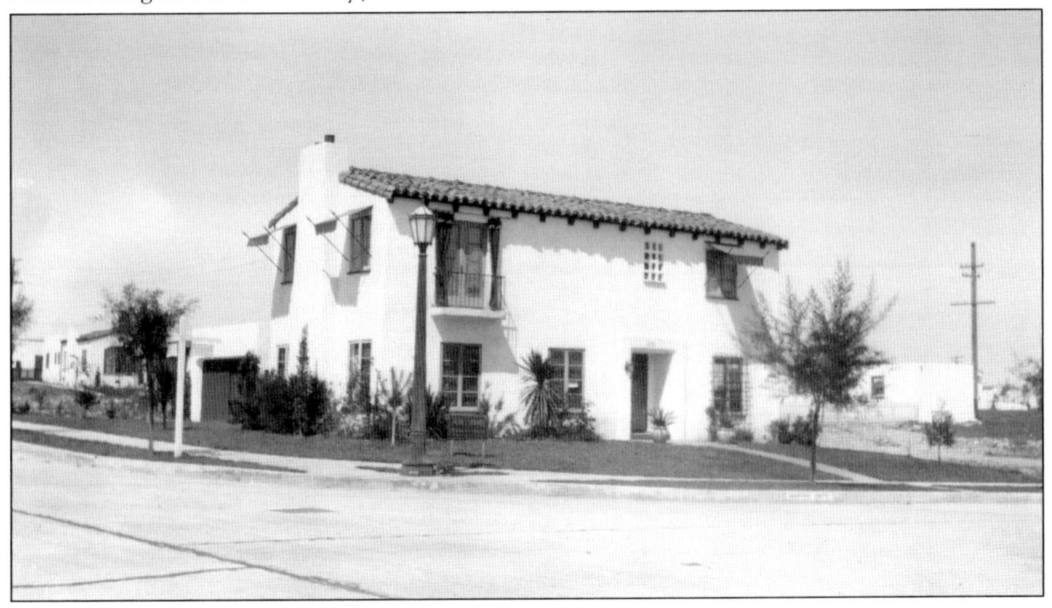

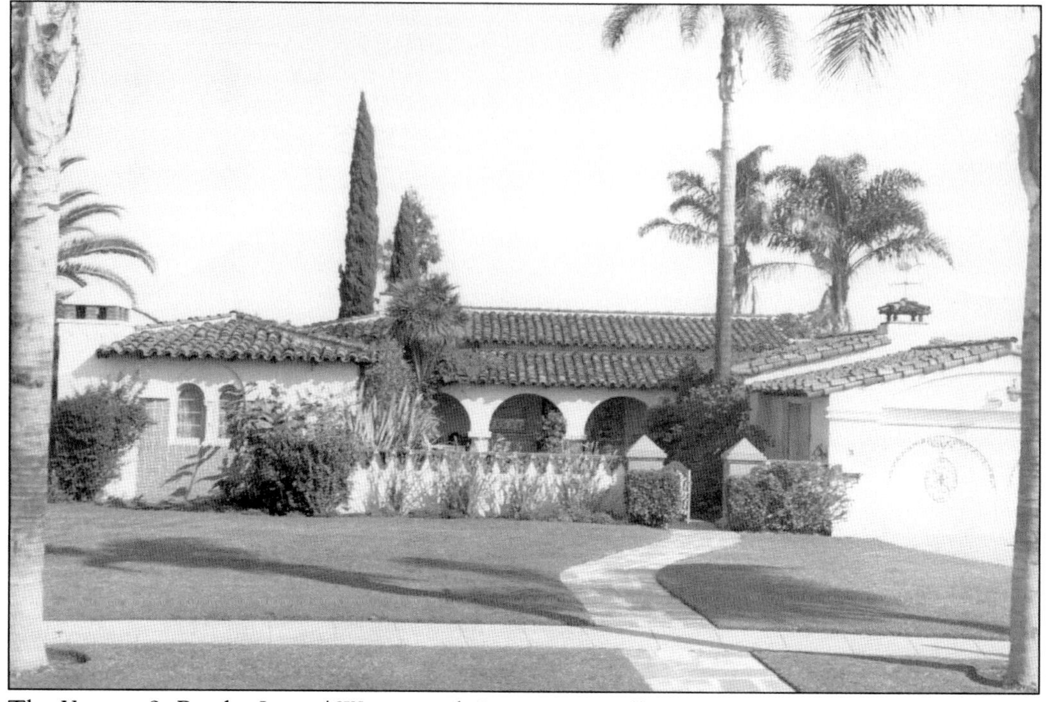

The Yngvar & Bertha Laws / Wayne and Corinne McAllister House was built in 1931 at the east end of Ridgeway. Designed by master architects Wayne and Corinne McAllister, and built by Ova F. Eckles, this Spanish Eclectic–style house was home to many notable people, among them Alphonse A. Burnand Jr., who used the house as his townhome during the period when he was developing Borrego Springs. Wayne McAllister's reputation grew after the couple moved to Los Angeles, and he is credited with designing the Brown Derby, the Pig n' Whistle, the prototype for the Kentucky Fried Chicken chain, and the famous McDonald's golden arches. In Las Vegas, he designed the Flamingo Hotel and the Desert Inn, among others. (Courtesy of San Diego History Center.)

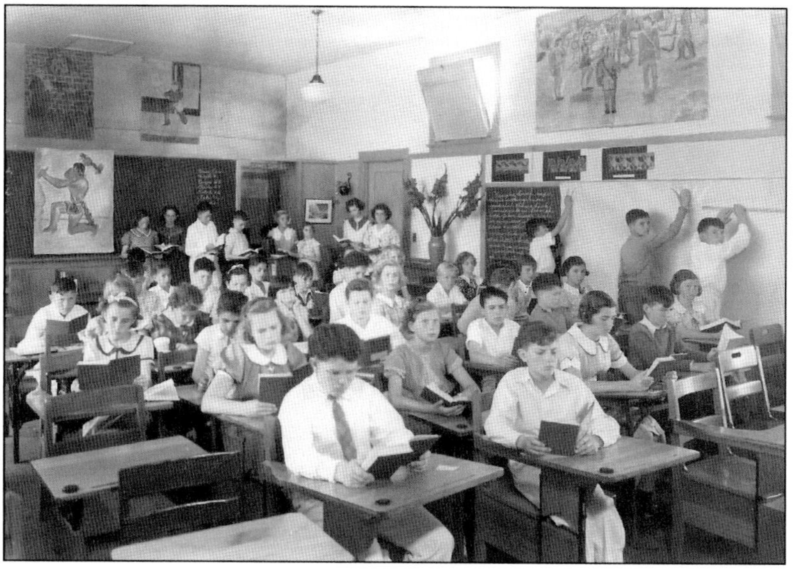

In 1935, the teachers at Benjamin Franklin School created a study unit on the upcoming California Pacific International Exposition held in Balboa Park. Students studied native cultures of the area and created tabletop displays for the exposition. (Courtesy of Franklin Elementary School.)

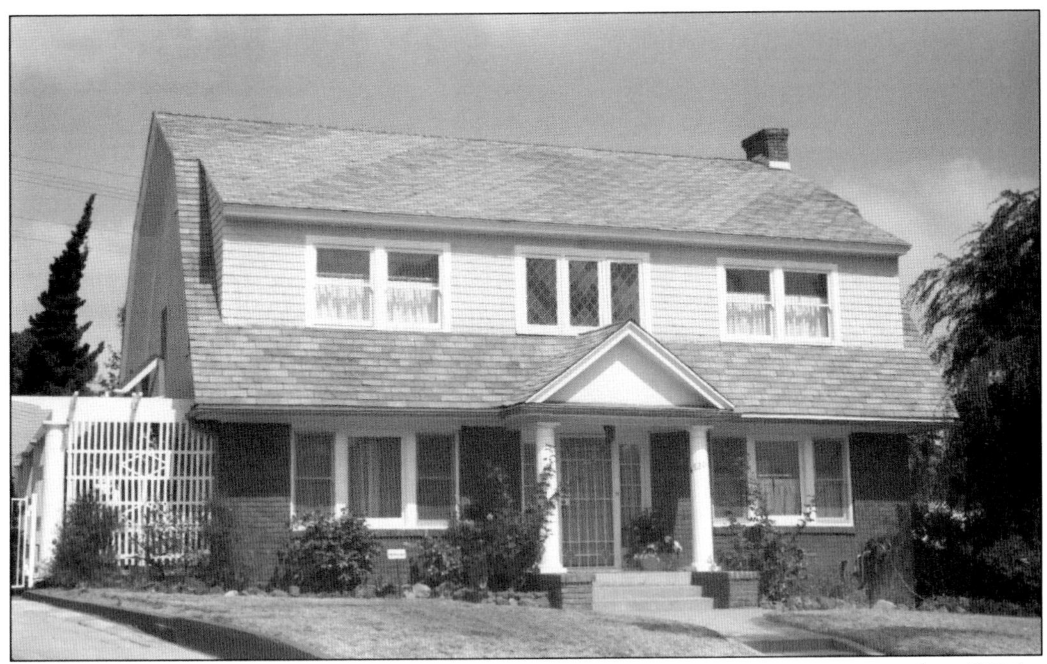

This Dutch Colonial Revival–style house at 4720 Van Dyke Avenue was constructed in 1929 by master builder Lewis Henry Dodge, who had moved his family from Rhode Island to Kensington Park in 1923. His son Edward remembered driving the old plank road across the desert from Yuma in a 1922 Dodge Touring car. Lewis Dodge built in a variety of styles, including Tudor, Spanish Colonial Revival, and Mission Revival. Dodge had a pattern of building a house and then moving his family into it while building the next house, and he built and lived in several other houses in Kensington, including another two-story Dutch Colonial Revival on Biona Drive. Lewis Dodge died in 1934, and his ashes were scattered near a memorial plaque located on a bench in Balboa Park, just west of the Botanical Gardens. (Courtesy of San Diego History Center.)

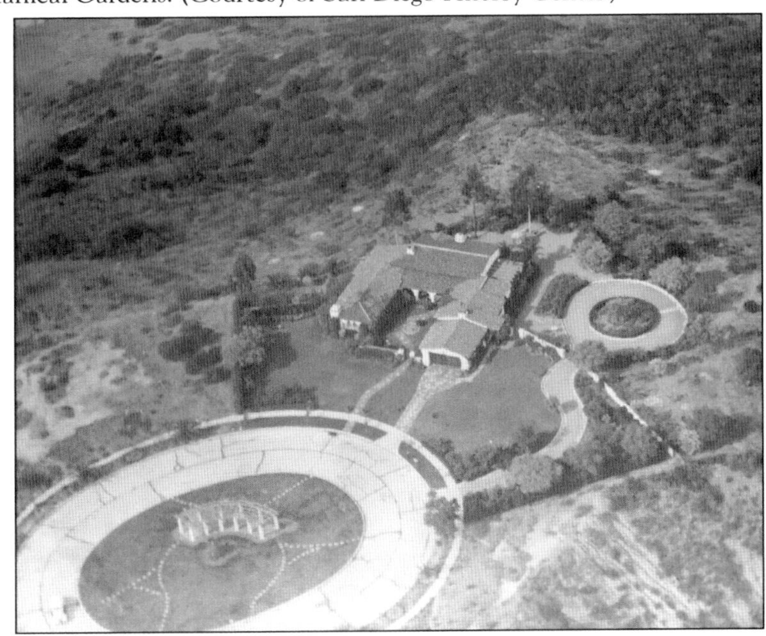

Yngvar and Bertha Laws, wealthy retirees from Minnesota, hired architect Wayne McAllister to design their Spanish Colonial residence at 4357 Ridgeway Drive, which was constructed in 1931. The couple purchased three lots on which to build, with the southernmost lot used as a rose garden. (Courtesy of San Diego History Center.)

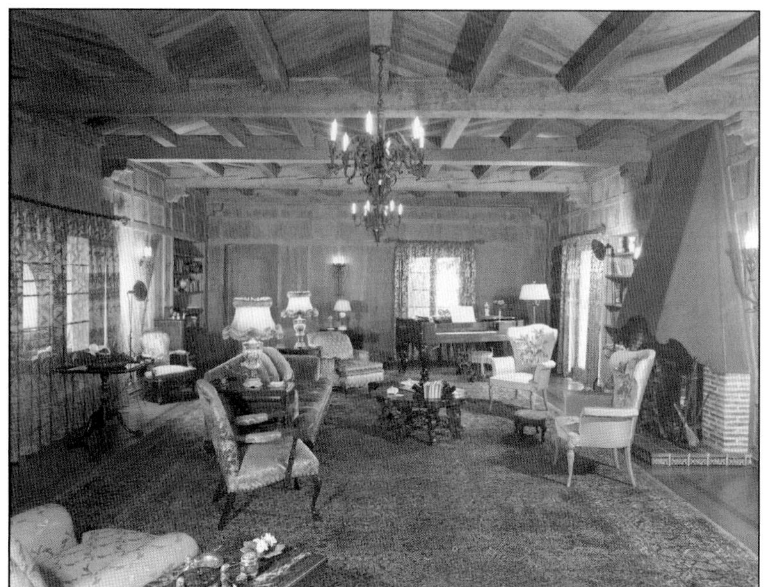

The great room of 4357 Ridgeway Drive was constructed of redwood, with rustic exposed wooden beams and herringbone patterned ceiling, which is contrasted by classical hanging chandeliers and wall sconces. The fireplace hood is made of hand-hammered copper. (Courtesy of San Diego History Center.)

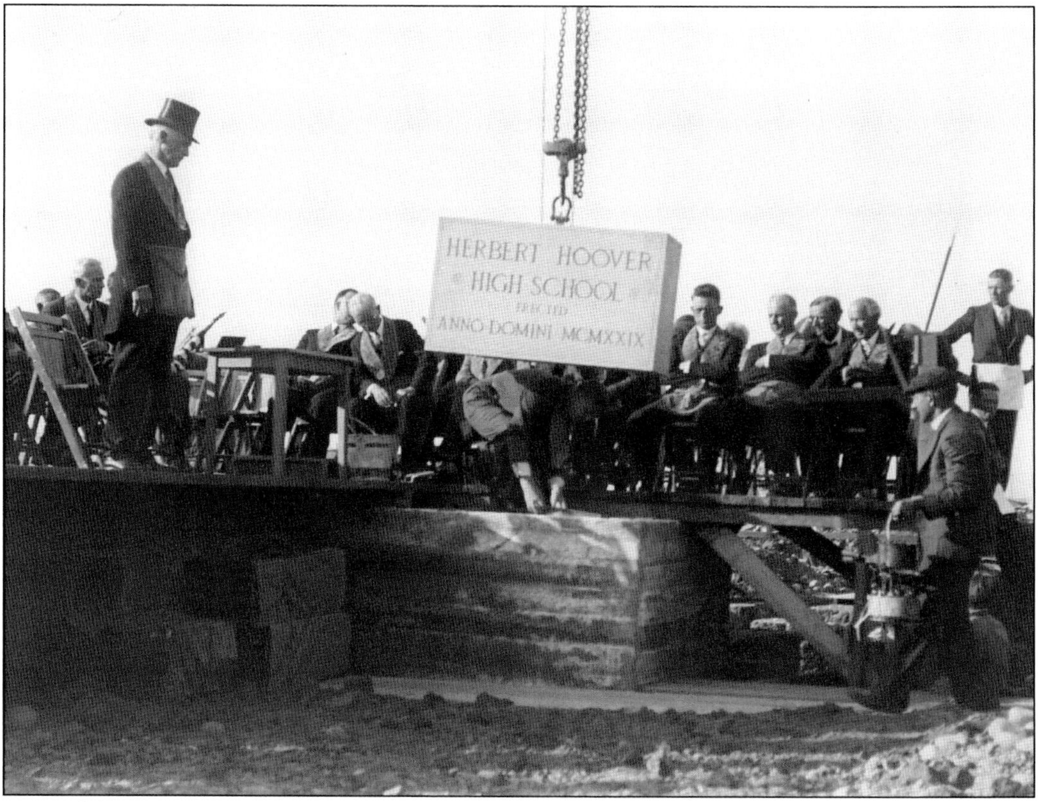

In an elaborate Masonic ceremony led by California grand master John Stewart Ross (standing left), construction of Herbert Hoover High School officially began on October 26, 1929. The crowd of nearly 1,000 watched as documents from the board of education were placed into a copper casket, which was sealed before the granite cornerstone, pictured above, was laid on top. (Courtesy of Herbert Hoover High School.)

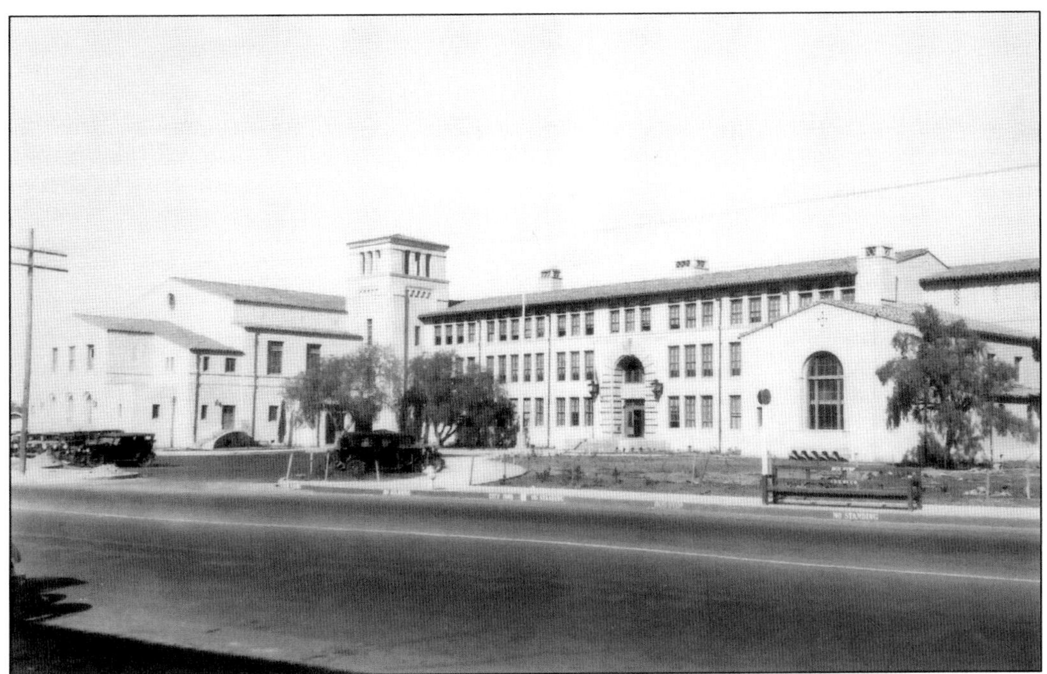

Herbert Hoover High School, pictured three years after its 1930 opening, served students from Kensington, Talmadge, and surrounding neighborhoods. A *San Diego Union* article from June 1, 1930, quotes area developer Roy Lichty as saying that the school gave these neighborhoods "the most complete and diversified educational facilities enjoyed by any section of the city." The first graduating class, in 1932, had 164 students. (Courtesy of Herbert Hoover High School.)

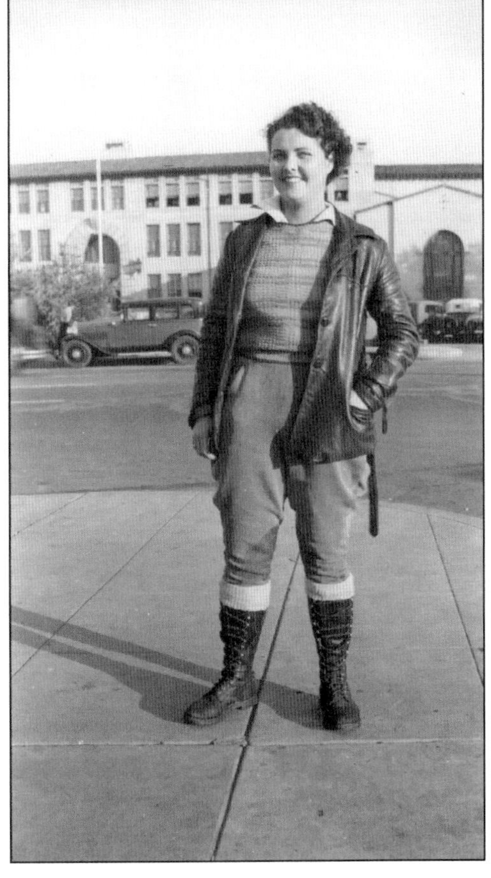

Dressed for a wintertime student field trip to Pine Valley in 1935, Marie Forbes stands in front of Herbert Hoover High School. Her father, George Forbes, was a prominent real estate agent and developer of Kensington Heights. Born in Montana, Marie spent her youth in Santa Monica, California, before moving to Kensington with her parents and siblings in the early 1930s. (Courtesy of Herbert Hoover High School.)

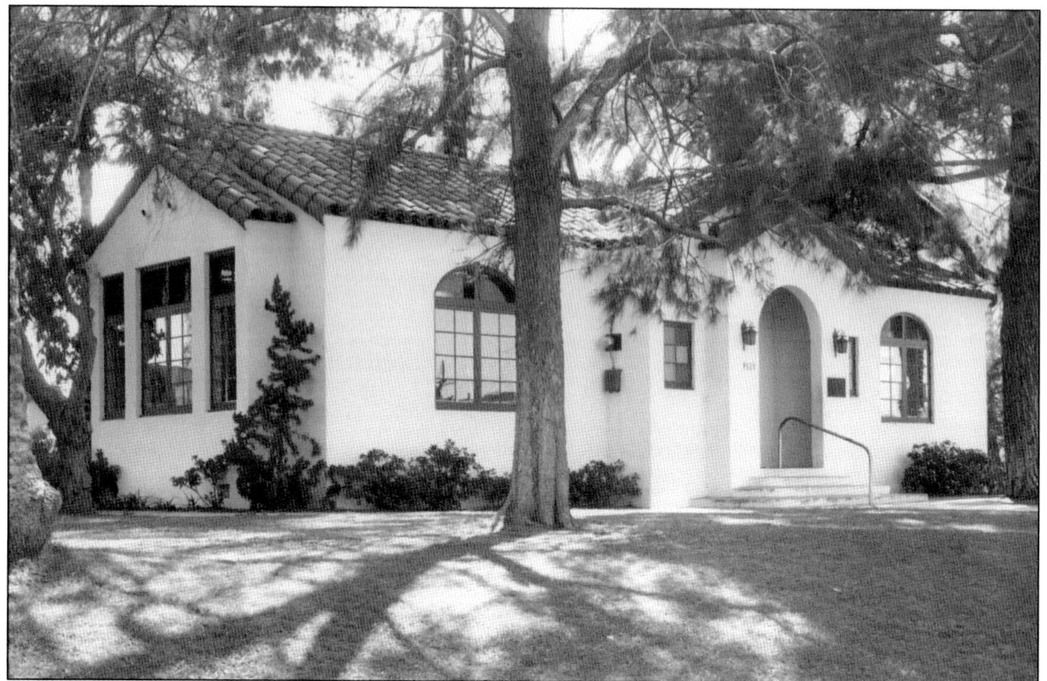

Sometime around 1935, the county constructed the Kensington–Normal Heights branch library on the grounds of the Pleasure Park, eradicating the landscaped pond. The style of this building reflected that of the residences being built throughout Kensington at this time. (Courtesy of Robert Sedlock.)

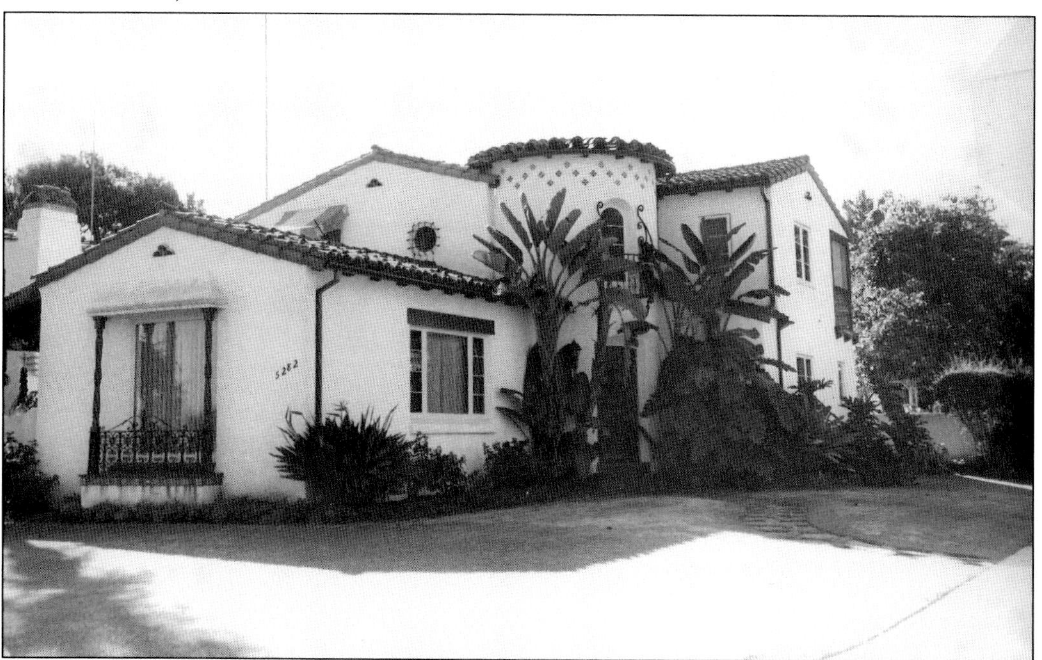

Built in 1927, this grand Spanish Colonial house features a large turret with inlaid tile detail at the top. The first occupants were Paul O. Vance, the president of Mission Pipe and Supply Company; his wife, Hazel; and their three children. (Courtesy of Estelle Milch.)

Four

WAR CHANGES EVERYTHING

By the early 1940s, the economy in San Diego began to improve from the dark days of the Great Depression. Construction in Kensington resumed, but residential designs had shifted from the elaborate Spanish and Tudor styles of the 1920s, and open lots were filled with more modest homes, many with traditional Colonial details. Residences in the sleek but short-lived Streamline Moderne style, popular in the late 1930s to early 1940s, were also constructed, with a pair built at the eastern end of Middlesex Drive.

The bombing of Pearl Harbor on December 7, 1941, brought several changes to Kensington. Herbert Hoover High School's roster of war casualties includes several students who left school to join the war effort. Women entered the workforce in unprecedented numbers, often employed as nurses and in local factories manufacturing airplanes and other essential items for the troops.

San Diego was rapidly transformed as servicemen and women from across the country streamed into local military bases, all within an easy commute from Kensington. San Diego's population swelled from approximately 203,000 people in 1940 to 308,000 by 1943. Residential house construction slowed dramatically after Pearl Harbor as the country utilized men and material for battle, resulting in a housing shortage. Renting to soldiers, contractors, and their families was encouraged, and many patriotic residents responded by converting detached garages to small apartments. Victory gardens, including one at Franklin Elementary School, were planted across Kensington.

After the war, numerous service members and contract workers who grew to love San Diego decided to stay permanently. Kensington was an ideal community and became home to several significant military leaders. Utilizing military surplus relocated from Camp Callan, the Kensington Community Church built its sanctuary in 1947. The Adams Avenue electric streetcar line ceased operating in 1949 and was replaced with bus service.

Despite the military's demobilization, San Diego's economy boomed. Home prices increased dramatically in the postwar era and the last remaining lots in Kensington were developed, finally completing the vision of the subdivision's original designers.

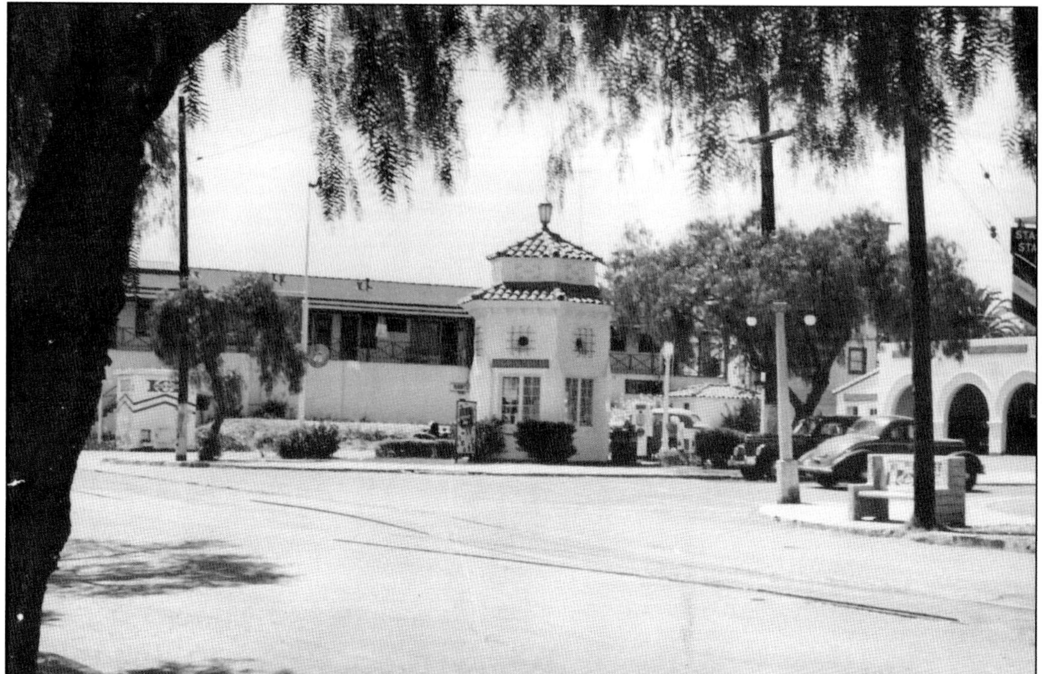

Al Bunnell's service station was located on the northwest corner of Adams Avenue and Marlborough Drive. In this photograph from the late 1940s, many original features of Kensington Park are visible, including the pepper trees that had been planted in the parkways in 1910, and double-headed street lamps. The streetcar tracks are visible running up the middle of Adams Avenue. (Courtesy of Margaret McCann.)

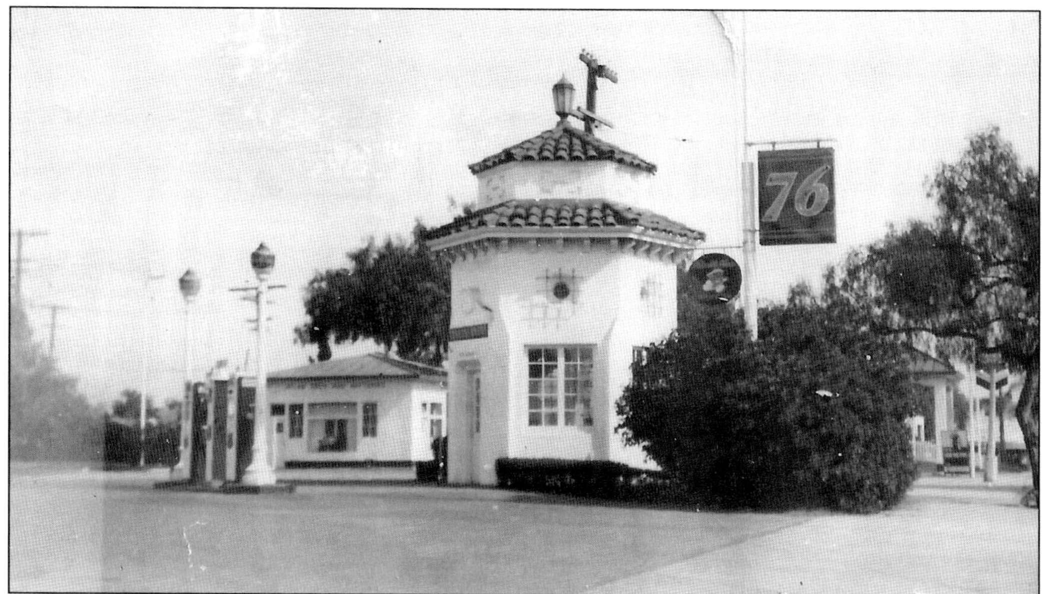

A closer look at Bunnell's service station shows that the builder emulated many of the features of the Spanish-style houses throughout the neighborhood, with clay tile roof, stucco finish, and empire-style lantern on the top. At one time, Kensington had five gas stations, although none remain today. (Courtesy of Margaret McCann.)

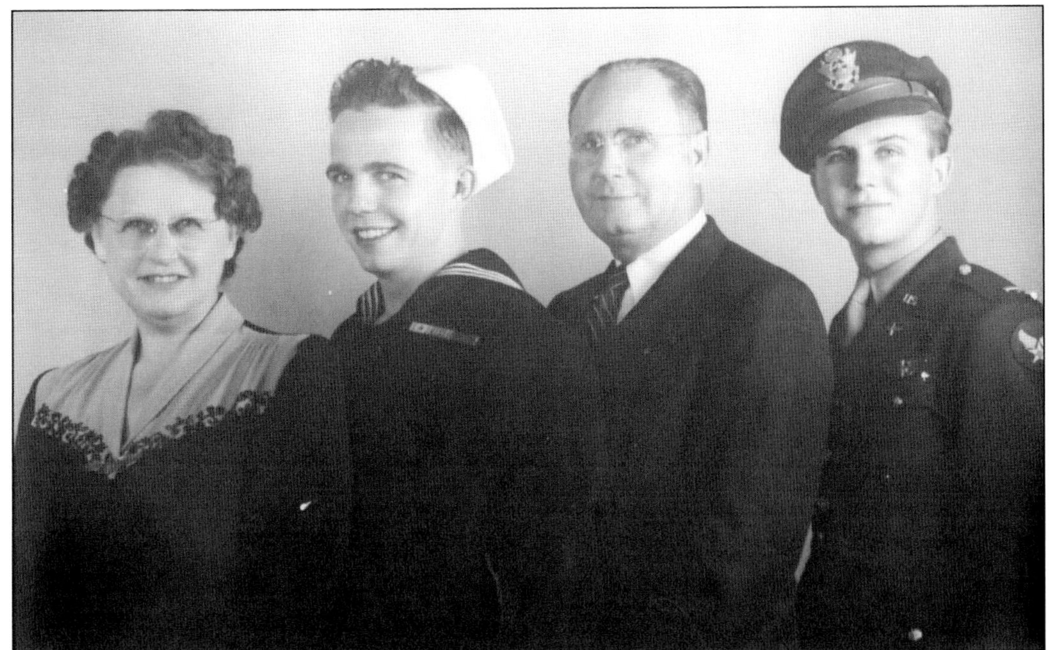

Many Kensington residents were called for duty in World War II. Leona Beilstein (left) and her husband, John (third from left), had sons in the military during World War II. Howard (second from left) served in the Navy while his brother Paul (right) was a lieutenant in the Army Air Corps. Both men returned safely and resided at 4952 Marlborough Drive with their parents before marrying and starting families after the war. (Courtesy of Debra Beilstein.)

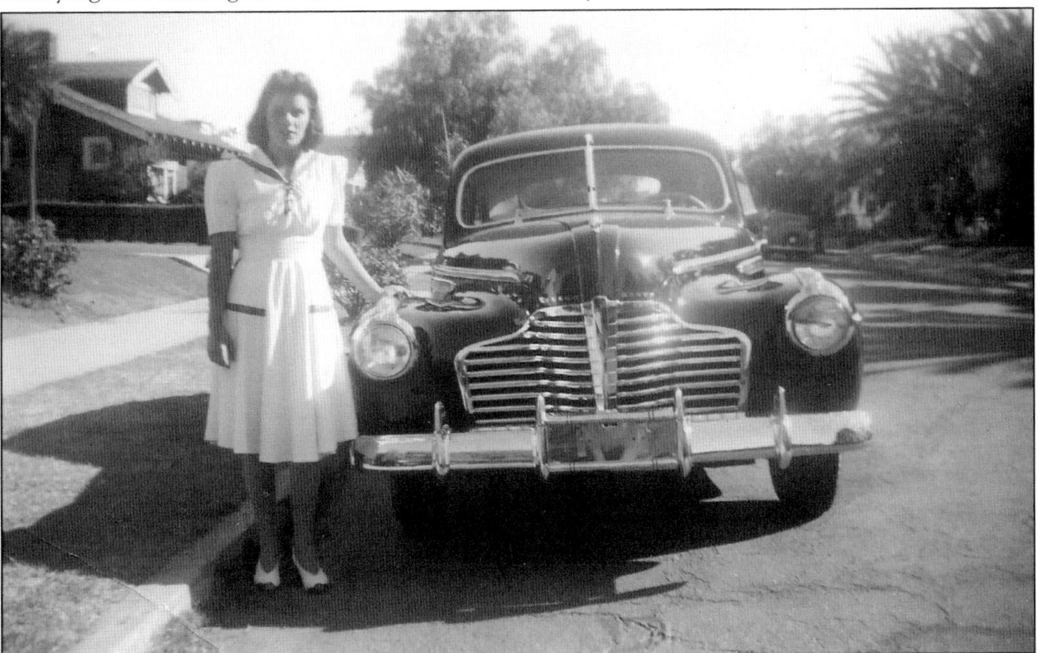

Eighteen-year-old Betty Anderson poses next to a new 1941 Buick parked in front of the family home on Edgeware Road. In a few years, the streetcar tracks would be ripped out, and cars became a necessity. (Courtesy of Don Generoli.)

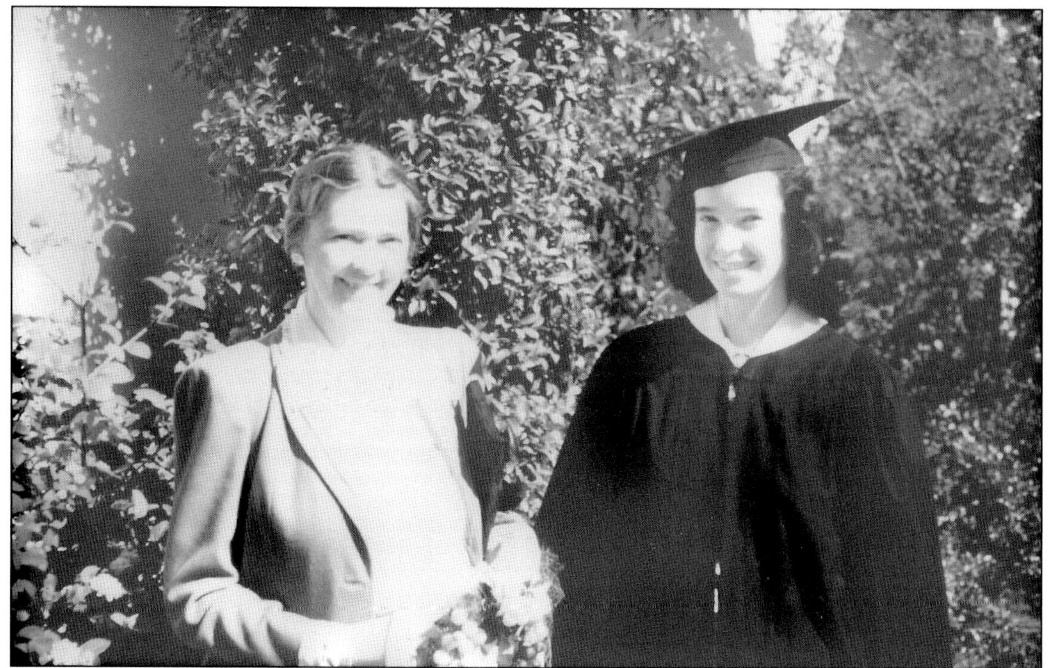

Alberta Marjory Dennstedt (right) and her mother, Cleveland Dennstedt, are pictured in 1942 on the occasion of Alberta's graduation from San Diego State College. Alberta was six years old when the Dennstedt family arrived in San Diego in April 1926. She recalled the trip west from Iowa, when the family drove their 1920 Franklin automobile over the infamous plank road across the Glamis sand dunes in Imperial County. (Courtesy of Larry Dennstedt.)

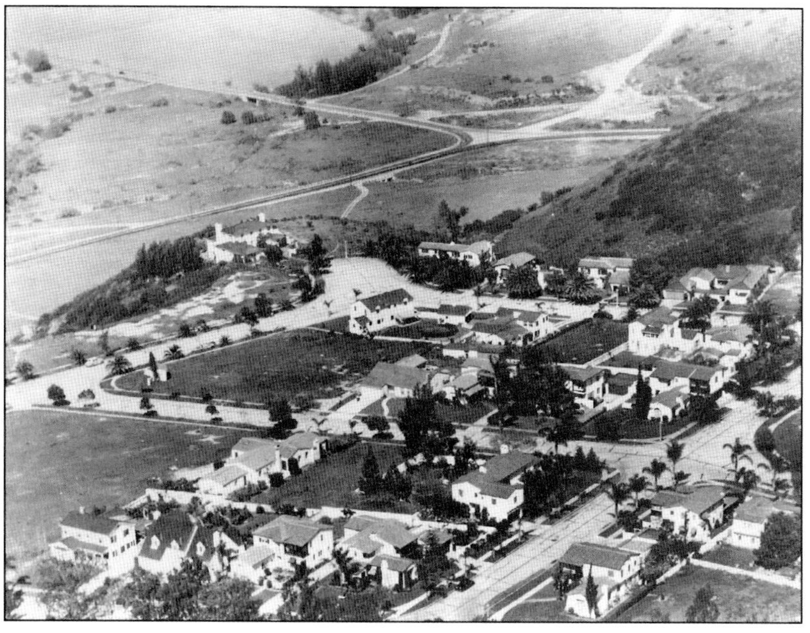

This aerial photograph of the Kensington Heights Unit No. 3 subdivision was taken sometime in the 1940s when the housing style was primarily Spanish Eclectic. Mission Valley, which was still an undeveloped agricultural area, can be seen in the background. (Courtesy of Richard Corder.)

Shoppers line up for the Kensington Community Church rummage sale in 1953. The church's Women's Guild held its first rummage sale in 1940 to raise funds for renovations and to establish a Sunday school building. The sale became tradition, raising proceeds for a variety of causes, including construction of additions to the church and for philanthropic efforts in the community. (Courtesy of Kensington Community Church.)

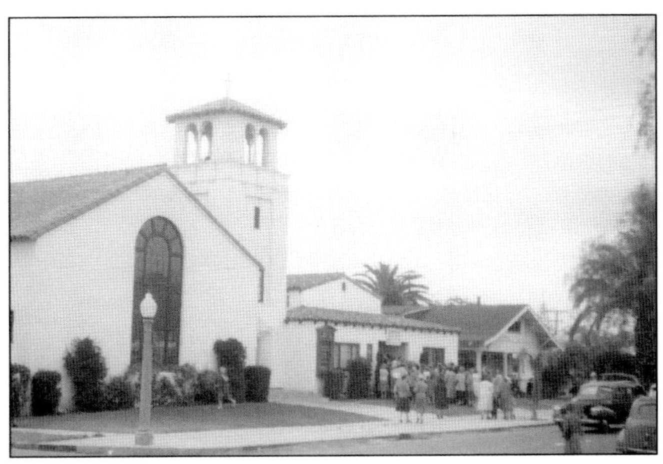

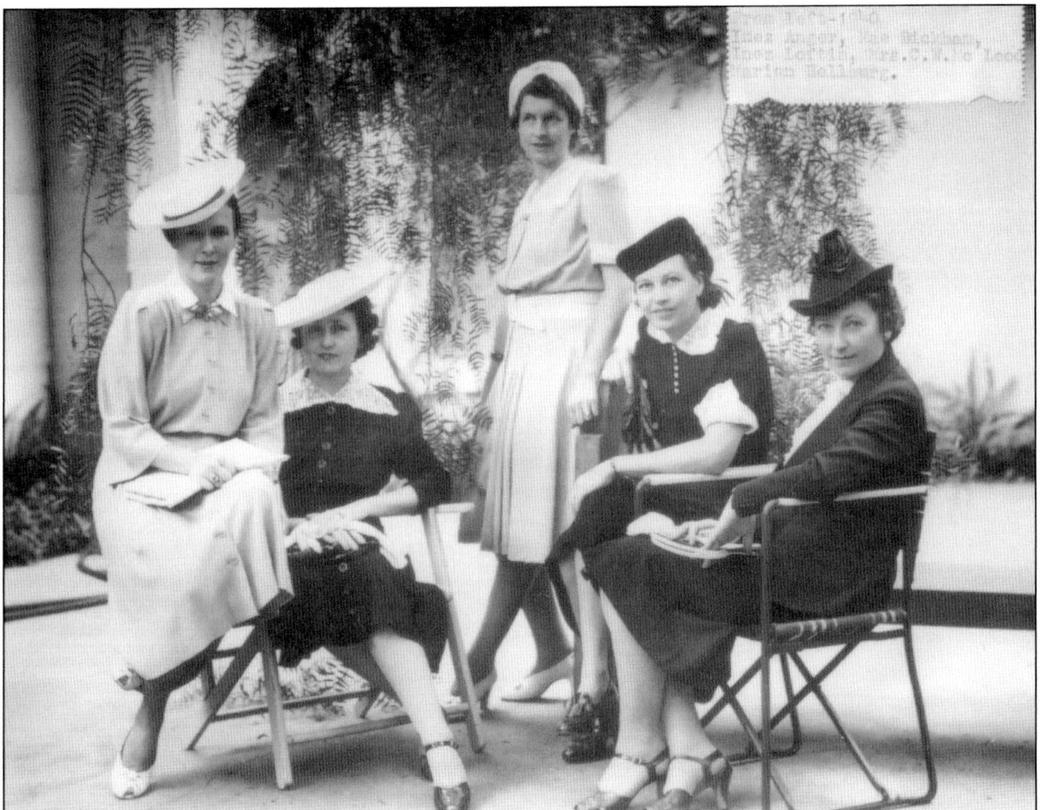

Officers of the newly formed Kensington Community Church Women's Guild are pictured in 1940. The guild was responsible for positively impacting many in Kensington and greater San Diego. They were instrumental in establishing a Sunday school at the church and pushed for the construction of a church recreation building for local youth. During World War II, they assembled care packages for wounded soldiers recovering in area hospitals. (Courtesy of Kensington Community Church.)

UNITED STATES OF AMERICA
OFFICE OF PRICE ADMINISTRATION

218453 EH

WAR RATION BOOK No. 3

Void if altered

NOT VALID WITHOUT STAMP

Identification of person to whom issued: PRINT IN FULL

E. R. Havens
(First name) (Middle name) (Last name)

Street number or rural route 4691 E. Talamadge Dr.

City or post office San Diego State California

AGE	SEX	WEIGHT	HEIGHT	OCCUPATION
32	Female	114 Lbs.	5 Ft. 4 In.	Housewife

SIGNATURE Evelyn Read Havens
(Person to whom book is issued. If such person is unable to sign because of age or incapacity, another may sign in his behalf.)

WARNING
This book is the property of the United States Government. It is unlawful to sell it to any other person, or to use it or permit anyone else to use it, except to obtain rationed goods in accordance with regulations of the Office of Price Administration. Any person who finds a lost War Ration Book must return it to the War Price and Rationing Board which issued it. Persons who violate rationing regulations are subject to $10,000 fine or imprisonment, or both.

LOCAL BOARD ACTION

Issued by .... (Local board number) (Date)

Street address ....

City .... State ....

(Signature of issuing officer)

OPA Form No. R-130

Book 4

Americans in World War II were issued a series of ration books that allowed the holder to purchase scarce food items such as sugar, meat, cooking oil, and canned goods. When one of these items was purchased, a stamp was torn from the book, and when a person's ration stamps were used up for the month, they could not buy any more of that type of food. Evelyn Havens held the family's ration book in 1942, which contained such advice as, "If you don't need it, don't buy it." (Courtesy of Franklin Elementary School.)

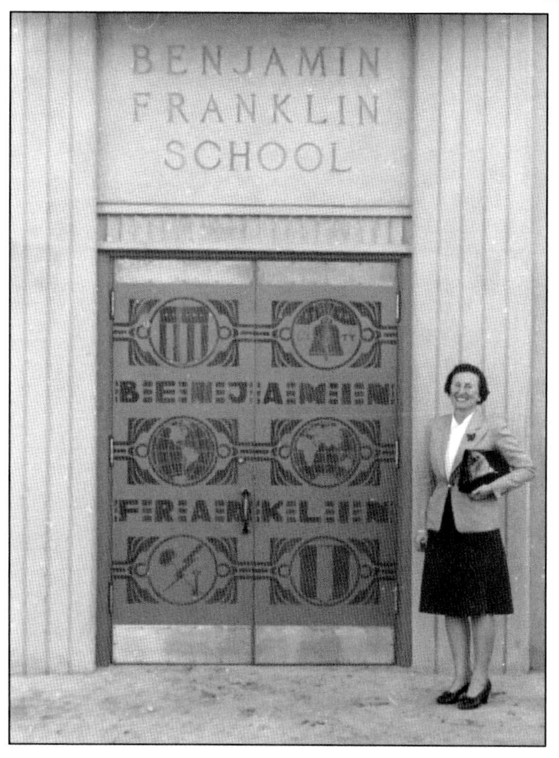

Benjamin Franklin School principal Louise Weller stands next to the school's doors, carved with symbols representing Benjamin Franklin, including lightning striking a kite string in this image from 1941. Miss Weller obtained her teacher's training at the San Diego Normal School in University Heights and was principal at Normal Heights Elementary School prior to becoming principal at Franklin. (Courtesy of Franklin Elementary School.)

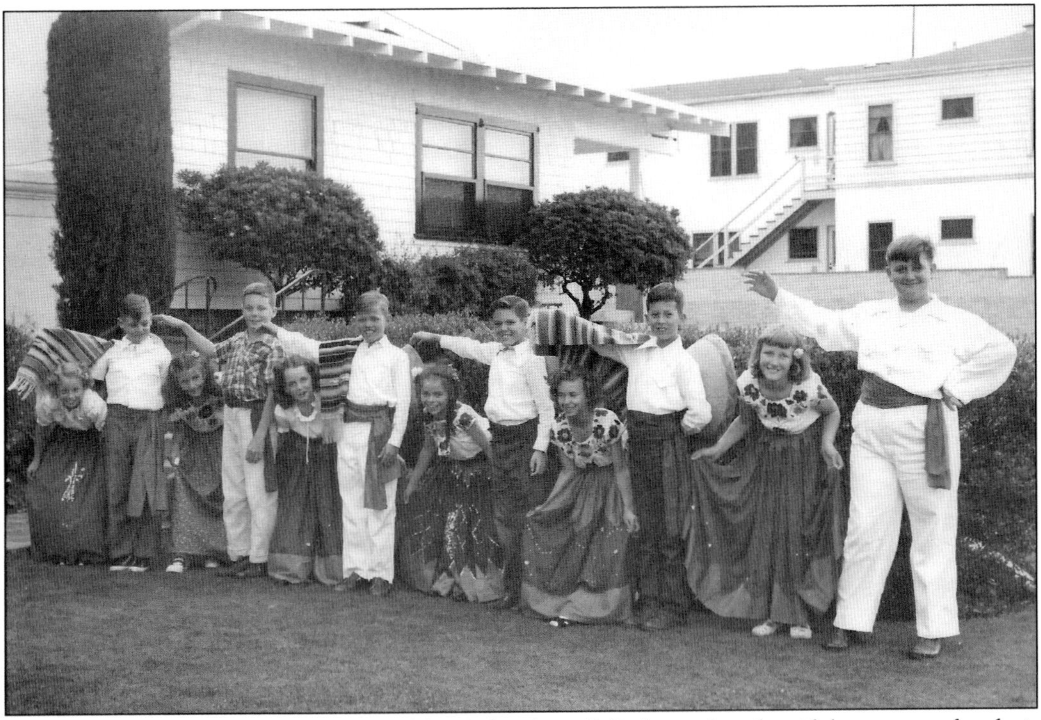

The fourth graders at Benjamin Franklin School in 1949 dressed in fanciful costumes for their studies of Mexico. The tall lad on the right is Victor Buono, who lived at 4317 Alder Drive. Buono would go on to fame as an actor, first at the Old Globe Theater, where he was spotted by a talent scout from Warner Bros. Studios in his role as Falstaff. He appeared in numerous Hollywood movies, including *What Ever Happened to Baby Jane*, for which he received a nomination for the Academy Award for Best Supporting Actor. His many television roles included playing King Tut on the series *Batman*. (Courtesy of Franklin Elementary School.)

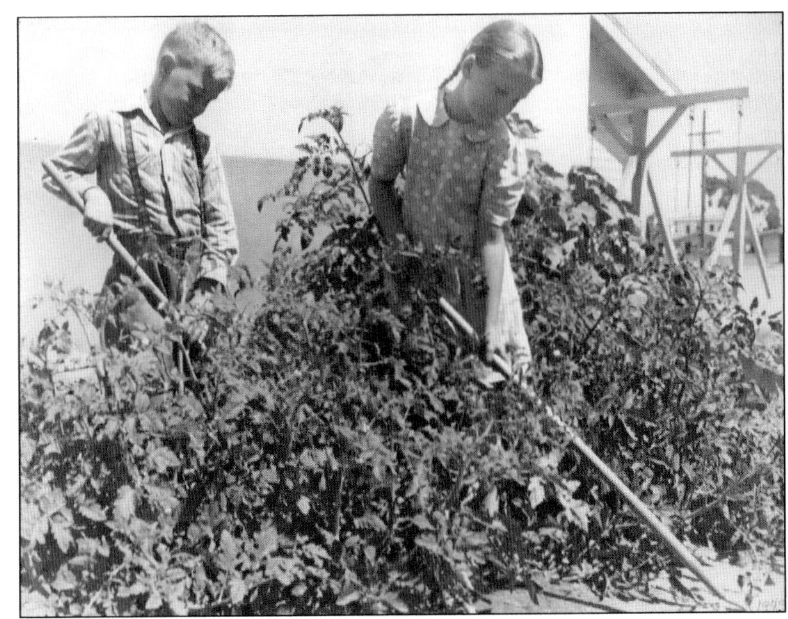

During World War II, Americans across the country planted Victory Gardens to help augment their rationed food goods and to support the war effort. The children at Benjamin Franklin School planted this Victory Garden on the school grounds in 1943, with the produce used in their school lunches. (Courtesy of Franklin Elementary School.)

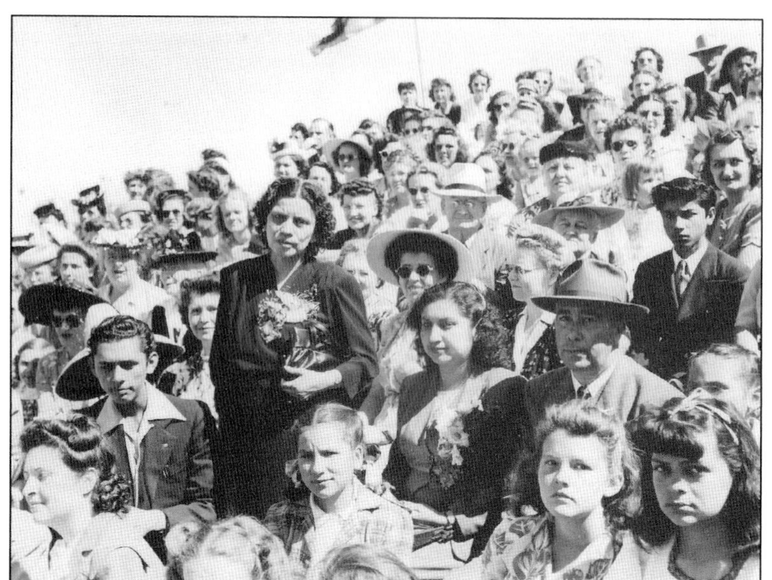

The Benjamin Franklin School Parent-Teacher Association's 1947 spring festival program included honored guests from the Álvaro Obregón School in Tijuana, Mexico. The woman standing in this photograph is Director Ramirez from the Obregon School. (Courtesy of Franklin Elementary School.)

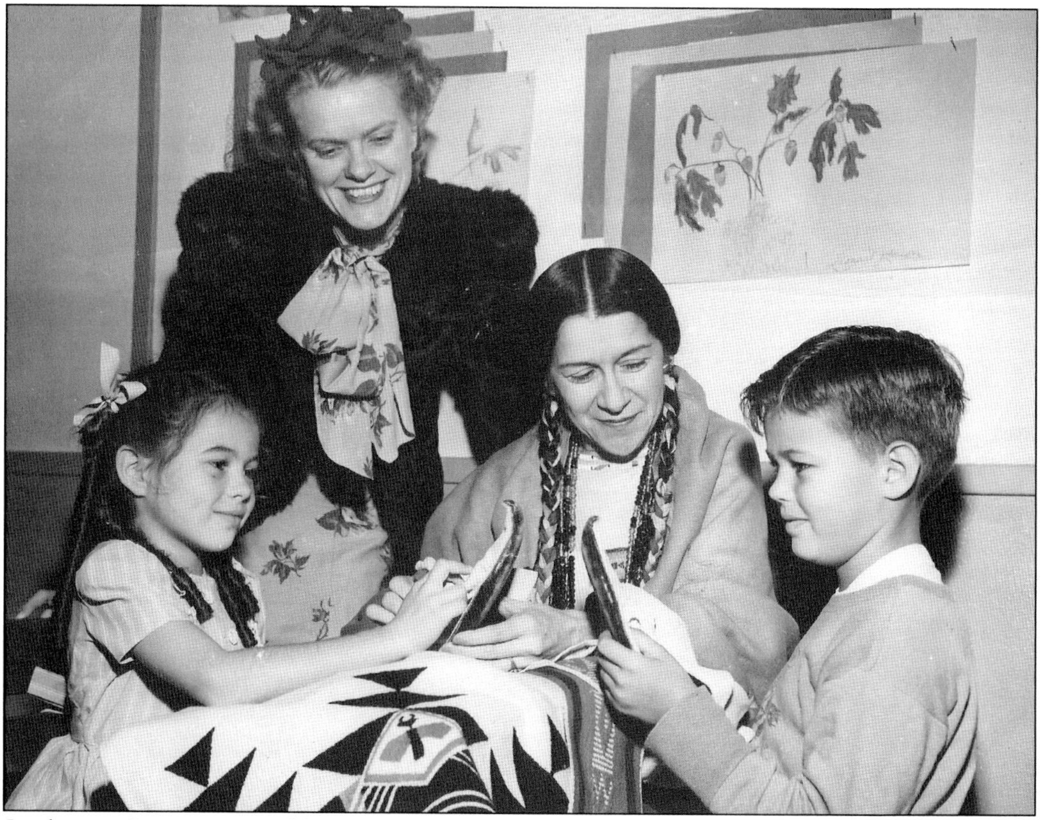

Students at Benjamin Franklin School were nourished by various teaching activities, such as this workshop on intercultural relations in 1947. Native American Mary "Ataloa" Stone McClendon of the Chickasaw Nation, a renowned concert vocalist, educator, and advocate of Native American traditions, shares artifacts and stories of her culture with the students as an unidentified woman looks on. (Courtesy of Franklin Elementary School.)

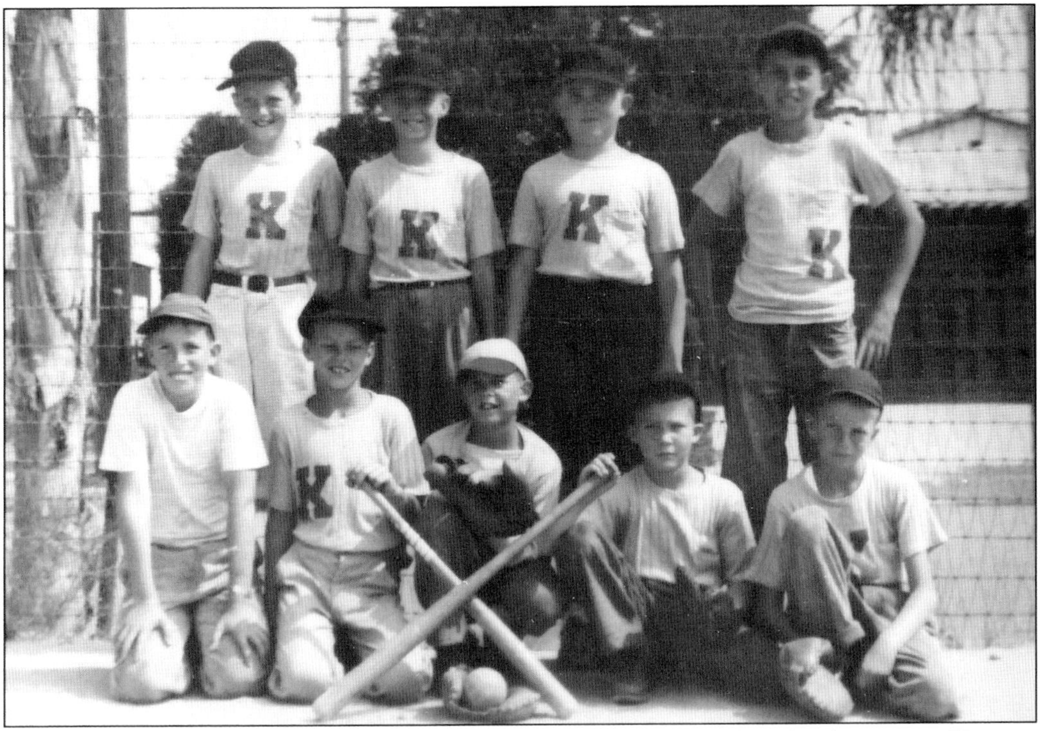

The playing fields at Benjamin Franklin School provided a perfect place for the summer Kiwanis softball team to play ball in 1943. As a nonprofit service organization, the Kiwanis Club sponsored many youth activities. (Courtesy of Franklin Elementary School.)

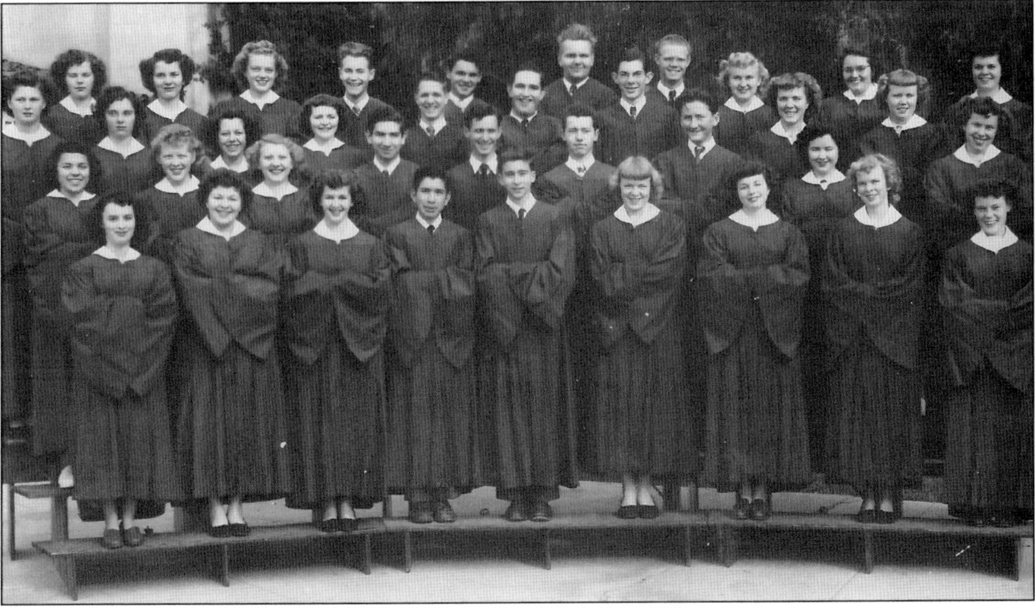

Benjamin Franklin School Parent-Teacher Association meetings were part business and part opportunity for socializing and entertainment. At one such meeting in December 1945, the a capella choir from nearby Herbert Hoover High School performed a collection of Christmas songs at Franklin. (Courtesy of Franklin Elementary School.)

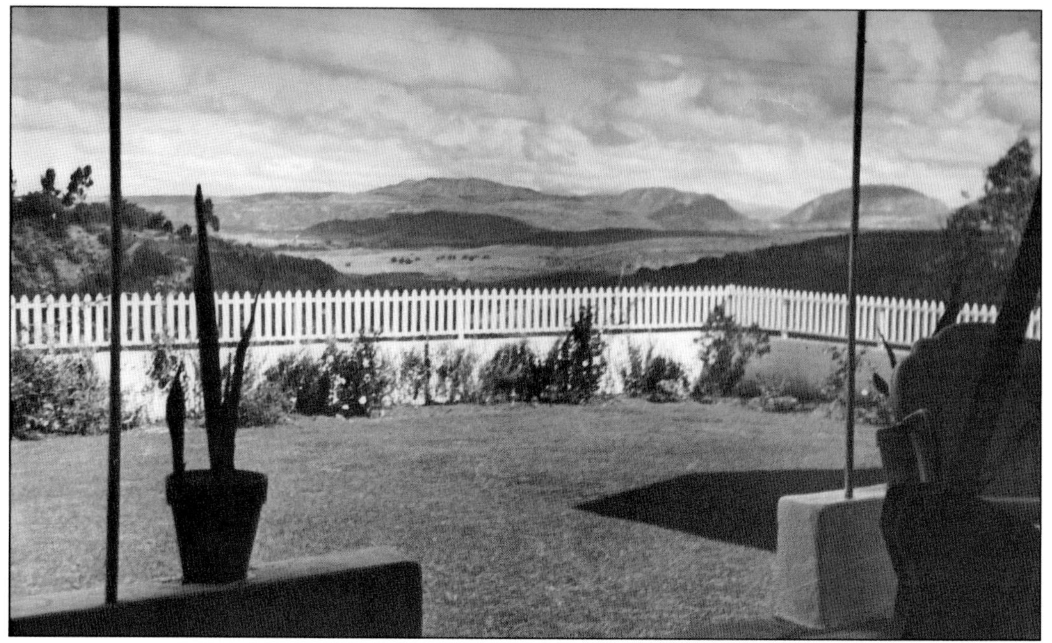

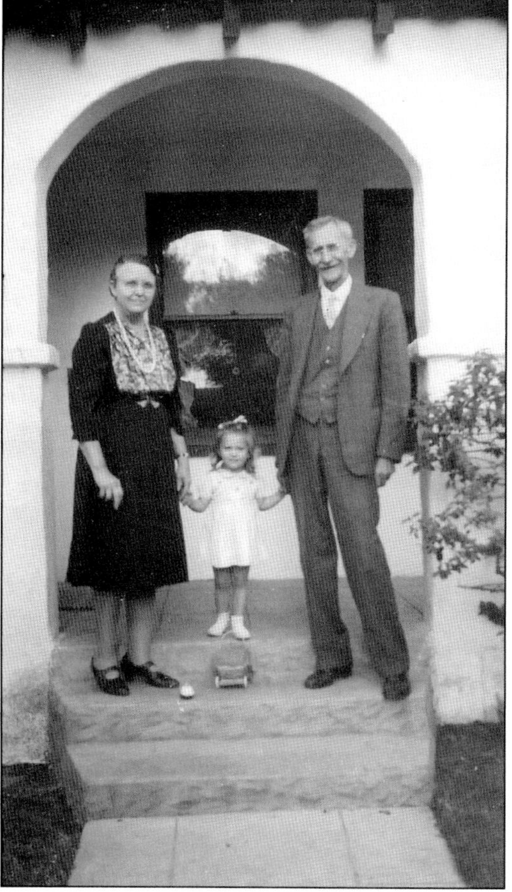

In 1940, the view to the north from the backyard of the home of Fred and Helen Morrison at 4274 Middlesex Drive showed only open space. This area would eventually be developed as Grantville. (Courtesy of Joann Morrison.)

Zella and Henry Sorkness visit with their granddaughter Sharon on the steps of the home of their son Ralph on Hastings Road in 1942. Henry Sorkness owned the Rarity Book Shop in downtown San Diego and lived in South Park. (Courtesy of Sharon Ballou.)

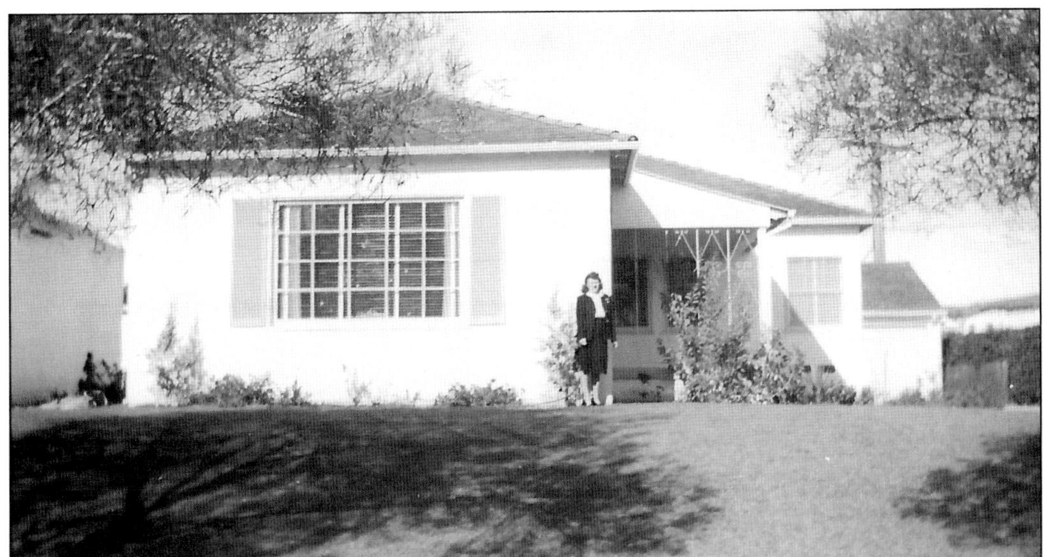

Hazel Van Harten, sister of Ray Perrigo, stands in front of the new house that her brother built for Hazel and her husband, Dale, at 4122 Bedford Drive in 1942. In the foreground are acacia trees that originally lined the streets of Kensington Heights. Hazel came to Kensington from Ohio in 1928 with her family and was a member of Hoover High School's first graduating class of 1932. (Courtesy of Joyce Gilchrist.)

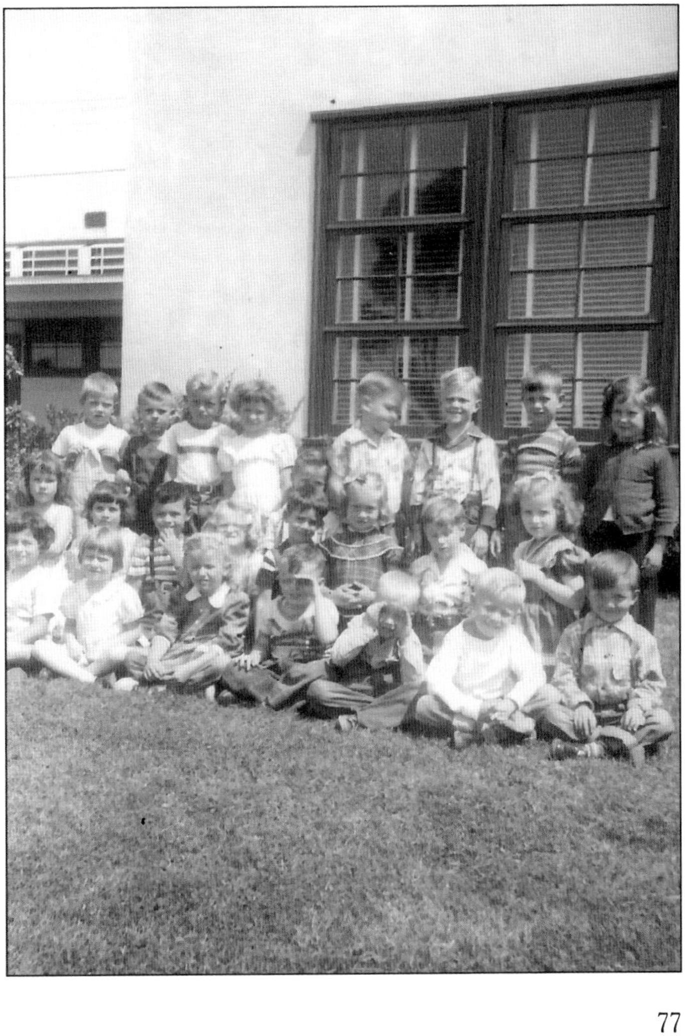

The kindergarten class at Benjamin Franklin School gathered for a class photograph in 1949. Franklin began in 1929 with three temporary classrooms obtained from Birney Elementary school and slowly added capacity as the surrounding population grew. (Courtesy of Joyce Gilchrist.)

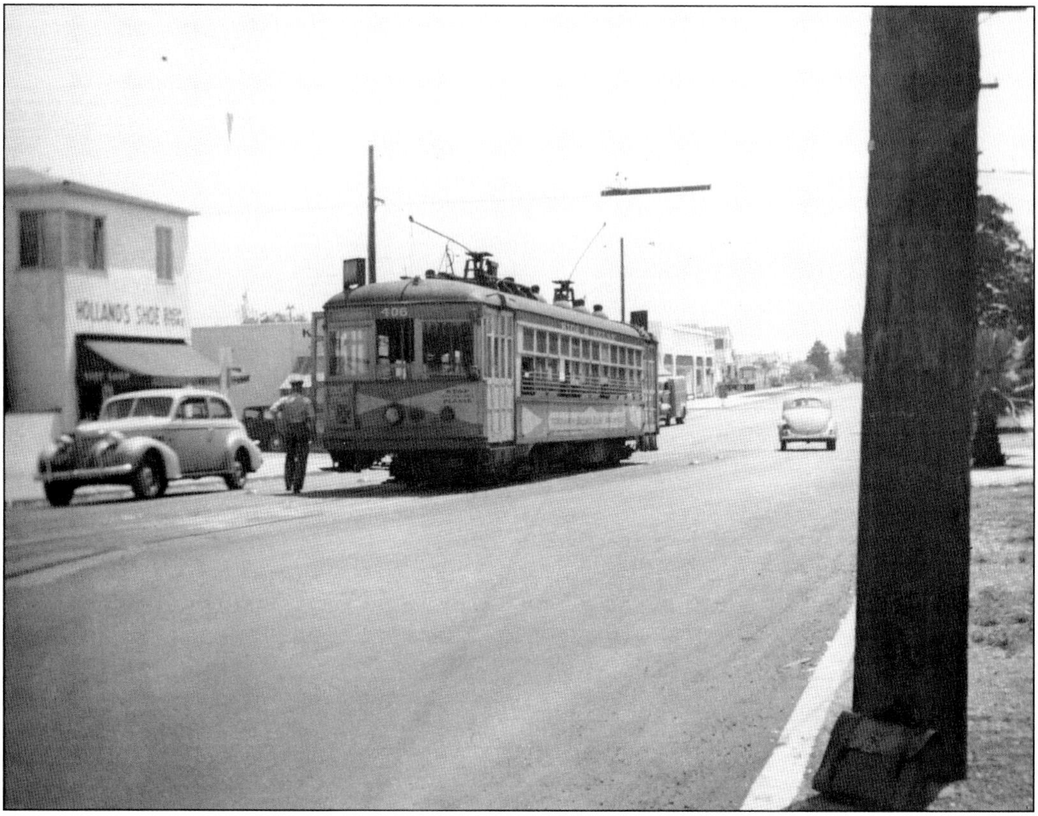

This early 1940s view looks east on Adams Avenue and Forty-Second Street, at the end of the No. 11 streetcar line. Holland's Shoe Store was operated by Kelley M. Holland and his wife, Marjorie, who resided at 4649 Biona Drive in the 1930s and 1940s. (Courtesy of San Diego History Center.)

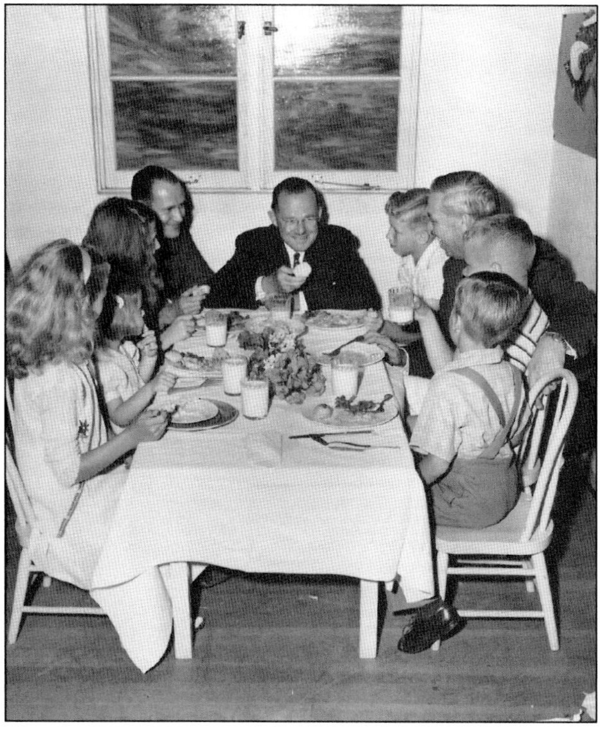

Dr. Lester E. Bond, a former Navy chaplain, accepted leadership of the Kensington Community Church in 1945, and during his 17 years of leadership oversaw the most ambitious building projects of the church's history. Pictured here around 1948, Reverend Bond is meeting with members of the Junior Hi committee in the social hall. (Courtesy of Kensington Community Church.)

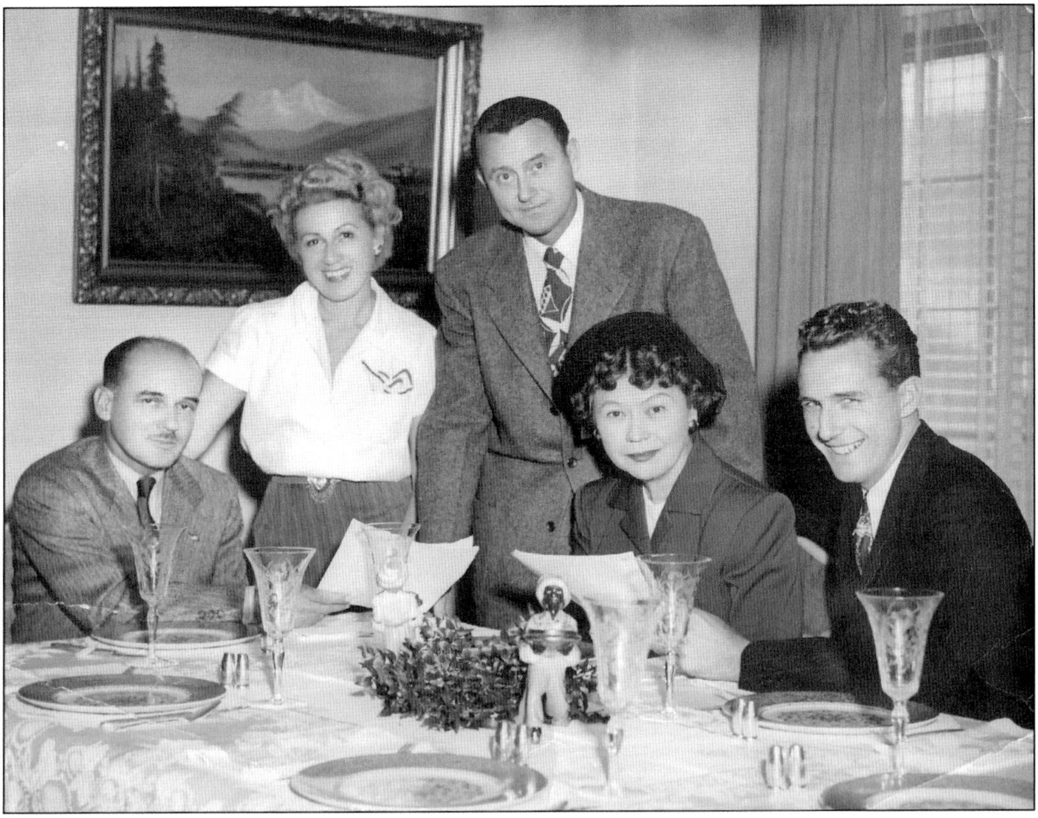

The Kensington Players were a short-lived theatrical troupe formed under the auspices of the Kensington Community Church, where the troupe put on plays. Members attended a board meeting in 1948 at the Buckland residence on Ridgeway. Pictured from left to right are Jack Buckland, Gladys Buckland, Dr. Thomas Baumann, Darlene Weise, and Judson Bradshaw. (Courtesy of Darlene Love.)

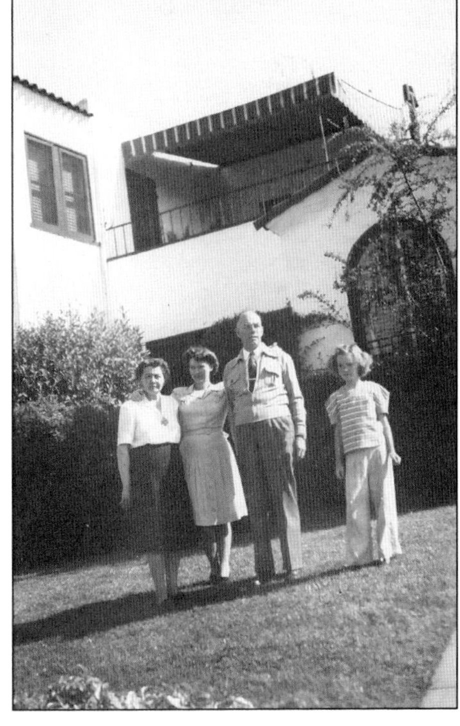

From left to right, Anna Gorsline, Bettie Gorsline Black, Lester P. Gorsline, and Bettie Black pose in the front yard of the Gorslines' home at 4195 Norfolk Terrace. Lester Gorsline was a tool designer at Convair. The house was historically designated by the City of San Diego as the Roy and Edith Rinehart House. The Spanish Eclectic–style house, located in the Kensington Manor subdivision, was built in 1929 by C.A. Turner. (Courtesy of Bettie Black.)

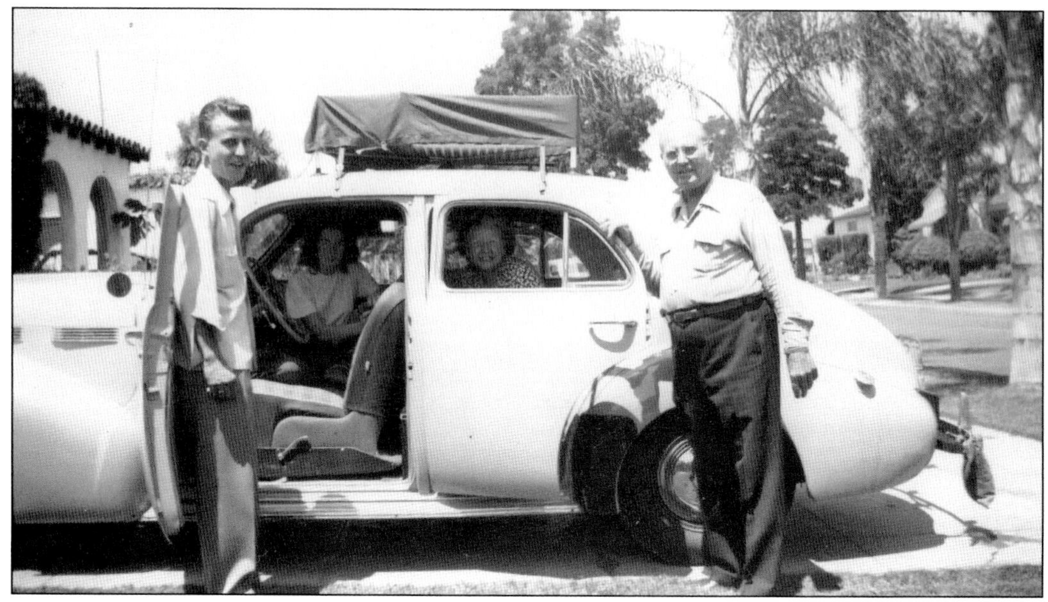

With their 1940 LaSalle packed for a trip to Iowa in 1949 are Paul Beilstein (left), wife Barbara (in front seat), and Paul's parents Leona and John in the driveway of 4952 Marlborough Drive. Originally from Iowa, Paul and his parents moved to San Diego in 1937, residing in the University Heights neighborhood before purchasing their Kensington home. (Courtesy of Debra Beilstein.)

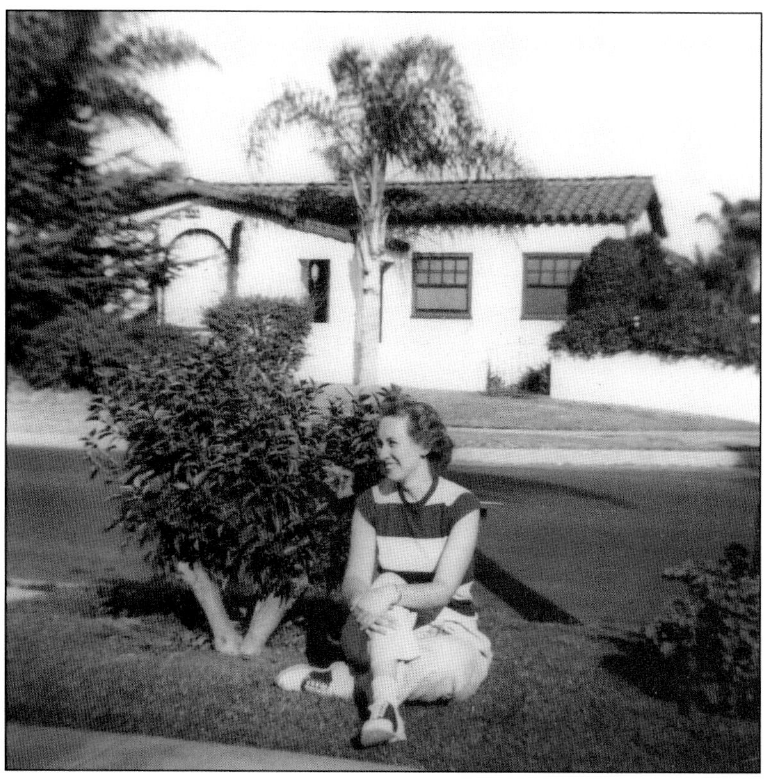

Patricia Beilstein, the daughter-in-law of John and Leona Beilstein, beams outside of their home at 4952 Marlborough Drive. Patricia married Howard Beilstein in 1949. Howard's brother Paul lightheartedly claims credit as being their matchmaker by giving her rides home from work when Howard was in the car. A talented organ player, Patricia played at several Catholic churches in El Cajon and Riverside. (Courtesy of Debra Beilstein.)

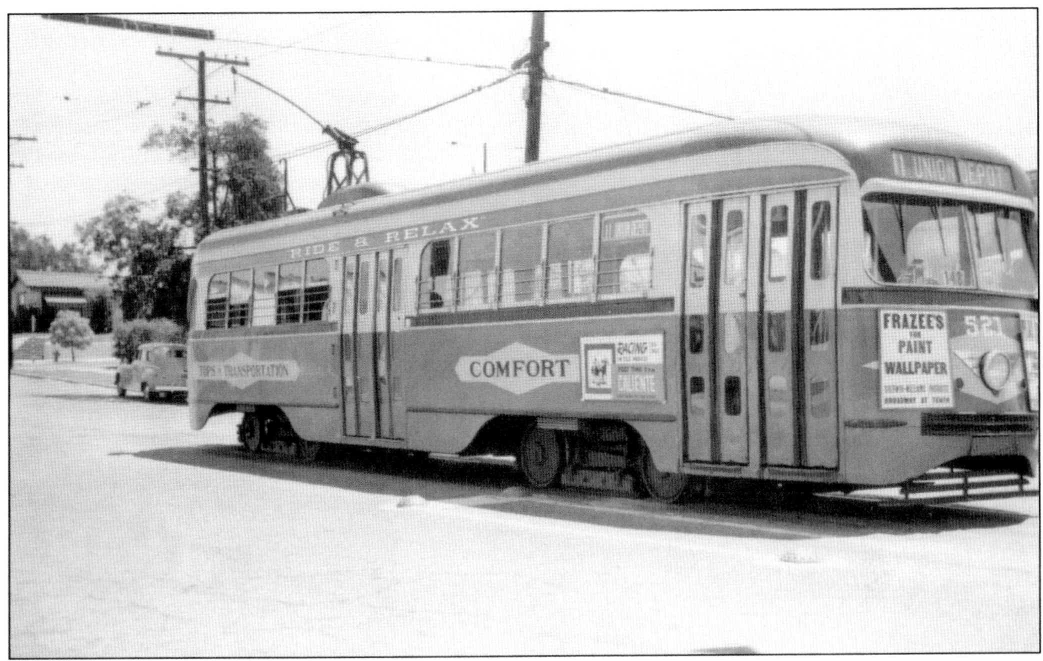

Pictured in 1948 on Adams Avenue, the streetcar has reached the end of the No. 11 line at Forty-Second Street. The following year, this route was eliminated and replaced with a bus route that extended north to Marlborough Drive between Hilldale Road and Middlesex Drive. (Courtesy of San Diego History Center.)

An annual tradition from 1932 until the Hoover High School tower was demolished in 1976, graduating students, such as these in the 1940s, dressed in their finest and waited in a long line to climb to the top of the tower. There, they signed pages from the tower register, which undoubtedly bears the names of numerous Kensington residents. (Courtesy of Herbert Hoover High School.)

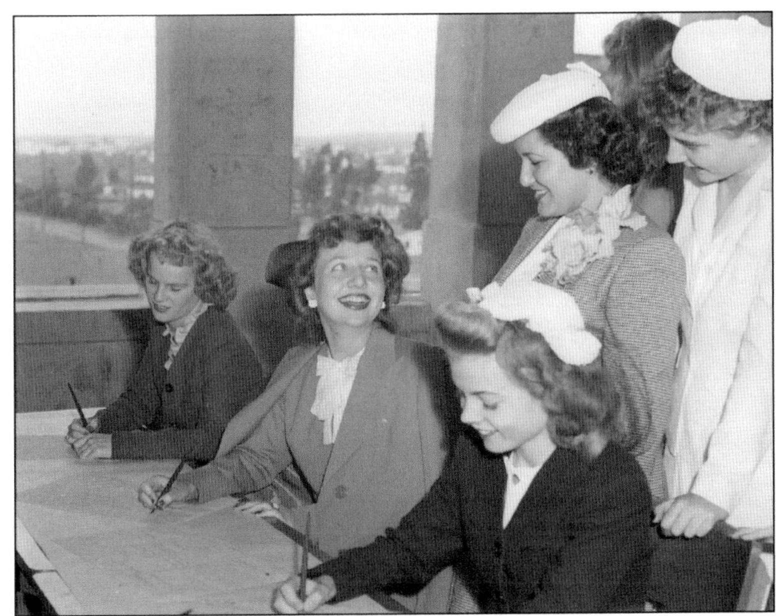

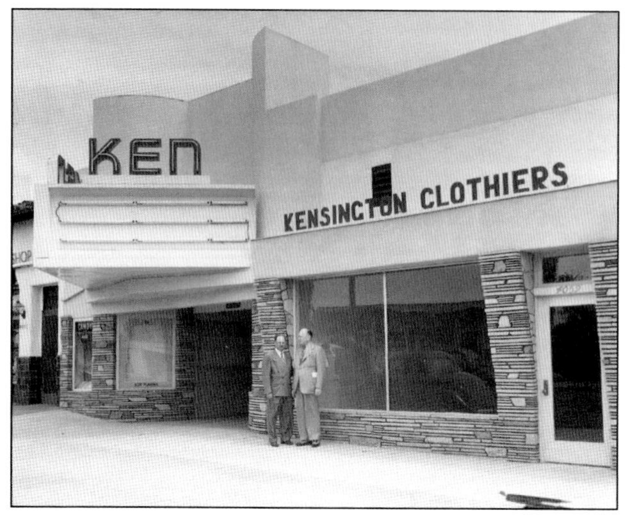

Kensington resident Chris Cosgrove built the Ken Theater complex, which includes the buildings to the west, in 1947. The theater was designed by renowned architect S. Charles Lee, pictured on the left with an unidentified man prior to the theater's opening on December 10, 1947. Lee is recognized as one of the most prolific and distinguished motion picture theater designers on the West Coast. Robert Berkun, who lived at 4568 Marlborough Drive, operated the theater and brought the first foreign films to San Diego. (Courtesy of University of California Los Angeles.)

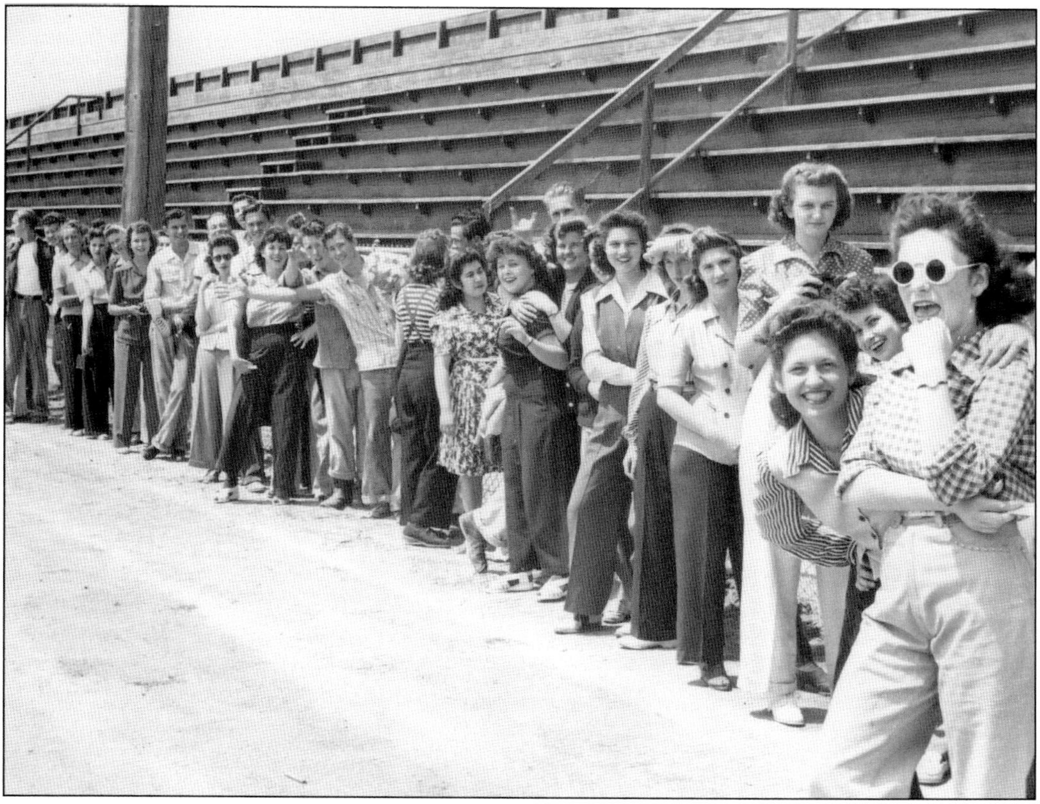

Herbert Hoover High School students celebrate the end of the school year with a picnic on campus in June 1942. Though summer vacation is normally a time to enjoy leisure time with friends and family, many graduating students enlisted in the military that summer or found work in factories manufacturing airplanes or other necessities for the war effort. (Courtesy of Herbert Hoover High School.)

Five

Coming Together

In the 1950s, San Diego's economy continued to boom. The post–World War II slowdown of local military operations was brief, and government and defense spending increased during the Korean War and rise of the Cold War. Gone were the rationing and supply shortages of the war years, and factories increased production to keep pace with consumer demand. Many veterans settled in Kensington and began to raise families during the postwar baby boom, and they were connected through church and other social clubs and activities in the neighborhood.

At the start of the 1950s, all of the subdivisions in Kensington, except one, were within the boundaries of the City of San Diego, having agreed to annexation in 1936. The lone holdout was Kensington Park. It was an island of the county surrounded by the city. This arrangement came to an end in 1953 when a house on Marlborough Drive, opposite the church, caught on fire and the county fire department could not reach it in time before it burned to the ground. That was the catalyst that caused the "island" to throw in the towel and agree to city annexation.

New home construction boomed, and gone were the earlier restrictions on building styles in Kensington. Homes were constructed on infill lots and were designed in the Colonial, Minimal Traditional, and Ranch architectural styles. Steep, canyon-edge lots that were previously considered almost unbuildable utilized advancements in construction materials and equipment to create modern residences with breathtaking canyon views.

This era also saw the growth of service and social clubs in Kensington. The Kensington Business Association was formed, and members came up with ways to promote their small businesses along Adams Avenue. Having admired the neon signs of surrounding neighborhoods, they set about raising funds for a sign of their own. Bake sales, lemonade stands, and contests were held and everyone pitched in, and the Kensington sign was erected over Adams Avenue in 1953. The accomplishment was celebrated with a Christmas festival on December 9, 1953, during which Anna McKinnon was chosen as the queen of Kensington.

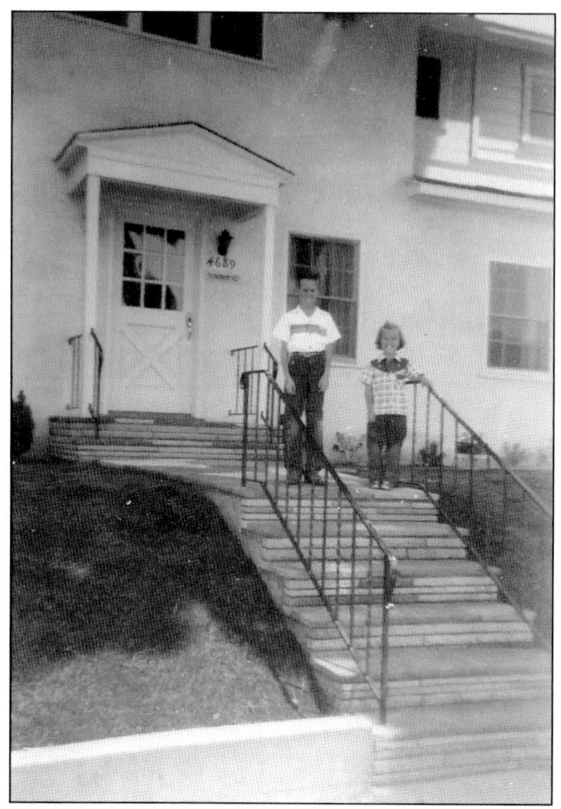

Howard and Darlene Baumann pose on the steps of their family home and their father's dental office in 1952. Dr. Baumann purchased the house at 4689 Marlborough Drive in 1950 and remodeled the original Craftsman house, adding space to the upper floor where the family lived. His dental office was on the first floor. (Courtesy of Darlene Love.)

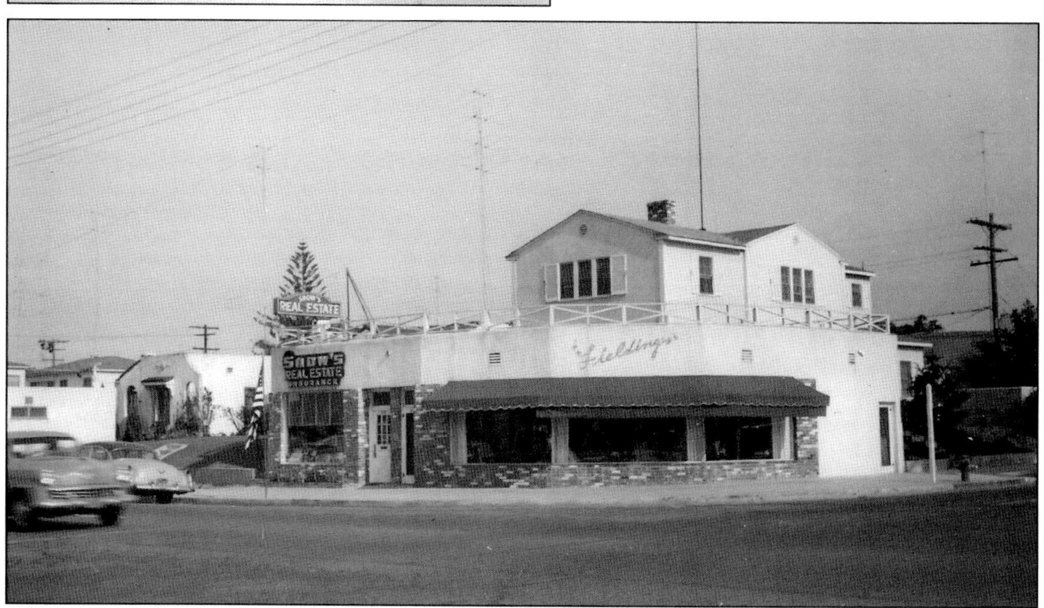

This house on the southeast corner of Adams Avenue and Marlborough Drive was built in 1911 as a Craftsman. Dr. Thomas Baumann added an auxiliary commercial structure around the north end of the house. Lillian and Kate Fielding operated Fielding's Dress Shop here from 1951 to 1984. It has been a coffee shop ever since. Malta Snow ran his real estate business out of the shop on the east side of Fielding's. (Courtesy of Darlene Love.)

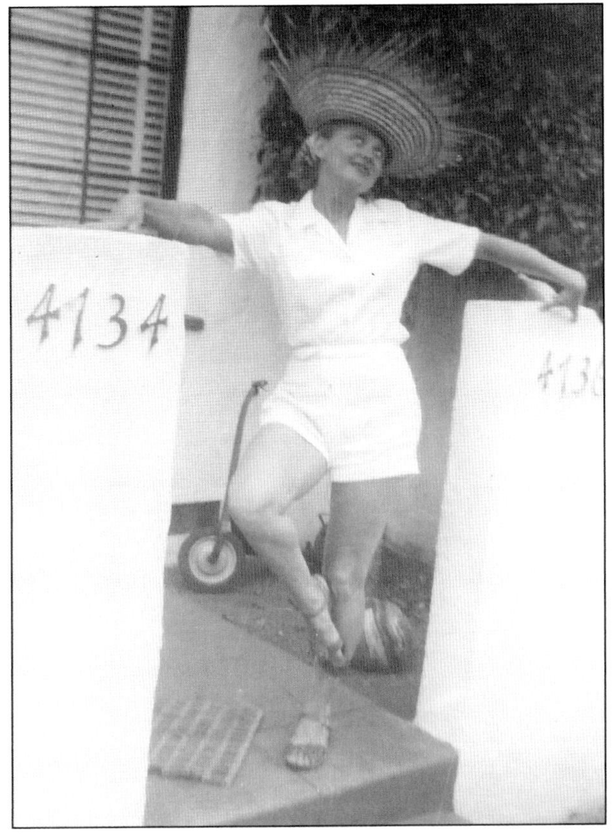

Bernace "Bea" Sickler models her straw sombrero in front of the family home on Biona Drive. The hat was a souvenir familiar to many San Diegans at the time, obtained in Tijuana during a trip with visiting relatives from Iowa. (Courtesy of Becky McMullen.)

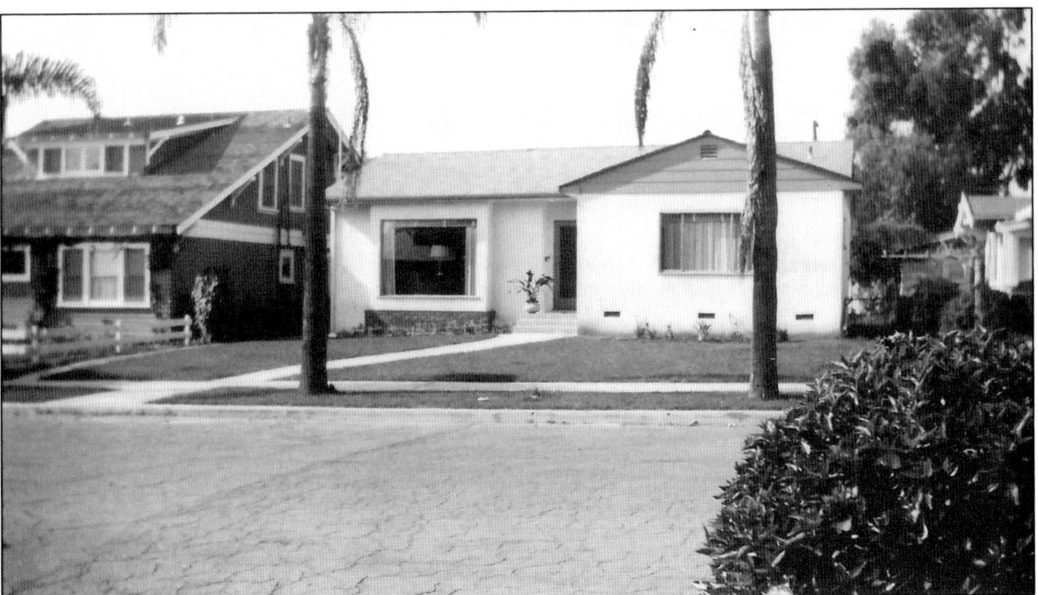

The home of Henry and Lena Van Harten at 4810 Edgeware Road was built around 1953 by Ray Perrigo. The Van Hartens were the parents of Dale Van Harten, Perrigo's brother-in-law. The elder Van Harten was a native of the Netherlands and was employed as a butcher at a meat market. (Courtesy of Joyce Gilchrist.)

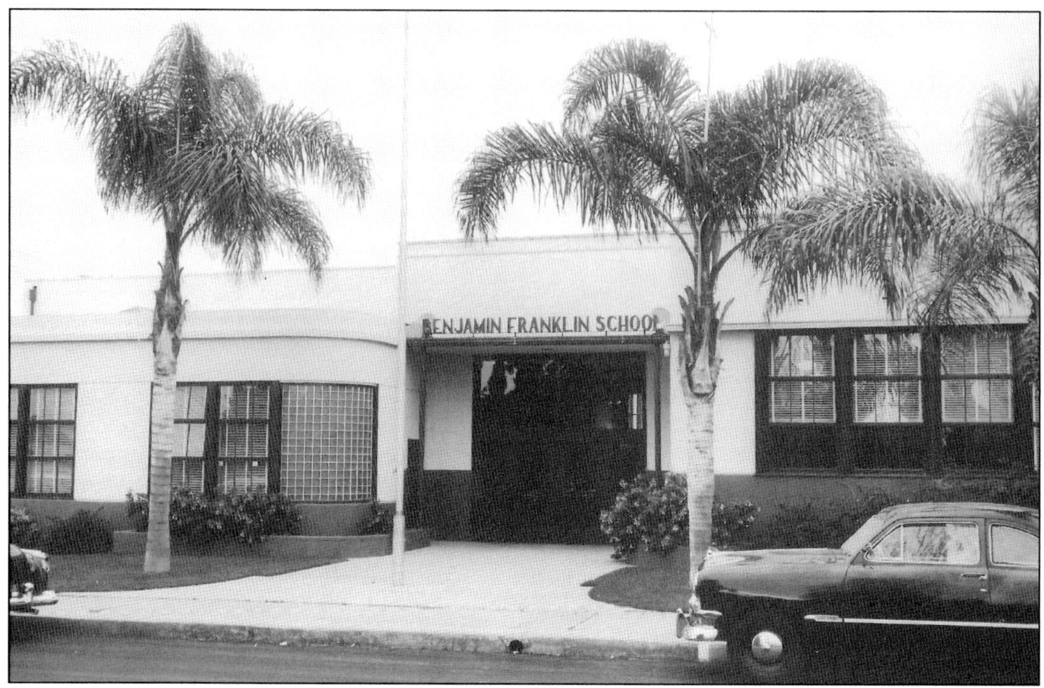

Benjamin Franklin School started in 1929 with three temporary wooden buildings. Additional space for classrooms, a library, a lunchroom, and administrative offices were added over time. The Streamline Moderne style that was popular in 1935 when this part of the school was constructed is evident in this photograph from 1953. (Courtesy of Franklin Elementary School.)

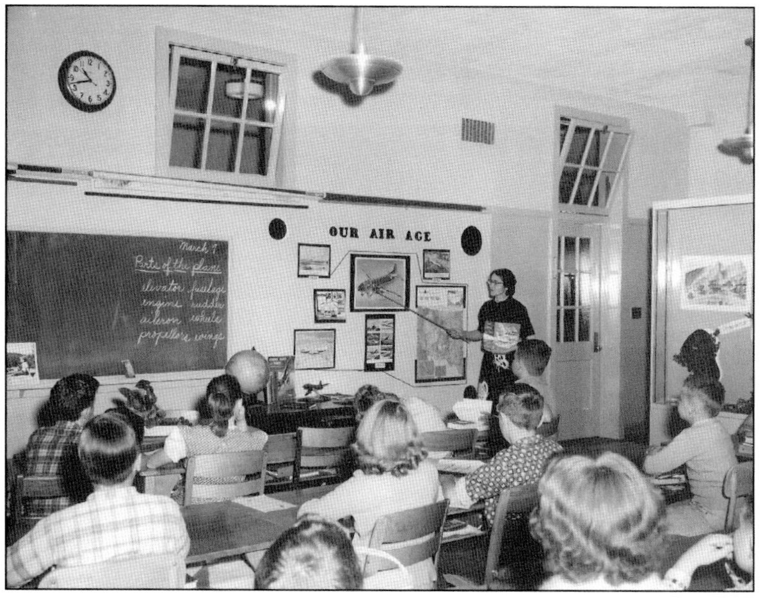

Staff at Benjamin Franklin School often teamed up with local companies to provide material for lesson plans. In March 1956, this class was studying the air age and learning how airplanes worked using materials provided by Ryan Aeronautical Company. (Photograph by Ryan Aeronautical Company, courtesy of Franklin Elementary School.)

Betty Anderson Generoli and an unidentified man pose with a group of children on the south lawn of the library park in 1954. In the background can be seen the Standard Oil station on the northeast corner of Adams Avenue and Marlborough Drive. (Courtesy of Don Generoli.)

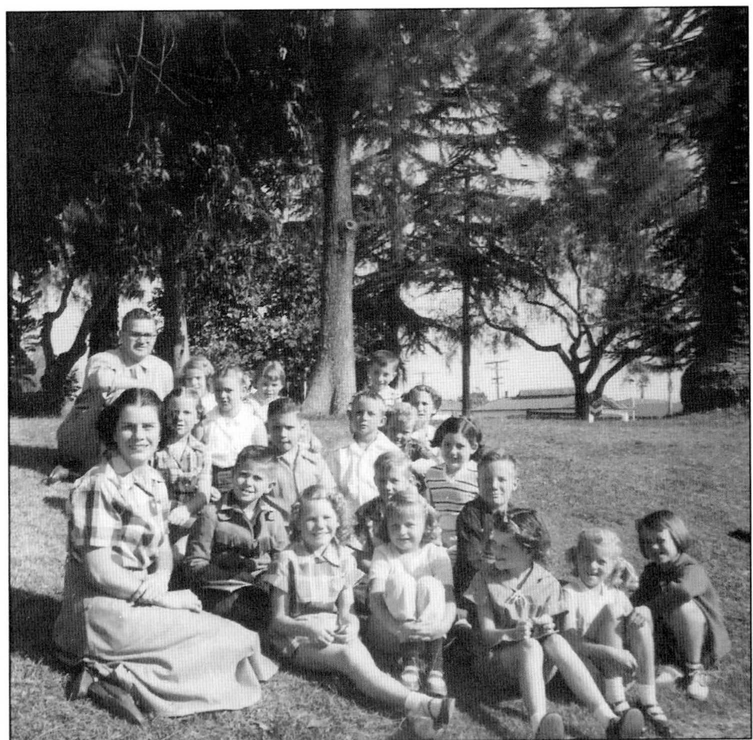

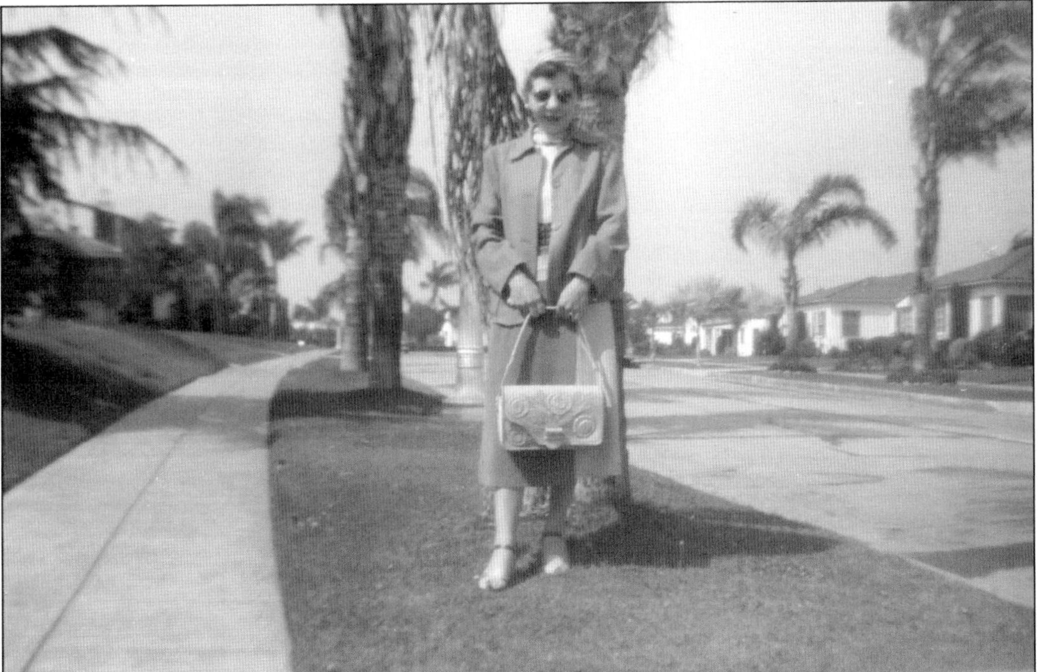

Aunt Red of the Mogavero family, visiting from New York, proudly shows off her new shoes and hand-tooled leather purse in front of 5232 Marlborough Drive around 1950. This view looks north on Marlborough and shows some of the later, post–World War II infill homes on the right side. (Courtesy of DeLayne and Devin Harmon.)

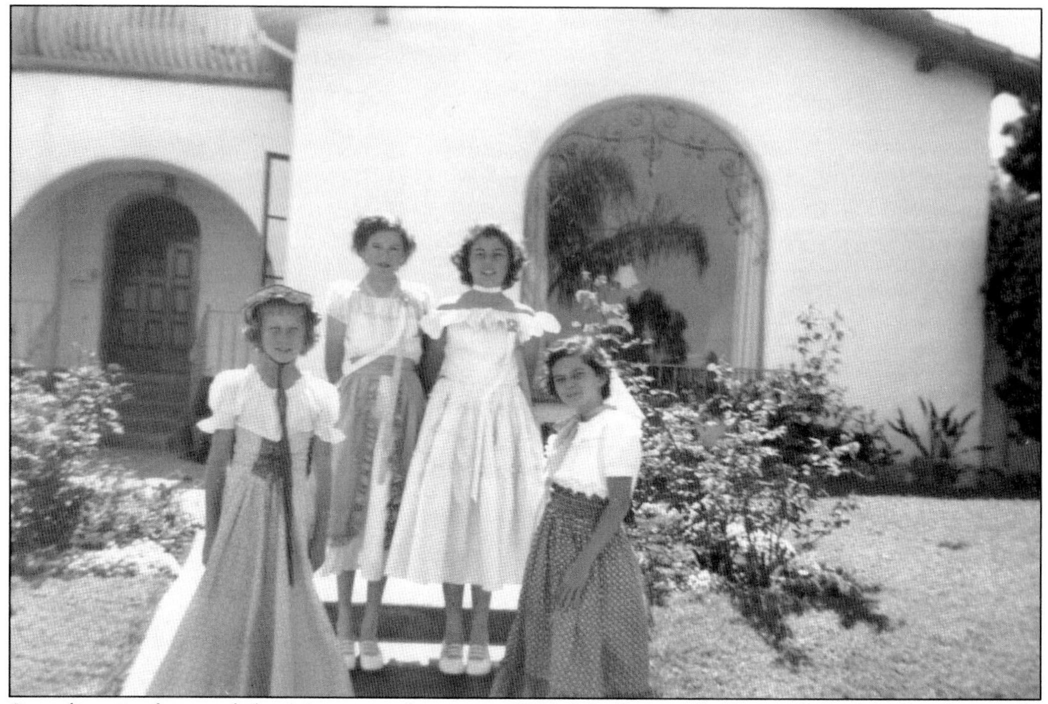

Standing in front of the Mogavero home at 5232 Marlborough Drive, Lois McCurdy, Linda Houghton, Judith Mogavero, and her sister Patricia are dressed for a May Day celebration at Franklin Elementary School. Marking the arrival of springtime, students participated in a maypole dance, sang, and played games. Many Kensington residents fondly remember partaking in this tradition. (Courtesy of DeLayne and Devin Harmon.)

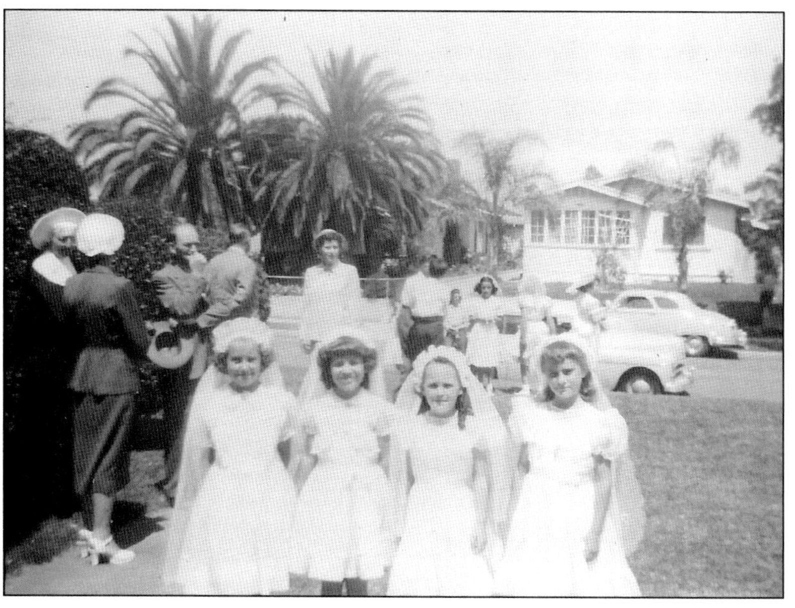

Kensington girls, including Marcia Sickler on the left, are all smiles after making their First Communion at St. Didicus Church in Normal Heights. St. Didicus Church was constructed on Felton Street in 1927. (Courtesy of Becky McMullen.)

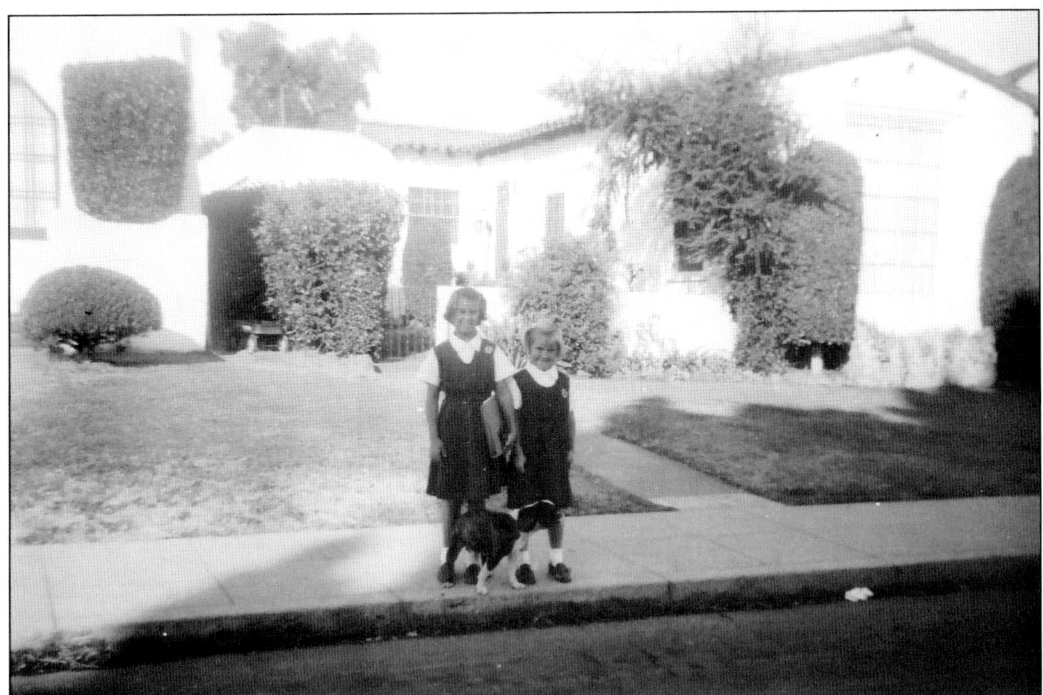

Marcia (left) and Becky Sickler, accompanied by their dog Billy, are dressed in their uniforms for the first day of school at St. Didicus Parish School in Normal Heights in 1954. The school was constructed in 1939 and served many Kensington families. (Courtesy of Becky McMullen.)

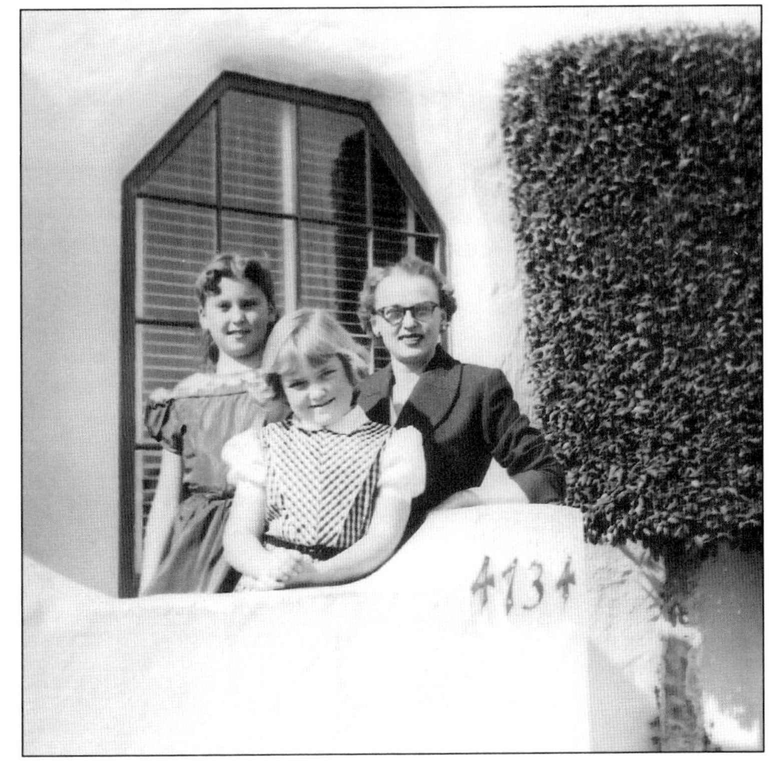

Bea Sickler and daughters Marcia (left) and Becky pose on the porch of their home on Biona Drive in 1953. After the death of her husband, Daniel, in 1949, Bea returned to her hometown of Carroll, Iowa, but was drawn back to Kensington shortly after. The Sicklers shared their duplex with Bea's sister Verna Mae Smith. (Courtesy of Becky McMullen.)

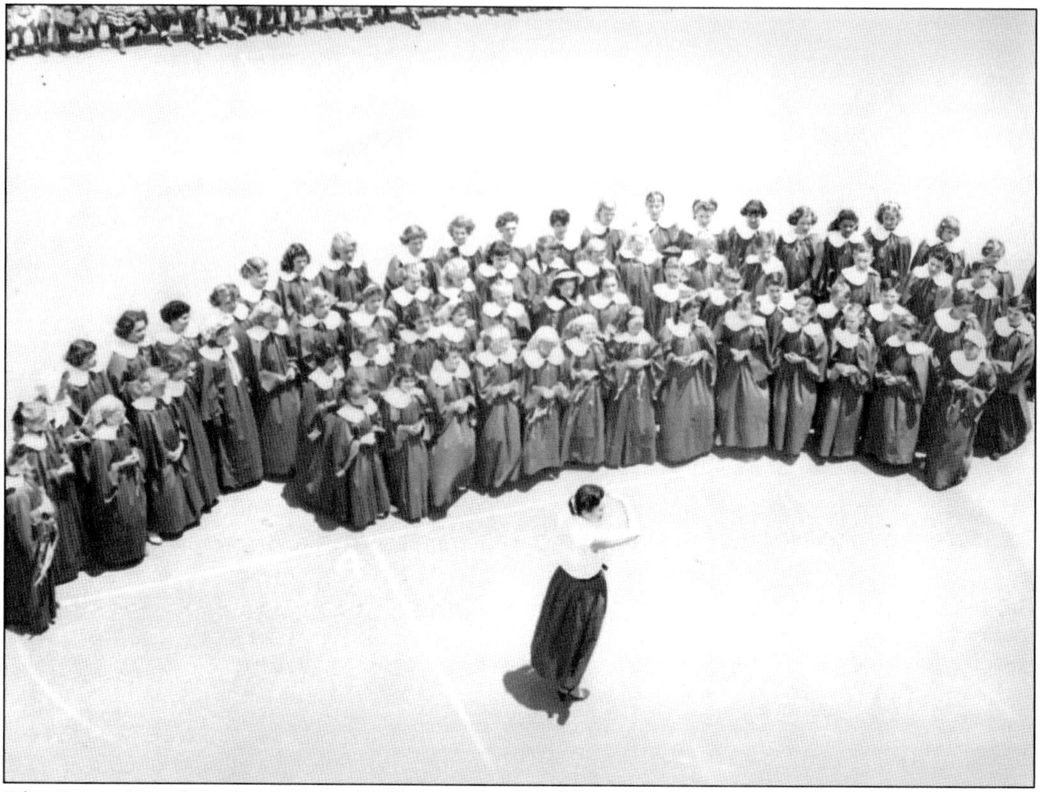

The Parent-Teacher Association at Benjamin Franklin School formed a Mother Singers Glee Club in 1947. By the time of this photograph in May 1953, the club had new robes and made appearances around the city. Here, the mothers perform a program of songs under the leadership of Mrs. G.C. Erickson during the spring festival on the school grounds. (Courtesy of Franklin Elementary School.)

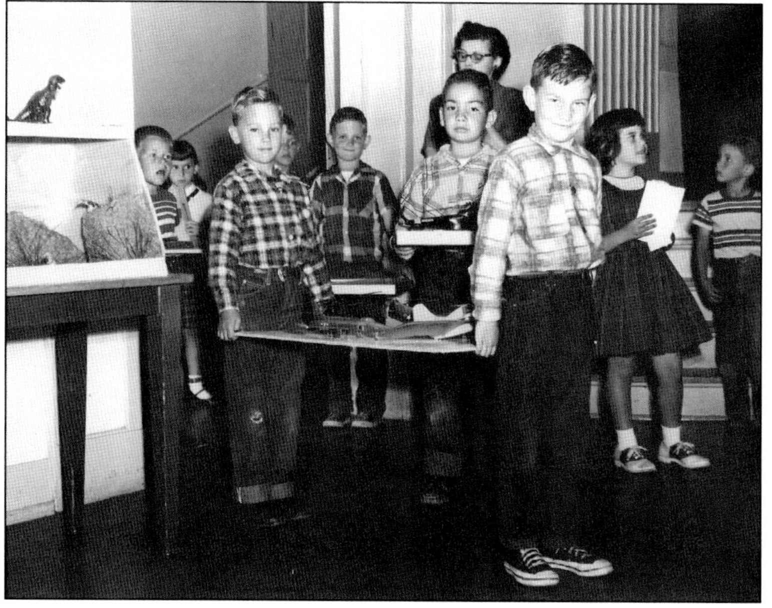

The Benjamin Franklin School PTA sponsored an annual hobby show at the school. In this 1957 photograph, the students are carrying their model airplanes into the auditorium for judging. (Courtesy of Franklin Elementary School.)

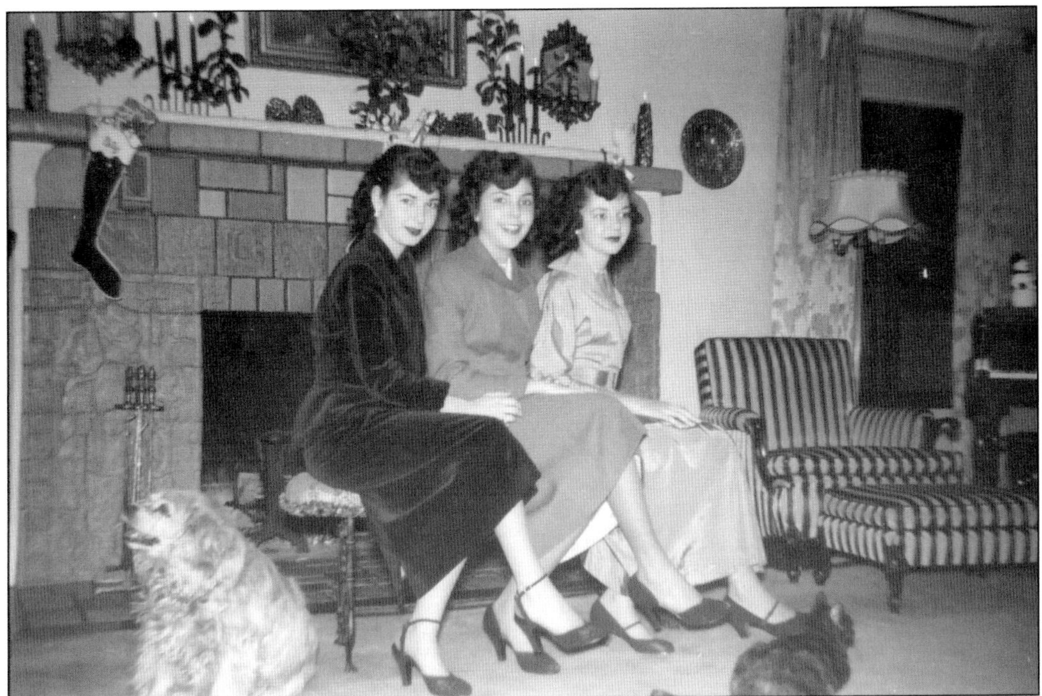

Three girls from the Mogavero family sit in front of the elaborate fireplace at 5232 Marlborough Drive around 1949. The fireplace and hearth utilize California Clay Products (Calco) art tiles with a Mayan motif. The irregularly shaped fireplace tiles were made to fit together as a puzzle. The tiles are in press molded relief and portray Mayan figures and symbols modeled after the figures on the ancient Mayan Temple of the Cross in Palenque, Mexico. (Courtesy of DeLayne and Devin Harmon.)

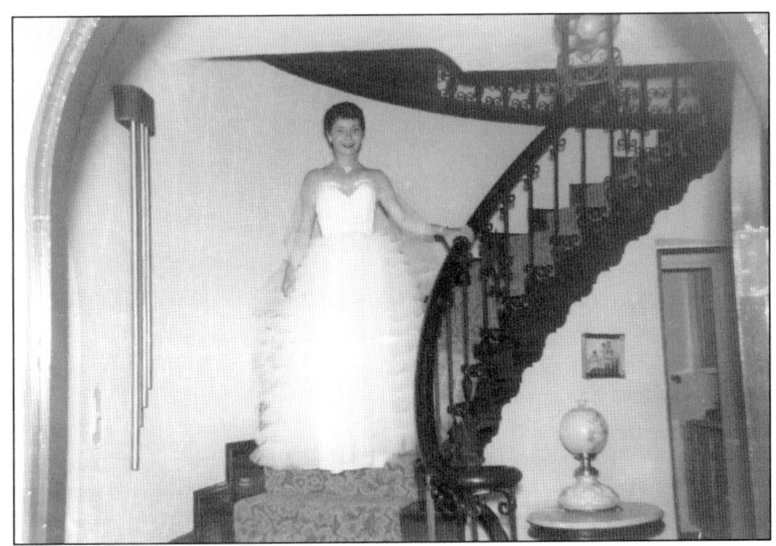

Barbara Mogavero stands proudly on the staircase of 5232 Marlborough Drive, dressed for her senior prom at Hoover High School, in the mid-1950s. The wrought-iron work and hanging light fixture are still in the home, and the original scored plasterwork on the walls has been restored by the current owners. (Courtesy of DeLayne and Devin Harmon.)

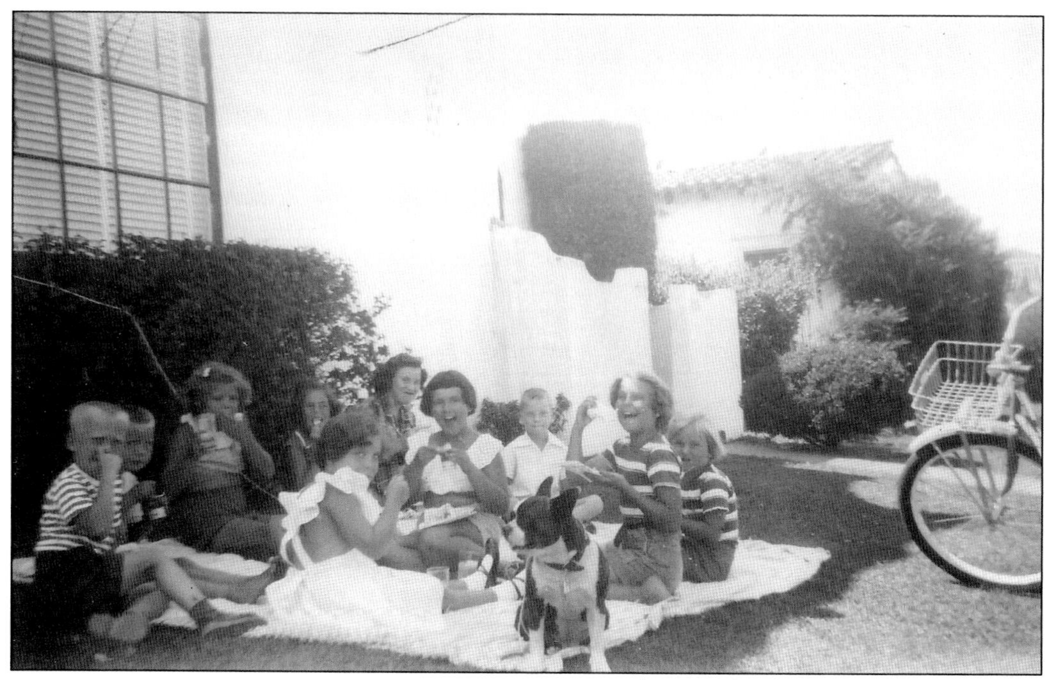

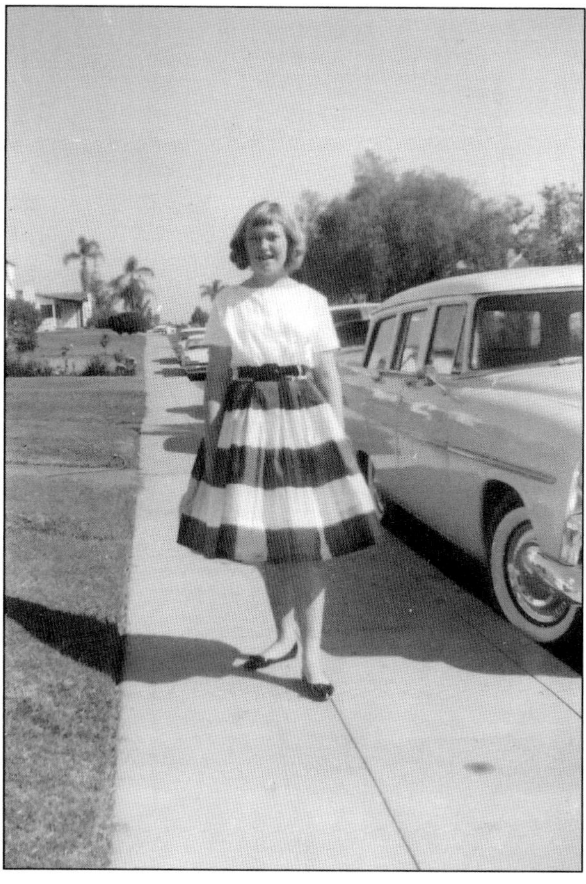

The 1953 birthday party of Becky Sickler brought the neighborhood kids to the Sicklers' front lawn on Biona Drive. No party in Kensington is ever without at least one dog, and this Boston Terrier mix's name was Billy. (Courtesy of Becky McMullen.)

The circle skirt was all the fashion in 1959 when Becky Sickler posed in front of the family home on Biona Drive. The family's 1956 Plymouth station wagon sits at the curb. (Courtesy of Becky McMullen.)

An embarrassed Nancy Walters hides her face as she is presented with a Christmas present from Hopalong Cassidy, also known as William Boyd, on December 25, 1951, as two unidentified girls look on. Nancy's father, James H. Walters, was a Navy lieutenant who died in 1951. The Navy hosted an annual Christmas party for children of deceased veterans at Naval Air Station San Diego. (Official US Navy photograph, courtesy of Nancy Walters.)

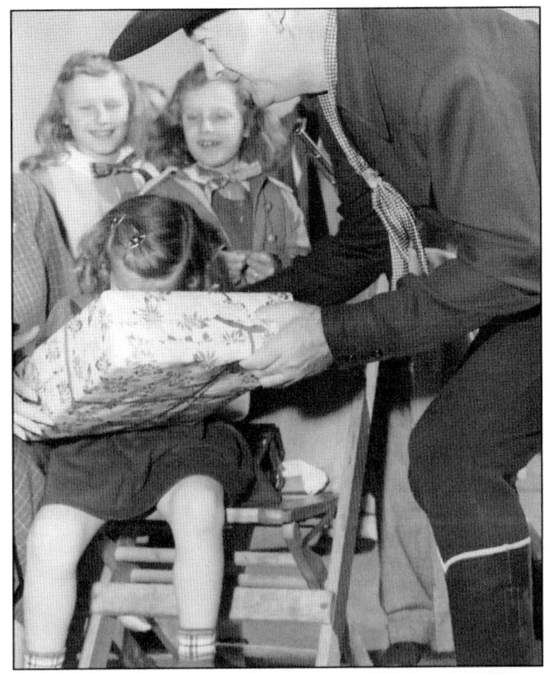

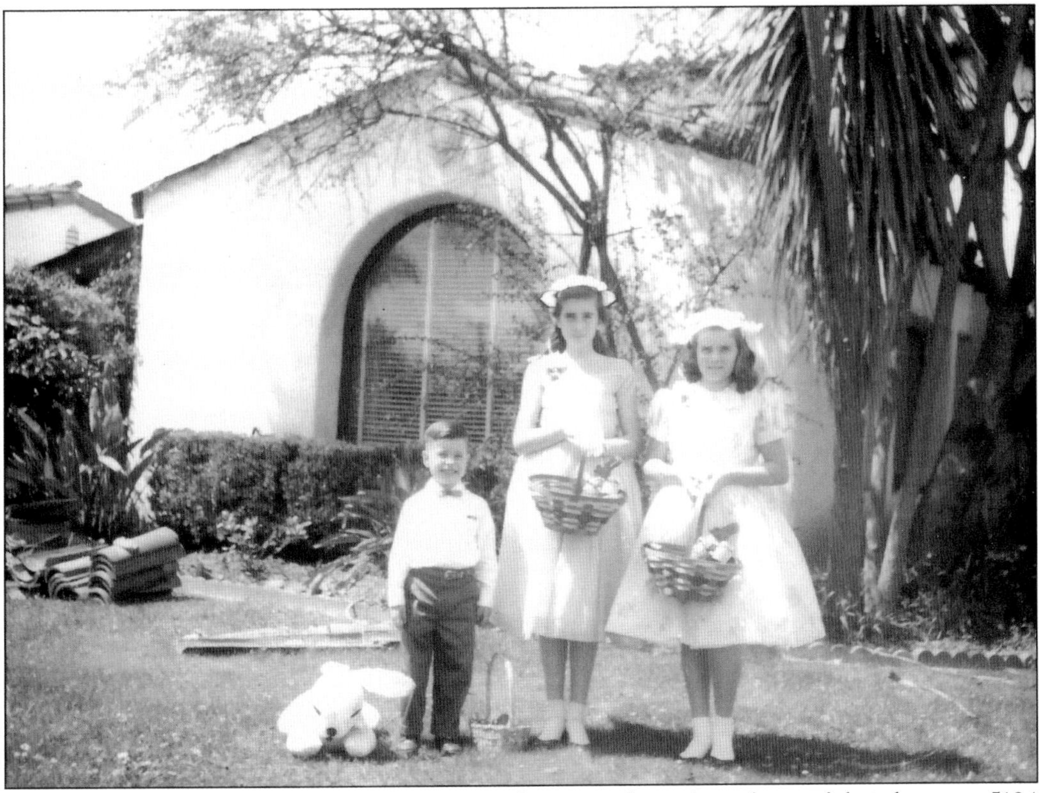

From left to right, Dick, Diane, and Nancy Walters pose happily in front of their home at 5194 Marlborough Drive on Easter Day, 1958. The Walters family moved into this home in 1950. (Courtesy of Nancy Walters.)

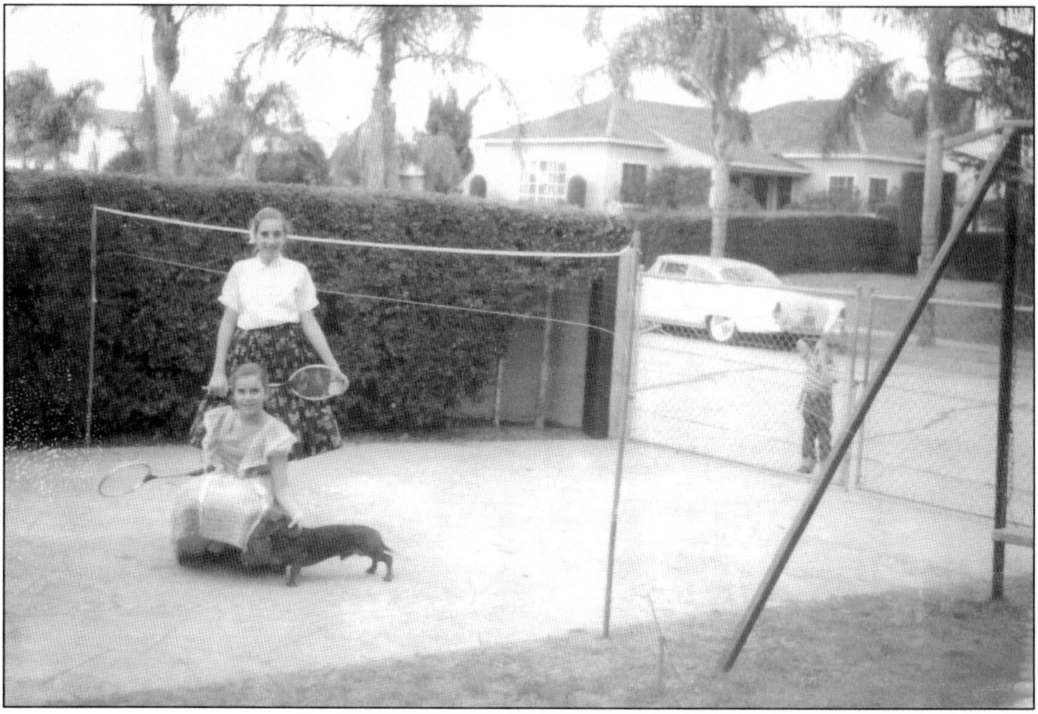

It's Christmas Day, 1958, and Diane (standing) and Nancy stop their badminton game long enough to pose with their dog Pierre while little brother Dick looks on. The house in the background is the Van Harten residence on Bedford Drive, built by Ray Perrigo. (Courtesy of Nancy Walters.)

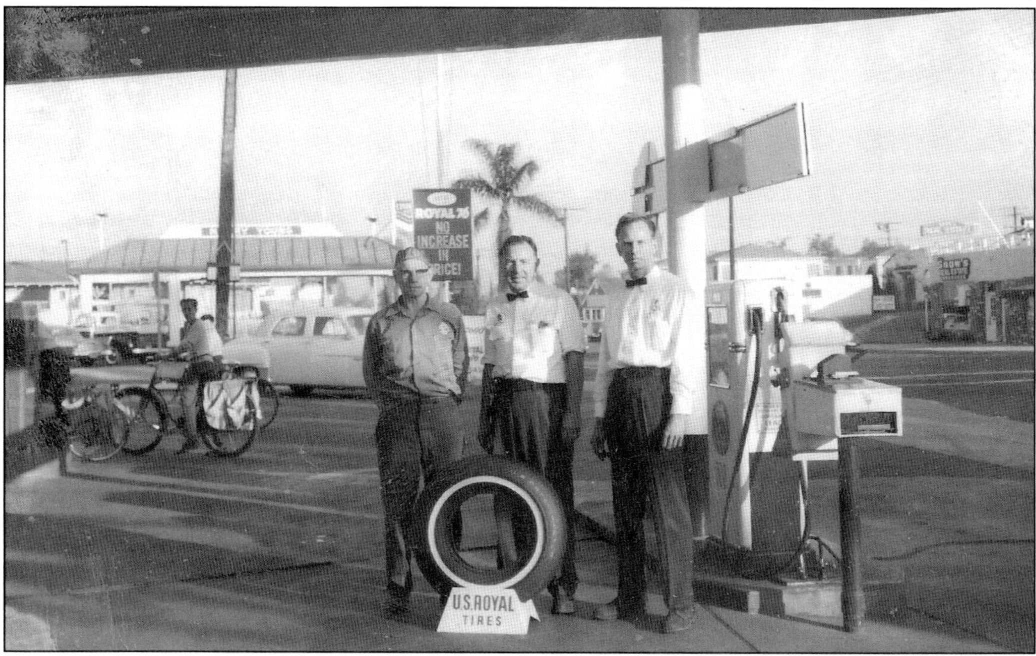

Al Bunnell (center) poses around 1955 with two unidentified employees at his service station on the northwest corner of Adams Avenue and Marlborough Drive. Across the street was Harry Young's service station. (Courtesy of Margaret McCann.)

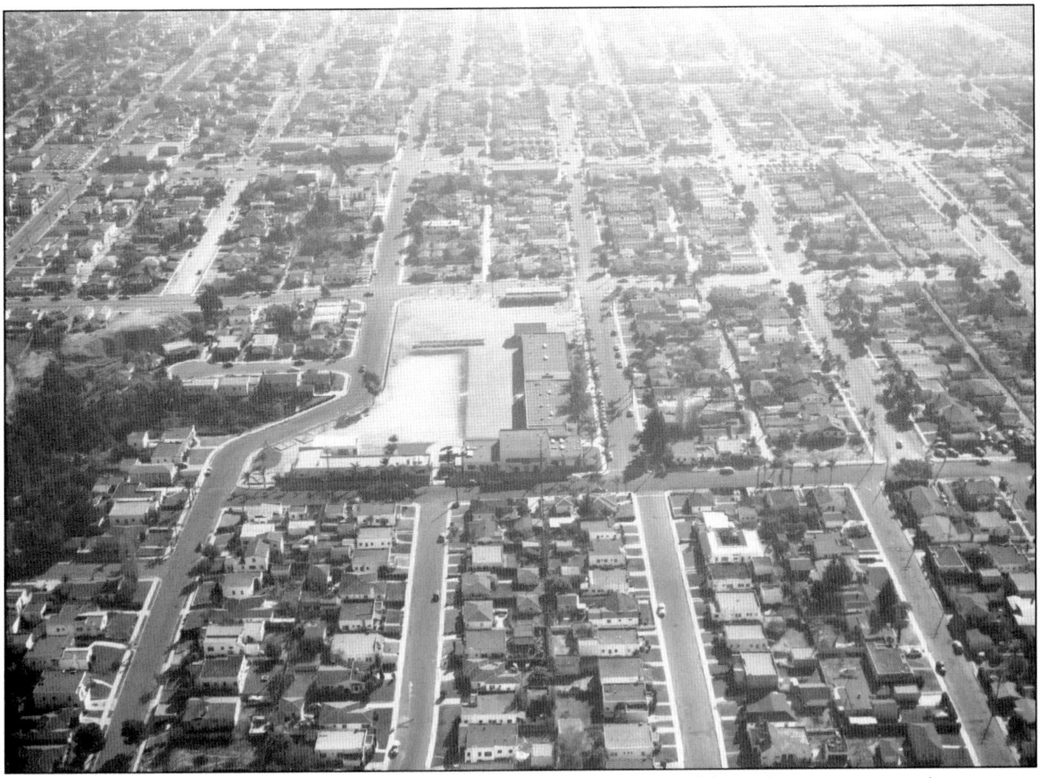

Basil Neil Webb Sr. moved to San Diego from Texas in 1953. Webb, a Kensington resident, was a private pilot who owned an aerial photography business, NAV-AIR Picture Company, and took this photograph of the neighborhood surrounding Benjamin Franklin Elementary school. The view is to the south and the crooked street on the left is Van Dyke Avenue. The north-south streets in this area frequently did not line up because East San Diego, immediately to the south, was mapped separately from Kensington. (Courtesy of Julia Webb.)

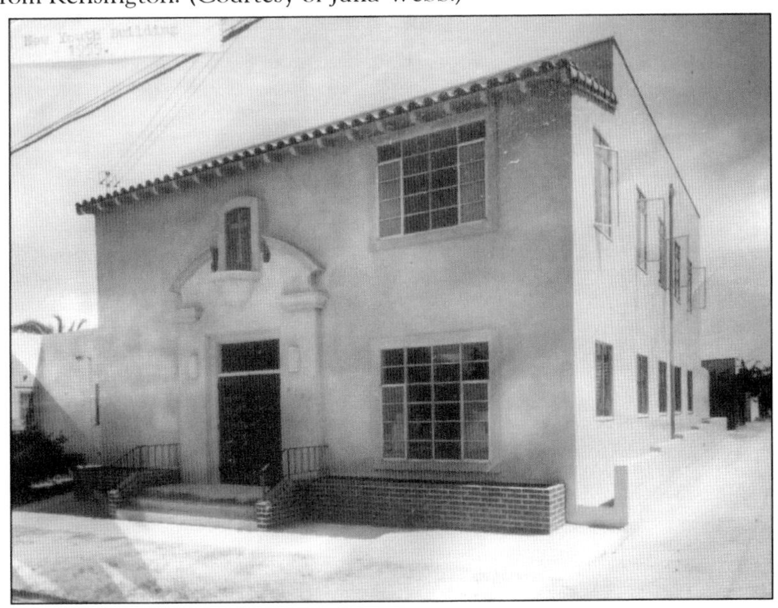

The Kensington Community Church took bids for the construction of a new youth hall, and the winning bid came from congregant Norman Dennstedt and his construction company. The building was constructed on Alder Drive in 1959 at a cost of $40,000. (Courtesy of Kensington Community Church.)

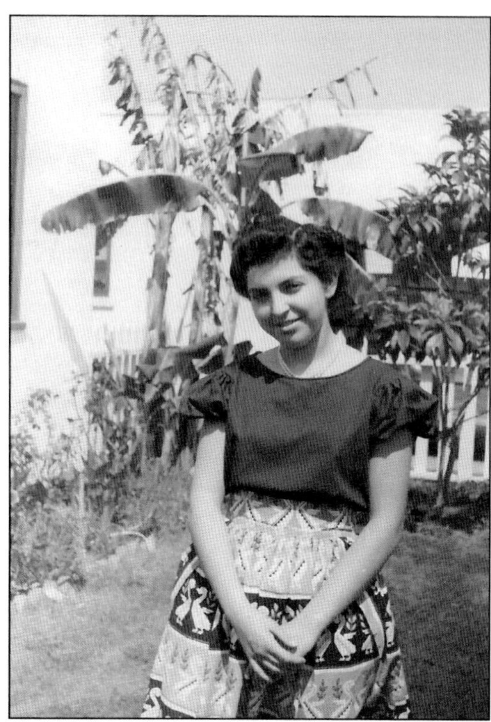

Geraldine Ottonello grew up on a hog ranch in El Cajon. When her father retired in 1950, he bought a house at 5282 Marlborough Drive, and Geri attended sixth grade at Benjamin Franklin School. She went on to junior high at Woodrow Wilson Junior High School, followed by Hoover High School, and finally San Diego State College. She was visiting her aunt, Vera Pavlovich, at her house on Edgeware Road in this photograph from 1951. (Courtesy of Geraldine Hodge.)

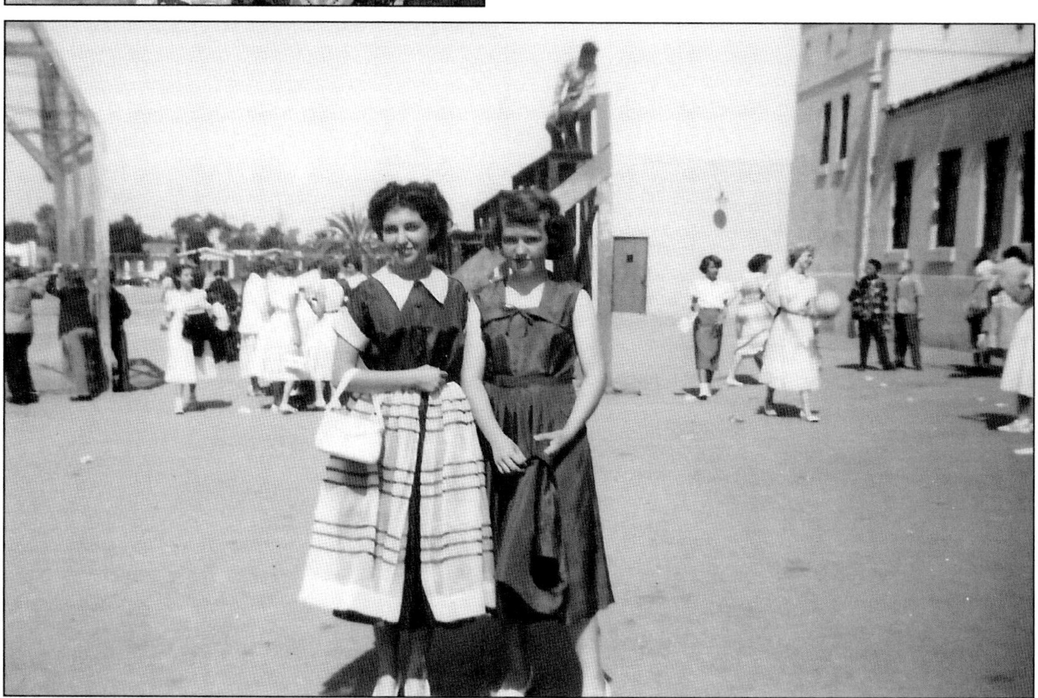

Geraldine Ottonello, left, and an unidentified friend are shown on the playground at Woodrow Wilson Junior High around 1952. Geri remembers her time at Wilson fondly, saying that there was an abundance of opportunities and activities for girls at the school, something she did not find to be true when she graduated and began attending Hoover High School. (Courtesy of Geraldine Hodge.)

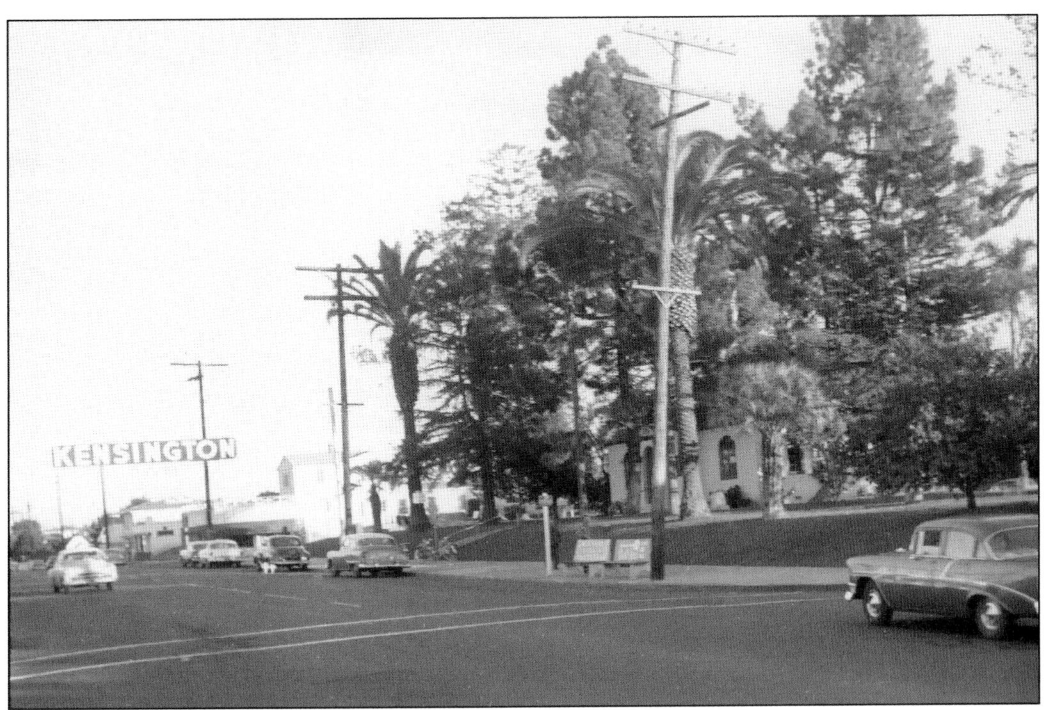

For three years, led by the Kensington Park Business Association, the neighborhood held bake sales, contests, and other fundraisers to purchase a neon sign to attract passing motorists to the shopping district and to put the neighborhood on the map. The sign was installed over Adams Avenue in 1953, and a celebration was held in December of that year. Thousands participated in the festivities, which included a parade of band music, gifts from Santa, and square dancing in Al Bunnell's service station lot. Anna Marie McKinnon was picked from 15 candidates to be crowned queen of Kensington. Geraldine Ottonello and Shirley Townsend were named princesses at a dinner held at the church. (Courtesy of San Diego History Center.)

Originally constructed in 1936, the Kensington–Normal Heights Branch Library is pictured here in 1959. Due to Kensington's population growth, an addition of approximately 1,700 square feet was constructed in 1962. (Courtesy of San Diego Public Library.)

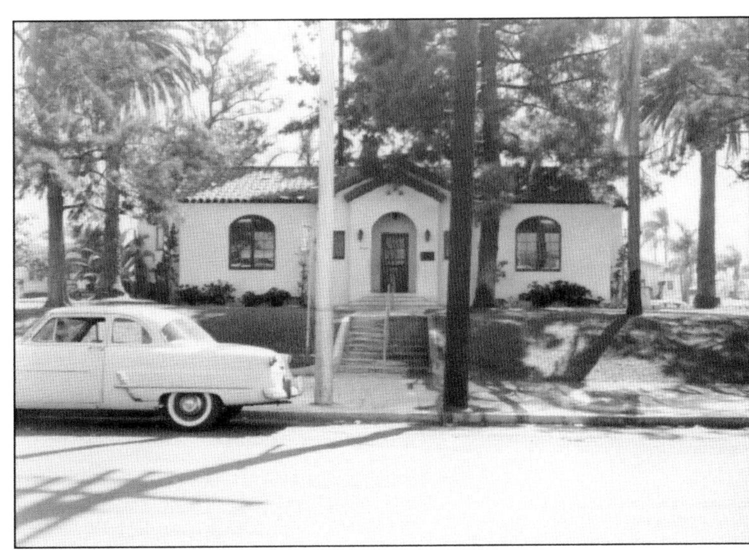

Howard Beilstein and his wife, Patricia, share a playful moment outside of the Marlborough Drive home of his parents, John and Leona. Although Howard and Patricia did not live in Kensington after their marriage in 1949, the home was the site of many family gatherings over the years. (Courtesy of Debra Beilstein.)

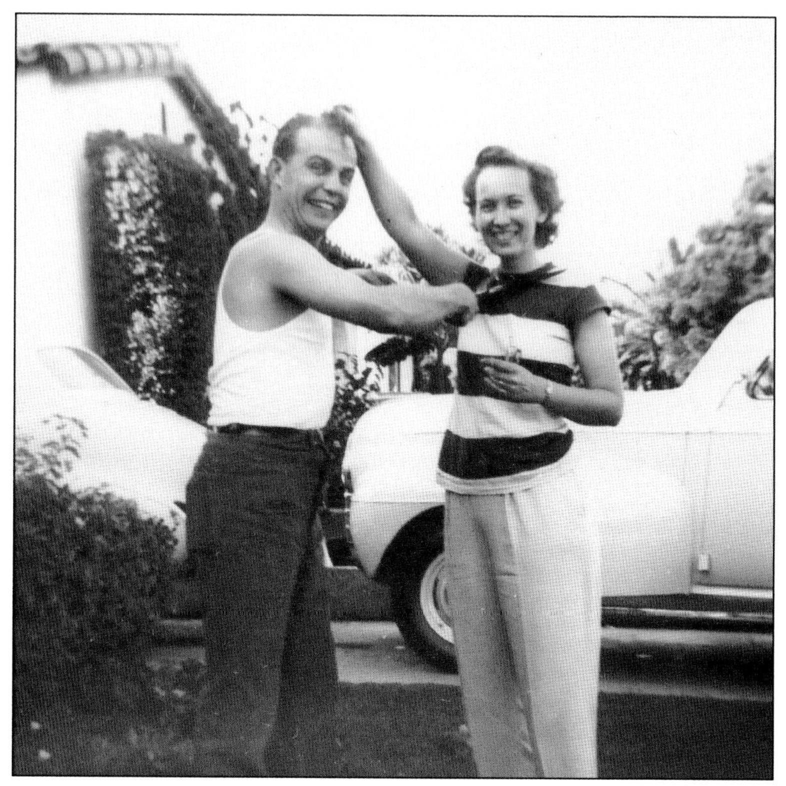

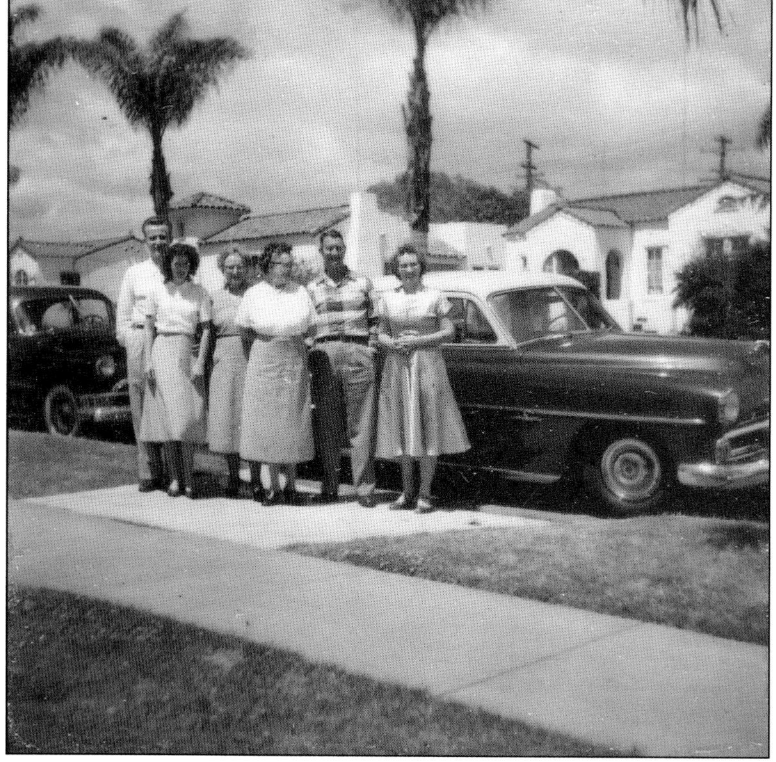

Members of the Beilstein and Barnes families gather outside of the Marlborough Drive home of recently widowed Leona Beilstein (third from left) in the 1950s. From the 1940s until the 1970s, the home was the site of many family get-togethers. (Courtesy of Debra Beilstein.)

Leonard Johnson (left) and wife Helga (center) relax with son Arne, daughter-in-law Mary Anne, and baby granddaughter Kathleen on the rear patio of 4343 Ridgeway Drive in the early 1950s. Originally from Sweden, Leonard arrived in San Diego in the 1920s and quickly established himself as a building contractor. He built several homes in Kensington, and in 1948 constructed the ranch style residence on Ridgeway Drive for Helga and himself. (Courtesy of Barbara Smith.)

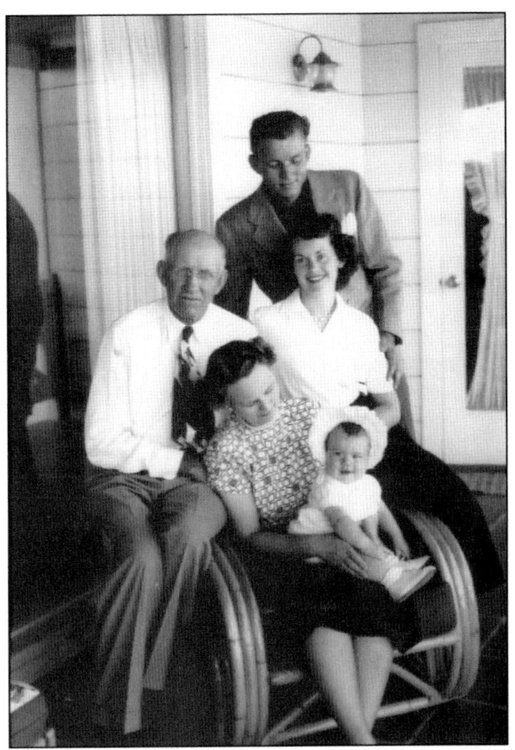

After the streetcar ceased operation, buses provided public transportation in the city. The bus route servicing Kensington retained the No. 11 name of the old streetcar line. On this day in the mid-1950s, people waiting for the bus were likely inconvenienced by an accident that drew the attention of the fire department. (Courtesy of Pacific Southwest Railway Museum.)

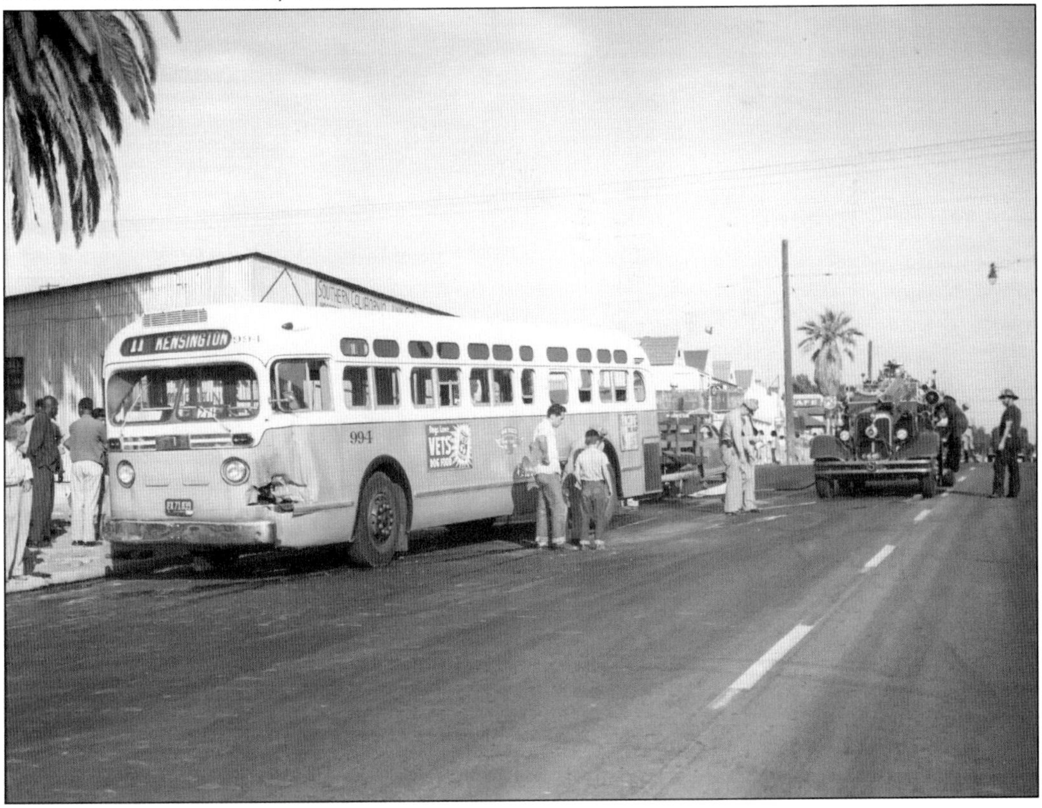

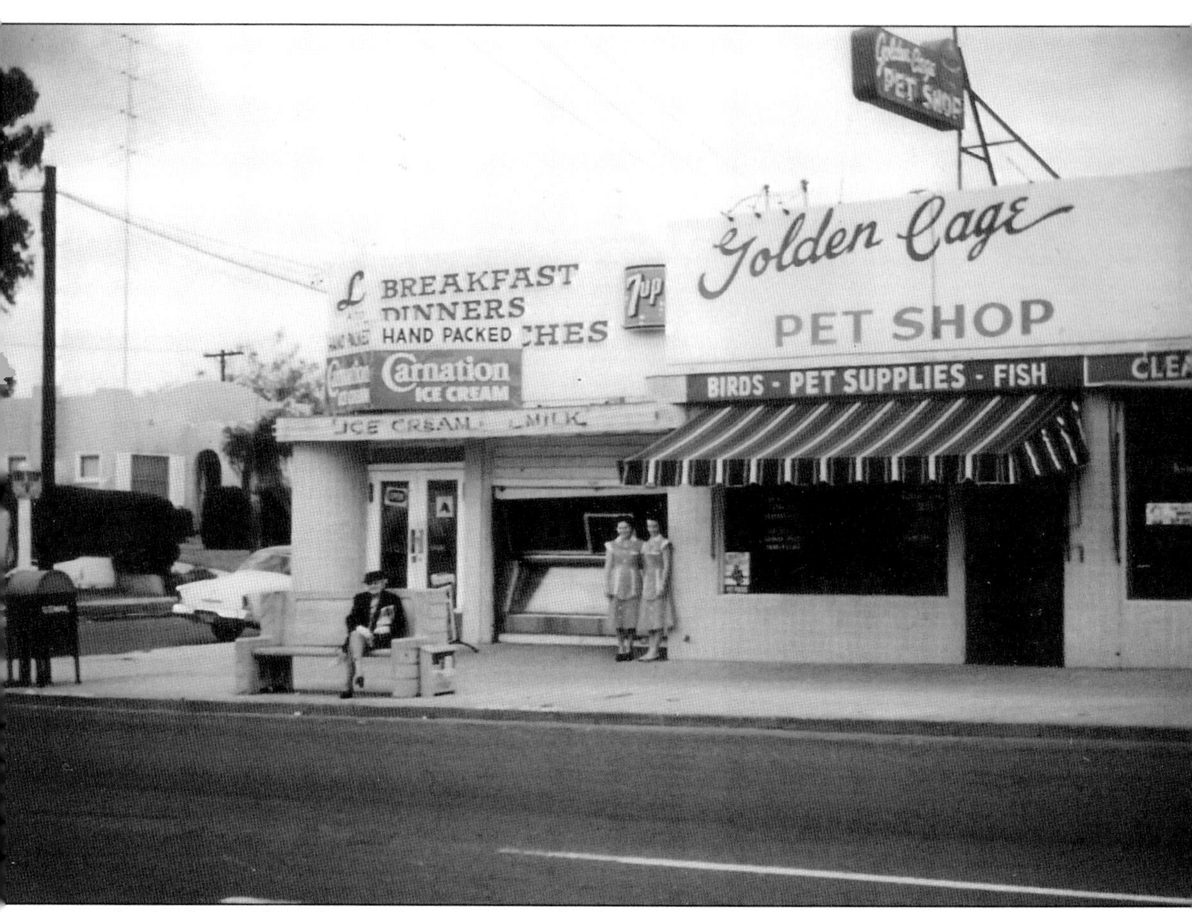

In the late 1950s, the northeast corner of Adams Avenue and Terrace Drive was home to two businesses, an ice cream parlor and a pet shop. The two buildings were later combined, and this location has been the home of Ponce's Mexican Restaurant since 1969. In the background on the left is one of the original houses that were demolished to make way for the State Route 15 extension. (Courtesy of Darlene Love.)

Six

Outside Pressures

The 1960s were a difficult time for Kensington. The old wooden trestle bridge that had served so well for 50 years was demolished and a new concrete bridge erected in its place. For over a year, Kensington could not be reached from the west via Adams Avenue. About the same time, the new Mission Valley Shopping Center, an automobile-centric mall, opened, the first of its kind in San Diego. Suddenly, everything anyone could want was a car ride away. The small mom-and-pop businesses along Adams Avenue went under one by one, leaving behind empty storefronts. The mall killed neighborhood businesses, and some of the commercial tenants that took their place, including a topless dance club, were less than desirable in the eyes of the community.

Another zoning ordinance in the 1970s allowed an influx of multifamily housing. Fine old Craftsman and Spanish-style houses were torn down or moved and replaced with "Huffman Six-Packs," unattractive apartment buildings with six units built on a lot intended for a single-family house. All over central San Diego, thousands of houses disappeared and apartment buildings were indiscriminately placed throughout the neighborhoods, leaving behind a trail of problems.

The final blow to Kensington came when the San Diego Association of Governments decided to complete the connection of the State Route 15 and Interstate 805 freeways by constructing a freeway segment through the mid-city neighborhoods of Kensington, Normal Heights, and City Heights. Once the project was announced in the late 1960s, houses in the proposed freeway area lost value, owners moved away, and the empty houses became attractive nuisances by drawing drugs, prostitution, gangs, and other seedy elements. When the project finally got underway around 1990, whole blocks of single-family houses were demolished or moved to make way for a six-lane freeway. In Kensington, almost all of the houses on the west side of Terrace Drive were lost.

Maybe these unwelcome changes awoke the preservationists in the community. In 1982, the first house in Kensington to be designated by the City of San Diego as a historical resource was the Duehn-St. John Residence at 4720 Kensington Drive.

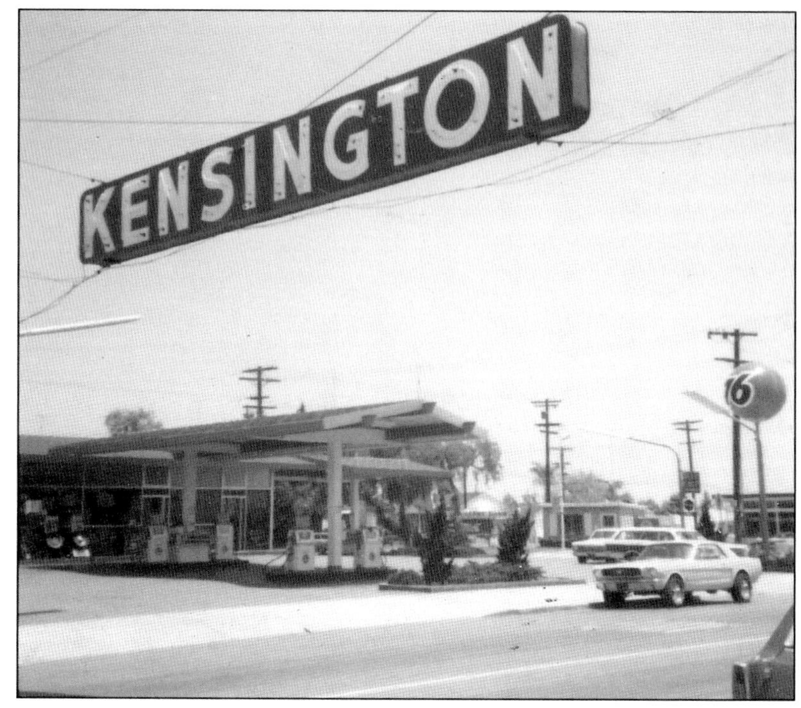

Al Bunnell continued to operate a service station on the northwest corner of Adams Avenue and Marlborough Drive. The old Spanish-style station was torn down and a new one, pictured here around 1965, took its place. The iconic Kensington neon sign was about 12 years old at the time. (Courtesy of Margaret McCann.)

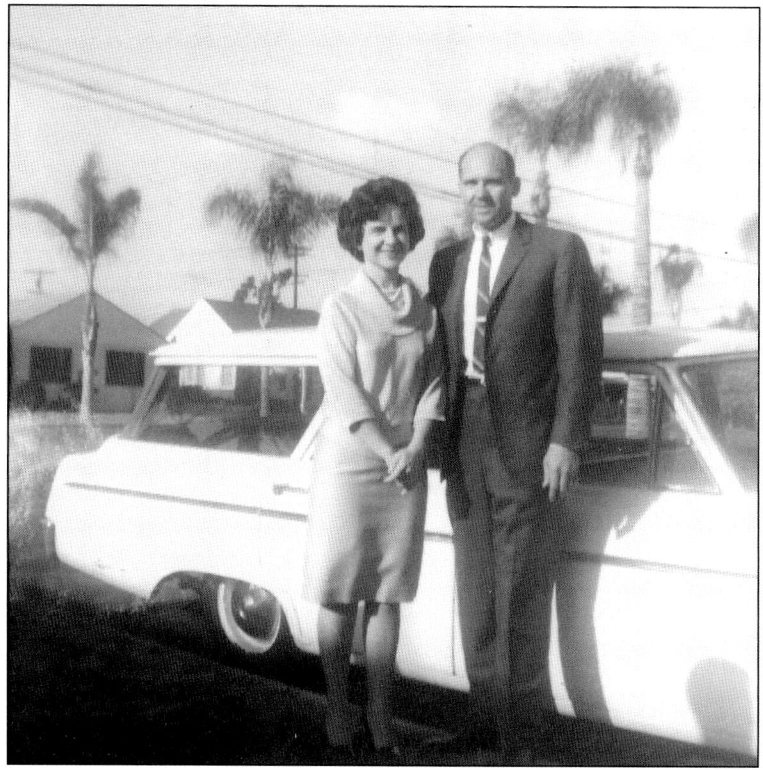

Winnie and Rich Hanford pose with their faithful station wagon in front of Beverly and Jim Sullivan's house on Vista Street. The very same automobile brought the Hanford family to Kensington from St. Louis in 1963. Jim Sullivan, Winnie's brother, moved his family to Kensington in 1960. (Courtesy of Winnie and Rich Hanford.)

Winnie and Rich Hanford arrived in Kensington in 1963, leaving their home in St. Louis. Winnie immediately took a job in sales at a Montgomery Ward store. On the store's "French Day" in 1963, Winnie stylishly attired herself in spiked heels and a fringed dress, looking the part for her shift on the sales floor. (Courtesy of Winnie and Rich Hanford.)

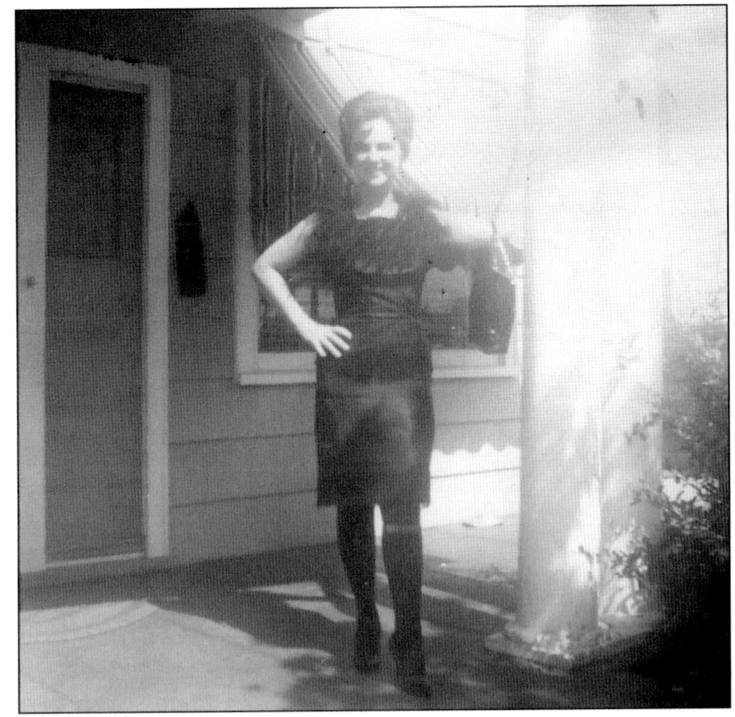

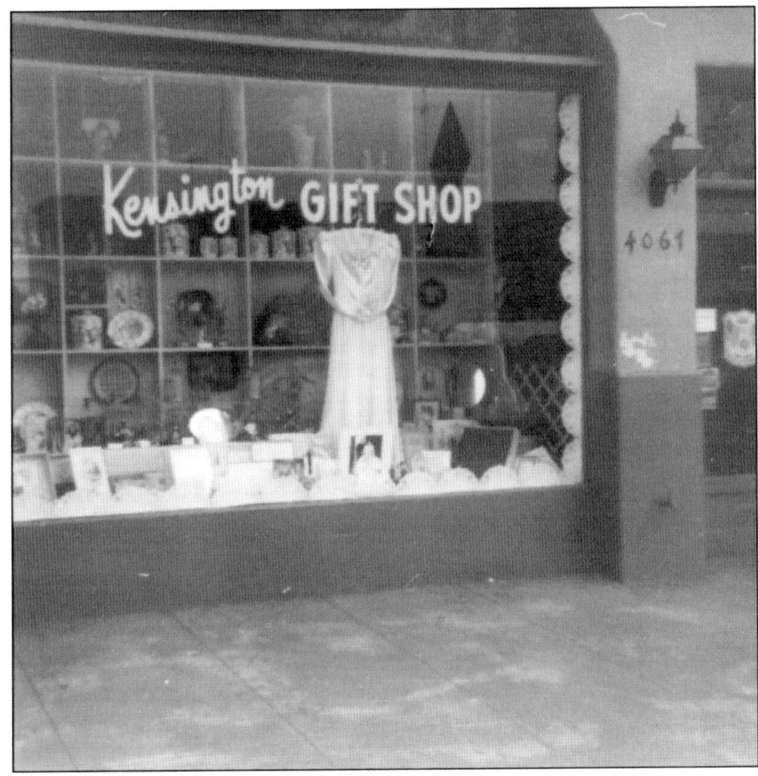

The Kensington Gift Shop at 4061 Adams Avenue was opened by Winnie and Rich Hanford in 1963. The original owner of the lot, Rose E. Fisher, hired Joseph Carlson Kelley, a building contractor, to construct the building in 1930. The first occupants were the Pack and Peterman building contractors, a firm that constructed many of the homes in the Kensington Park Extension subdivision along Biona Drive. The dress hanging in the window was Winnie's wedding dress. (Courtesy of Winnie and Rich Hanford.)

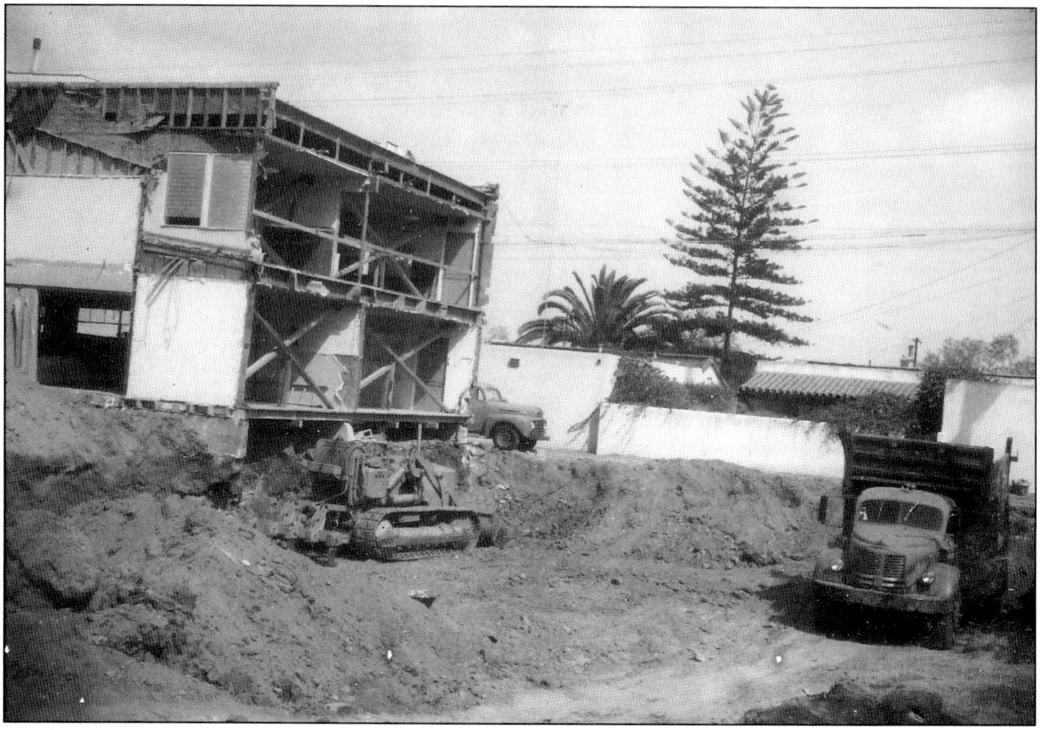

Work is progressing on the demolition of the Kensington Community Church Sunday school building that was severely damaged in a 1965 fire. The fire was started by a few small children who lit the robes on fire in the choir room. From the time of its inception, the church building fund was put to good use as the congregation grew. (Courtesy of Kensington Community Church.)

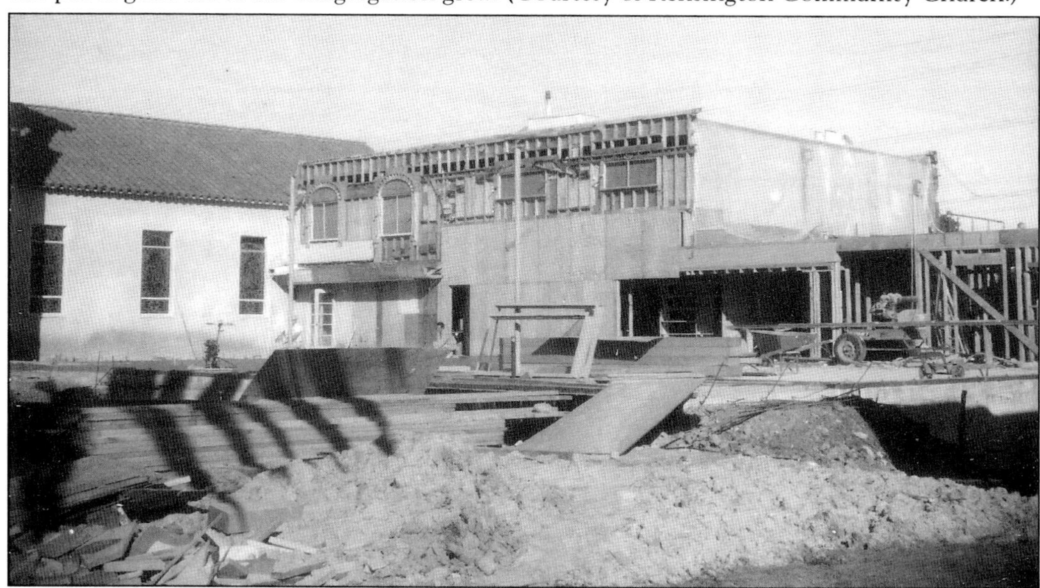

Construction of a new social hall and classrooms is underway at the Kensington Community Church after it was severely damaged in a fire in 1965. The church has undergone many renovations since its inception shortly after the Southern California Conference of the Congregational Church purchased the land in 1929. (Courtesy of Kensington Community Church.)

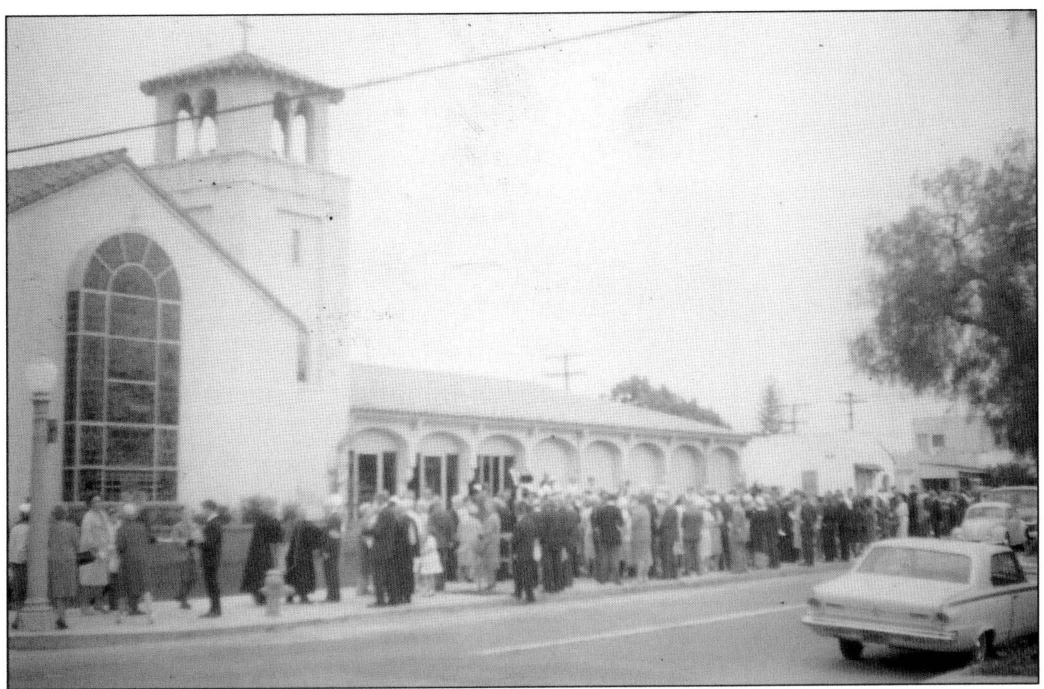

Throngs of people turned out for the May 1966 dedication of the new Kensington Community Church buildings on Marlborough Drive. The large stained-glass window in the sanctuary was made and installed by the American Art Glass studio. (Courtesy of Kensington Community Church.)

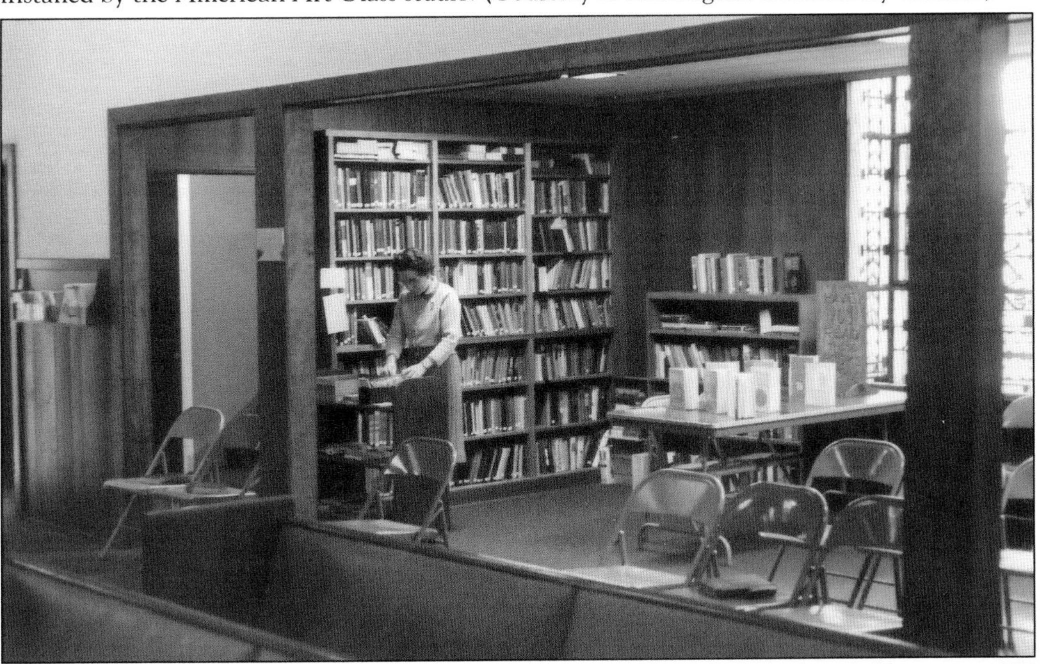

Kensington Community Church librarian Ruth Cole established the church library in 1957 beginning with devotional books and expanding over the years to include fiction and nonfiction for youths and adults. Ruth was the church librarian for 31 years. In this photograph from 1965, Cole organizes the card catalogue. (Courtesy of Kensington Community Church.)

Teenagers Becky Sickler (left) and her neighborhood friend Sandee Rose look ready for a day as California surfer girls in this photograph from December 1961. (Courtesy of Becky McMullen.)

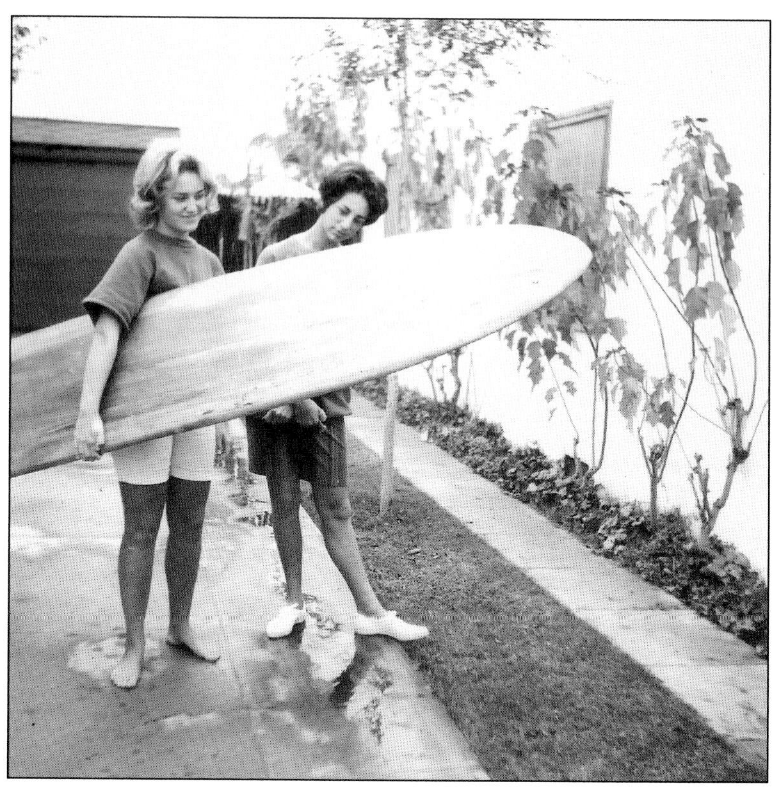

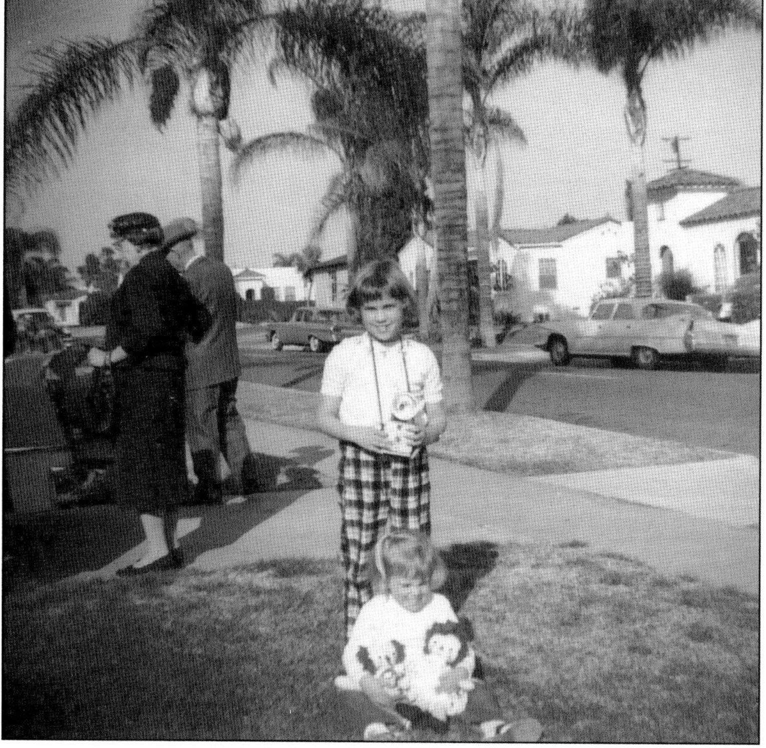

Sharon Beilstein shows off her new camera, while sister Debra is thrilled about her Raggedy Ann and Andy dolls during this December 1960 visit to the Marlborough Drive home of their great uncle and aunt, Frank and Clara Peck Wood. The Woods, seen in the background, moved from Iowa and into the home earlier that year. It had previously been occupied by Clara's sister Leona Beilstein. (Courtesy of Debra Beilstein.)

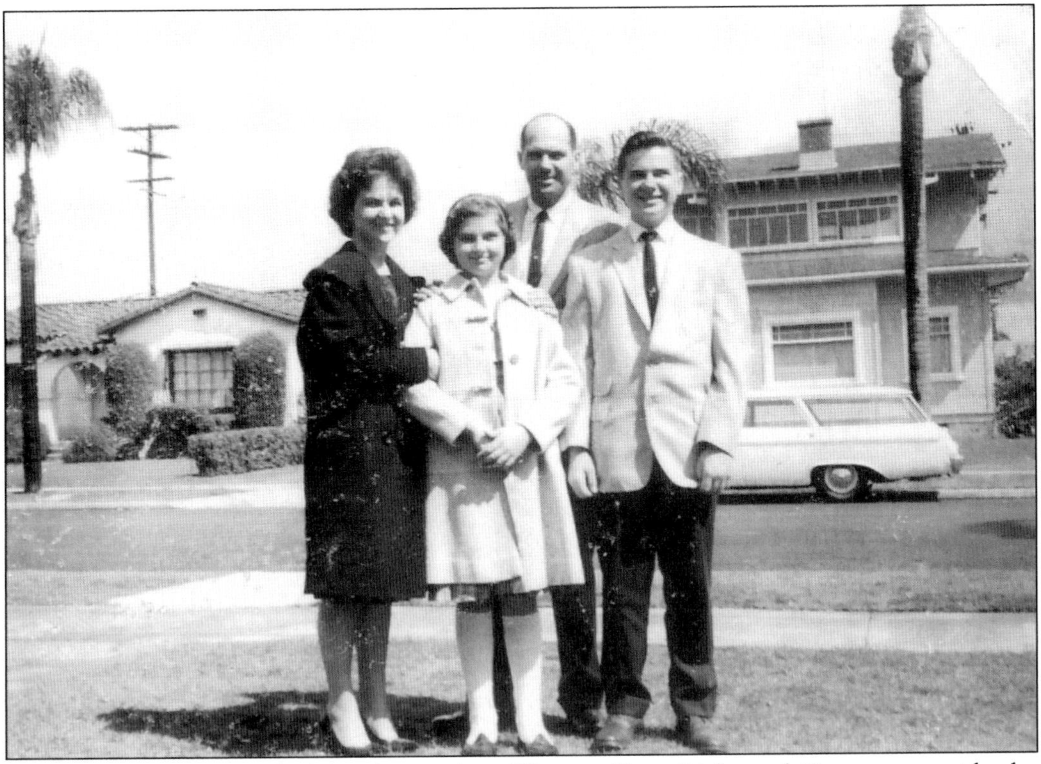

From left to right, Hanford family members Winnie, Pam, Rich, and Guy pose outside the Sullivans' house on Vista Street in 1965. The two-story Craftsman house in the background is the historically designated Oscar Grunert House, built in 1912 and moved to this location from the northeast corner of Adams Avenue and Marlborough Drive in 1926 to make way for a gas station. The charming house on the left was later rendered unrecognizable by a remodel, and became a dental office. (Courtesy of Winnie and Rich Hanford.)

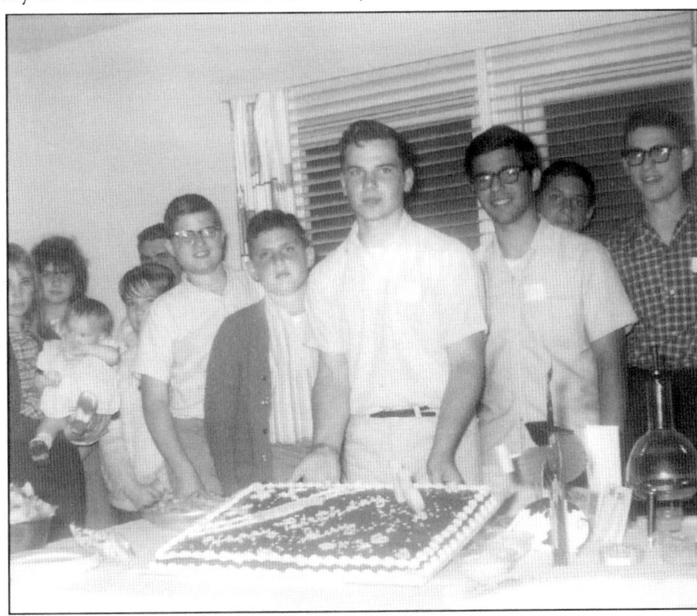

Future schoolteacher Guy Hanford celebrates his 16th birthday in 1965, surrounded by unidentified friends. His sister Pam is in the background, second from left. A lover of movies, Guy convinced his parents to convert their gift shop to a video store that was renowned throughout the county. (Courtesy of Winnie and Rich Hanford.)

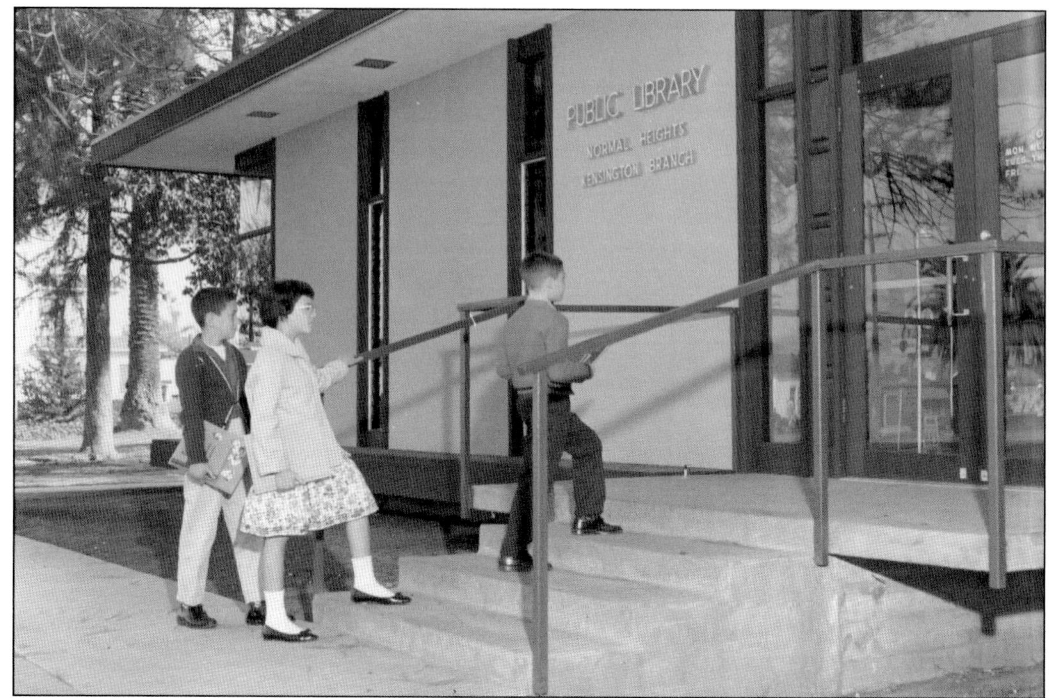

Children climb the steps of the remodeled Kensington–Normal Heights Branch Library in 1963. Architect Richard Lareau designed the approximately 1,700-square-foot remodel, which was completed in 1962. San Diego mayor Charles Dail officially dedicated the addition on October 29, 1962. Its sleek appearance was a departure from the Spanish style of the original building but reflected Lareau's design philosophy of structure as a building's decorative program. Lareau also designed the East San Diego Library and the Mission Bay Visitor Information Center. (Courtesy of San Diego Public Library.)

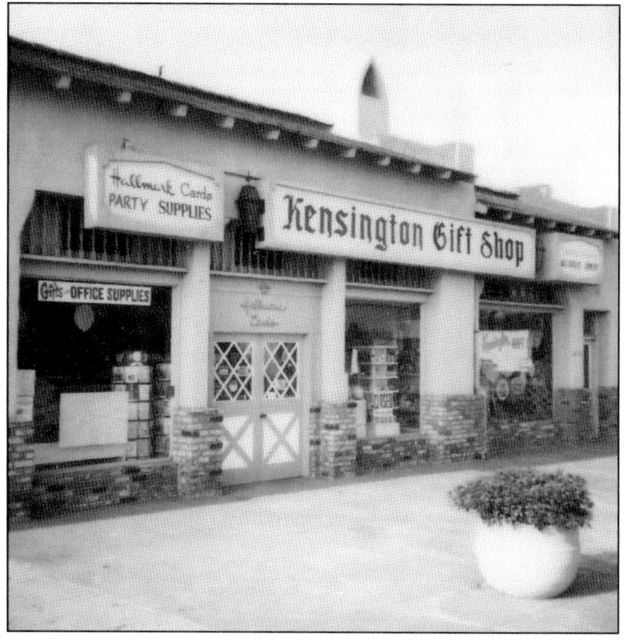

The Kensington Gift Shop at 4061 Adams Avenue was opened by Winnie and Rich Hanford in 1963. The original owner of the lot, Rose E. Fisher, hired Joseph Carlson Kelley, a building contractor, to construct the building in 1930. The first occupants of the building were the Pack and Peterman building contractors, a firm that constructed many of the homes in Kensington. (Courtesy of Winnie and Rich Hanford.)

Very little has changed at Benjamin Franklin School since this photograph was taken in 1961. The school safety patrolman watches as children cross Copeland Avenue, headed for a day at school. (Courtesy of Franklin Elementary School.)

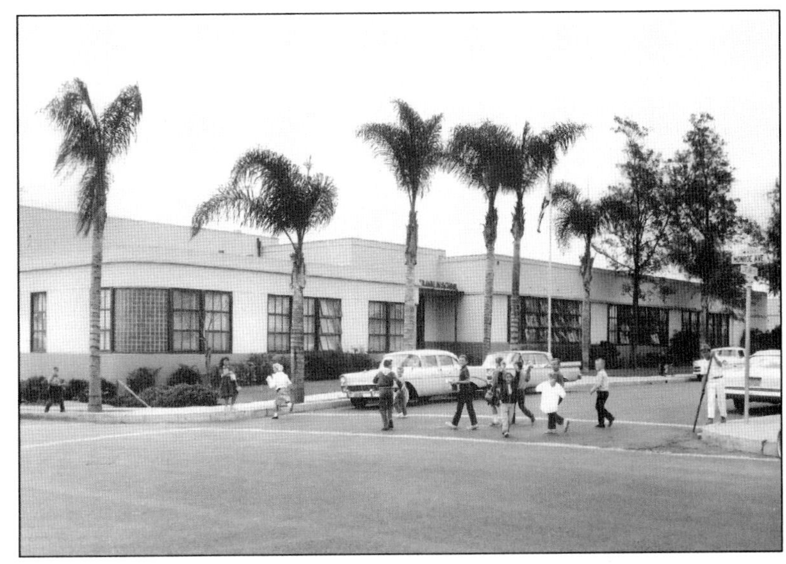

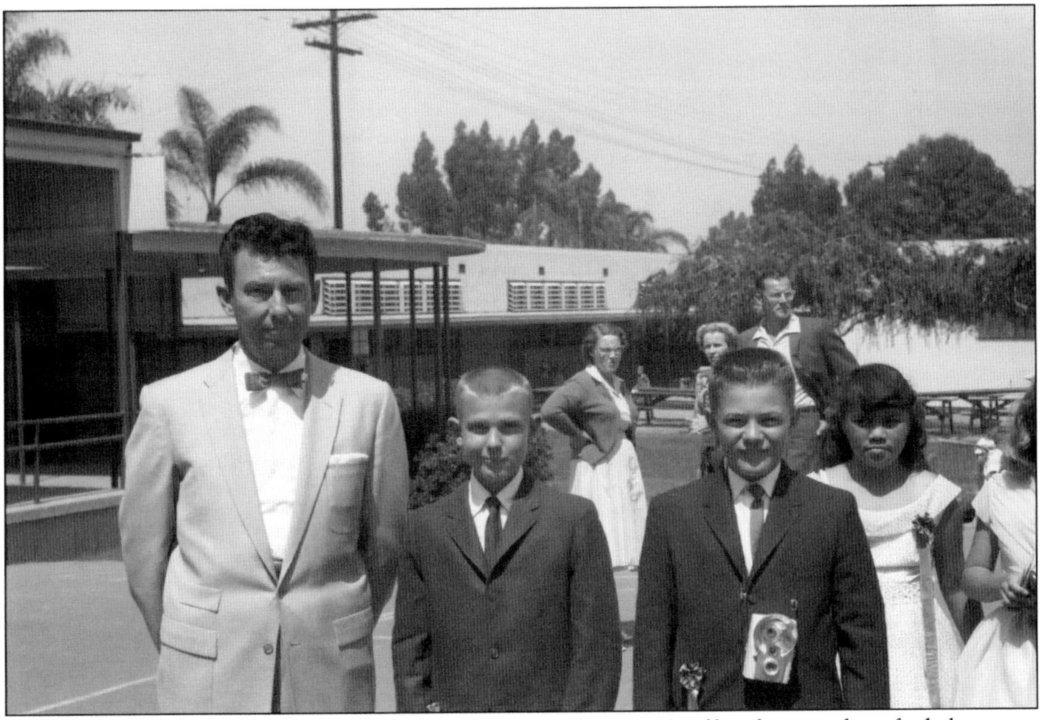

Neil Webb Jr. (center) stands with his sixth grade teacher Mr. Stuff and an unidentified classmate on the grounds of Benjamin Franklin School on the occasion of Webb's graduation from sixth grade in 1966. Neil Webb went on to become a teacher with the Riverside Unified School District, and for 20 years taught German, Latin, and early English literature at Riverside Polytechnic High School. The couple behind the unidentified classmate are Julie and Hank Jeitler, the original owners and creators of Adams Avenue Bookstore. (Courtesy of Julia Webb.)

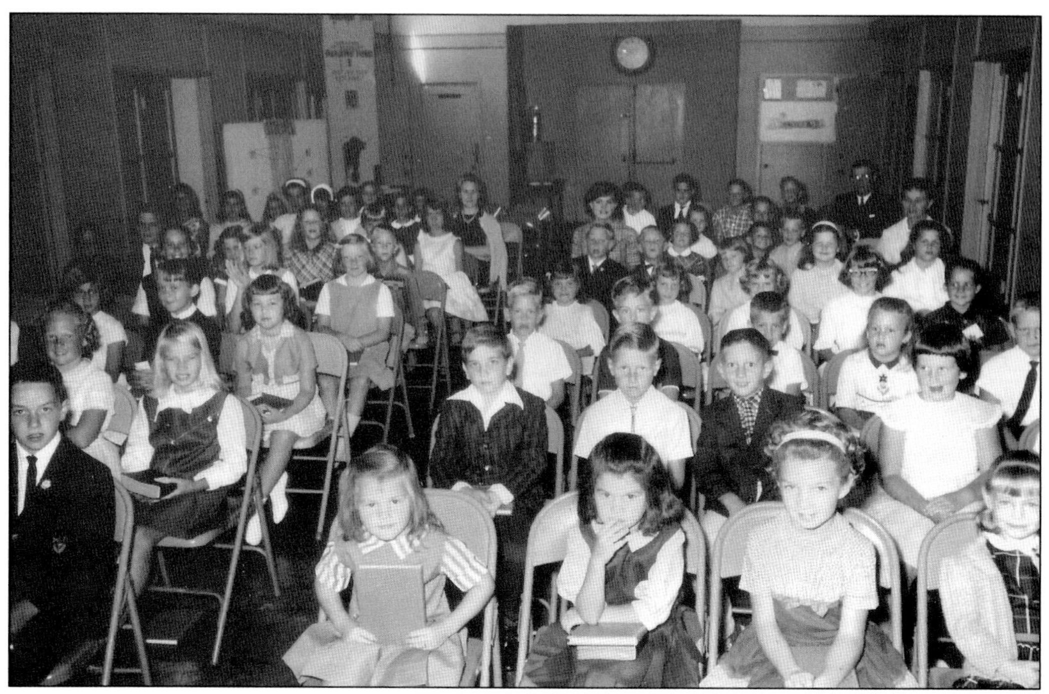

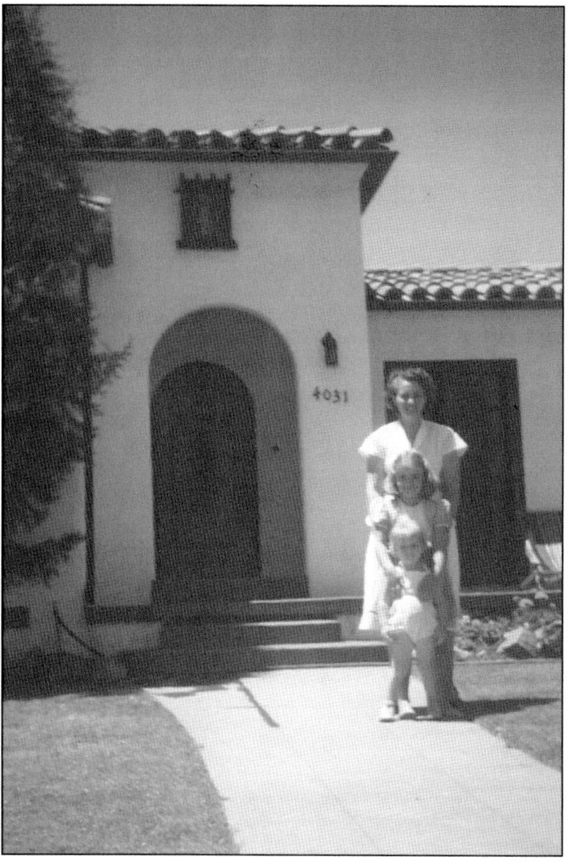

Sunday school was full at the Kensington Community Church in this image from the early 1960s. The church's board of trustees hired architect Victor Wulff in 1964 to design a new building, which was constructed in 1965 after a fire severely damaged the social hall and school building. (Courtesy of Kensington Community Church.)

Marjorie Nelson Greer poses in the front yard of her sister Stella Dupree's house on North Hempstead Circle with her nieces Marilyn Dupree (center) and Patricia Dupree in the mid-1950s. (Courtesy of Gail Greer.)

Gail Greer is ready for the Hoover High School prom in 1963. Her hairstyle and dress show the change in style from the previous era. Gone are the bouffant hairdos and Cinderella dresses, replaced by short, natural hair, and a sleek, sleeveless dress decorated with a paisley pattern. (Courtesy of Gail Greer.)

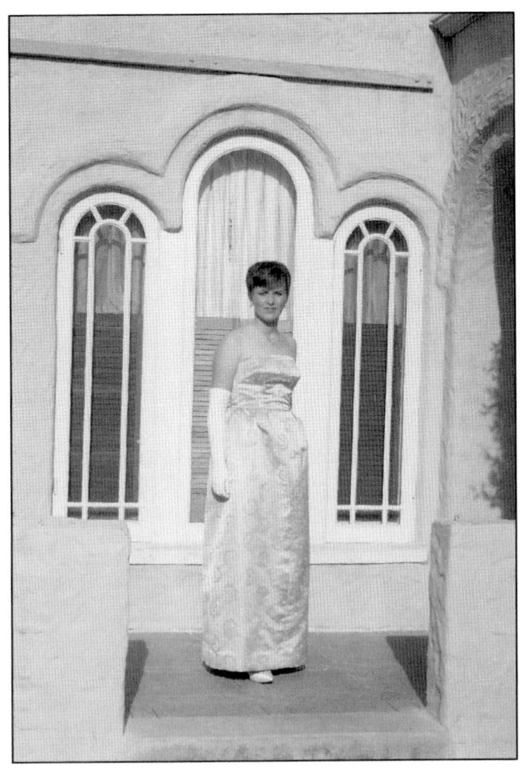

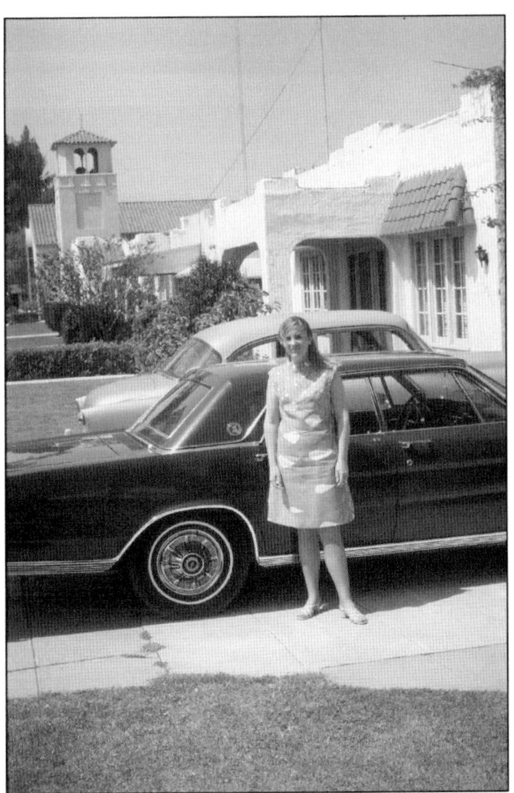

Gail Greer Lombardo poses in the driveway of her family home at 4725 Marlborough Drive in 1967 next to her Ford Galaxie. The Kensington Community Church can be seen farther north in the background. (Courtesy of Gail Greer.)

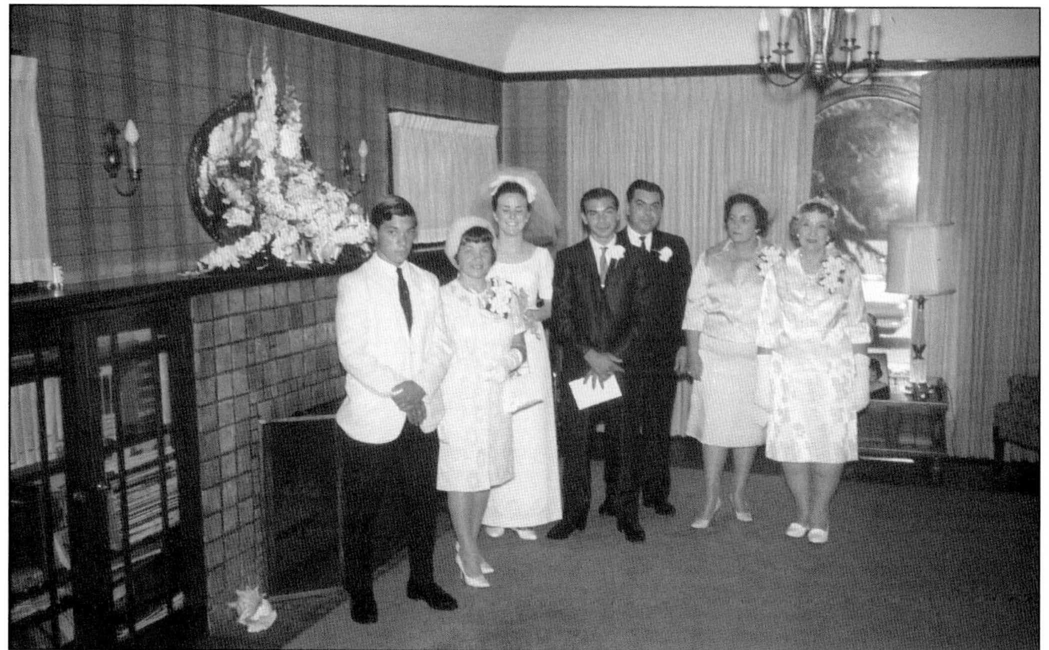

A floral arrangement decorates the fireplace mantel in the living room of the Greer home on Marlborough Drive on the occasion of Gail Greer's wedding in 1966. On the far right is the bride's grandmother Corrine E. Nelson, who lived across the street. On her right is the bride's mother, Marjorie Jane Nelson Greer. The groom and his family round out the wedding party. (Courtesy of Gail Greer.)

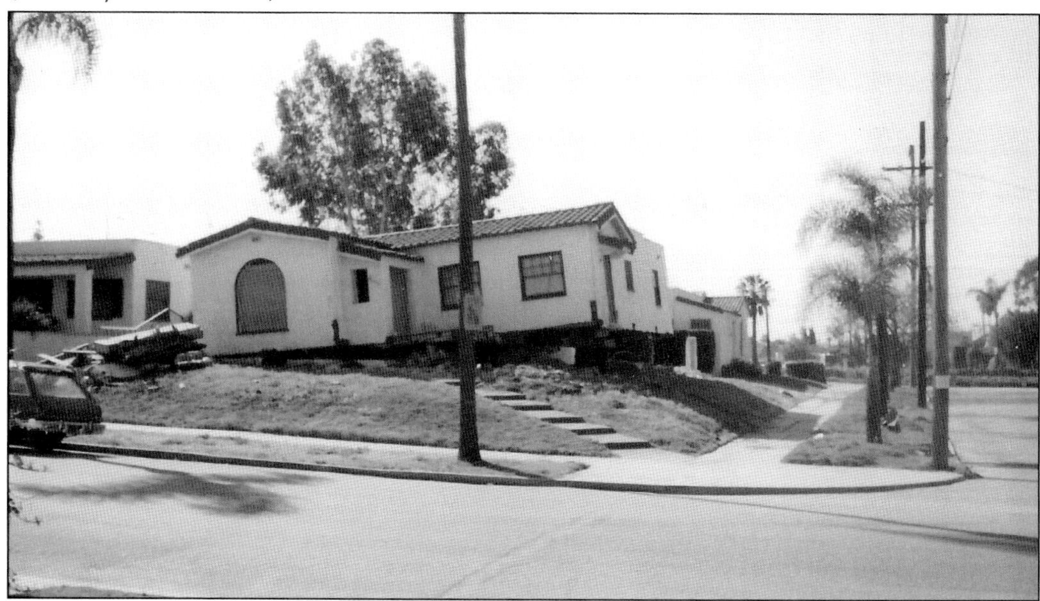

Kensington and the surrounding neighborhoods of City Heights and Normal Heights lost dozens of fine old houses when State Route 15 replaced Ward Road and Fortieth Street. Sibyl Crossman, owner of the Tom Thumb Market, lived in this Spanish Eclectic house on the southwest corner of Terrace Drive and Madison Avenue. The house was moved to another location to make way for the State Route 15 off-ramp to Kensington. (Courtesy of Winnie and Rich Hanford.)

Seven

Continuing Their Legacy

From its inception, Kensington has been home to pioneers of all stripes. It began with Silas St. John, who drove the first eastbound mail stagecoach for the Great Overland Mail Company out of San Diego from Carriso Creek to Fort Yuma in 1857. St. John survived a massacre at the Dragoon Springs Stage Station with only the loss of an arm, and after subsequent work as a federal Indian agent and agricultural editor, retired to 4720 Kensington Drive in 1914, where he lived until his death in 1919. On his grave marker in Mount Hope Cemetery is inscribed, "Of His Stuff the West Was Made."

The spirit of the architects, builders, neighbors, and business owners that shaped this community shines through today in community organizations and events. The Kensington Social and Athletic Club's (KSAC) volunteers put on a pretty darn good parade and relay race every year on Memorial Day weekend, and the club's KSAC Litter Pickers help keep the roadways and canyons clean. The Kensington-Talmadge Community Association maintains the historic Kensington neon sign that hangs over Adams Avenue and sponsors the Garden Angels, volunteers who use their own time and money to plant attractive water-wise gardens in the parkways around the neighborhood. The last of the single screen movie theaters in San Diego is the iconic Ken Theater on Adams Avenue, which has been saved from oblivion time and again by residents kicking up a fuss. Dozens of homeowners have invested in voluntarily obtaining historical designation for their houses, ensuring the charm and character of the neighborhood remains intact for all to enjoy.

Kensington has a sizable LGBT population that includes pioneers in the struggle for human rights. One of the earliest gay bookstores was located on Adams Avenue, and the Ken Theater regularly showed films as part of Outfest, The San Diego Gay & Lesbian Film Festival. Other residents helped found the first Pride March in San Diego, and the nation's second oldest LGBT community center, The Center, in Hillcrest.

Over 100 years since its founding, Kensington today is a delightful neighborhood because of everyone who came before us, and everyone who calls this place home today.

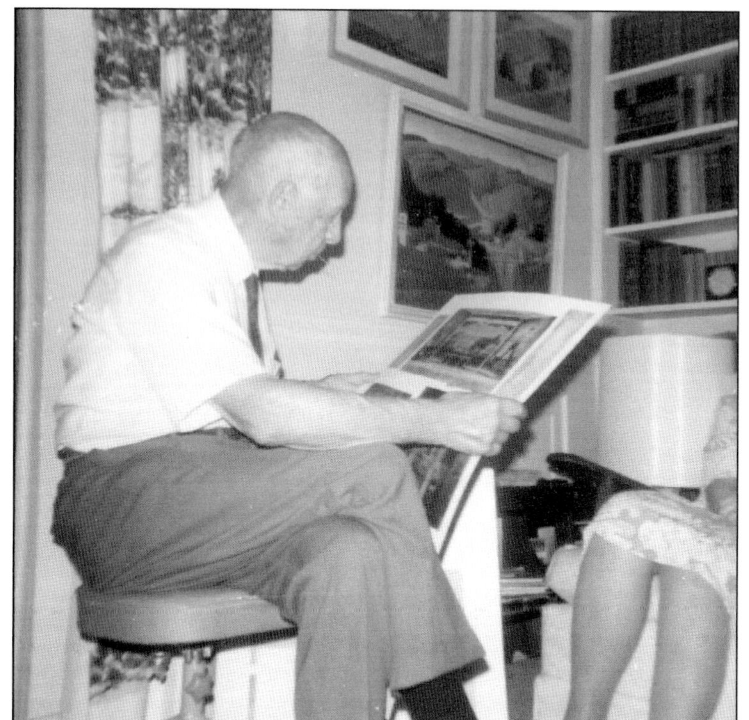

Frank Wood studies a scrapbook of his late brother Grant Wood's artwork in this 1960s photograph taken in the den of 4952 Marlborough Drive. In 1930, Grant painted the iconic *American Gothic*. Nan Wood Graham, sister of Frank and Grant, was the painting's female model and frequently visited Frank in Kensington. Several of Grant's pieces, many of them original, were displayed in the home. (Courtesy of Debra Beilstein.)

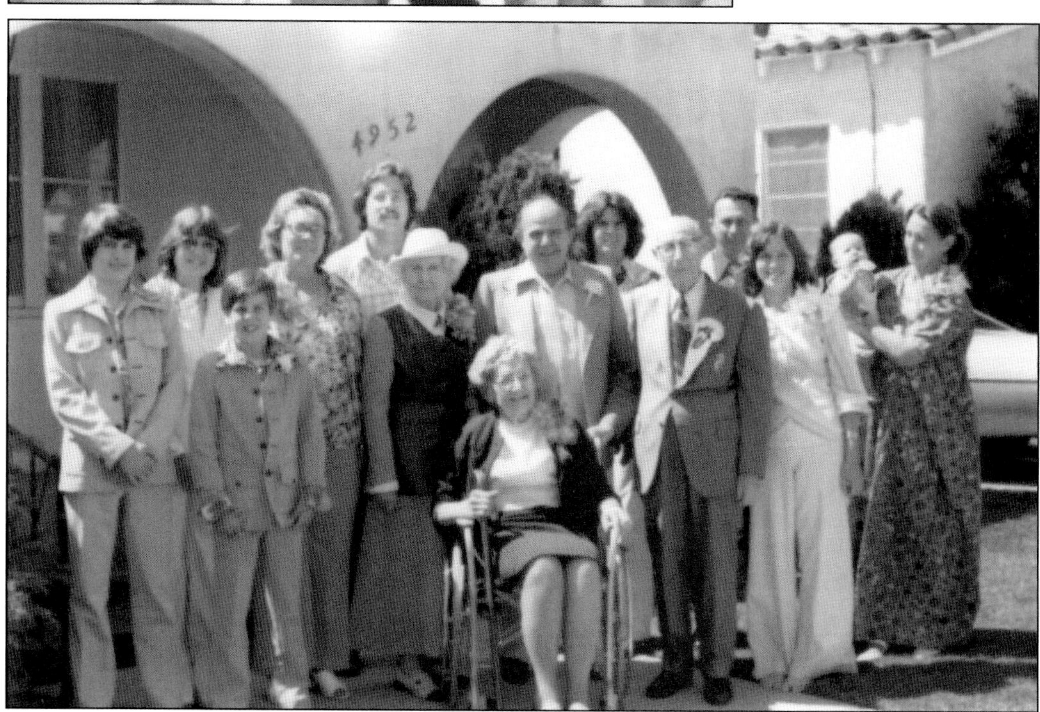

Celebrating their 65th wedding anniversary in 1976, Frank Wood (fourth from right) and his wife, Clara (seated), gather with family members in front of the Wood home. The woman wearing the hat is Frank's sister Nan Wood Graham, the model for their brother Grant Wood's *American Gothic*. She was visiting from Riverside. (Courtesy of Debra Beilstein.)

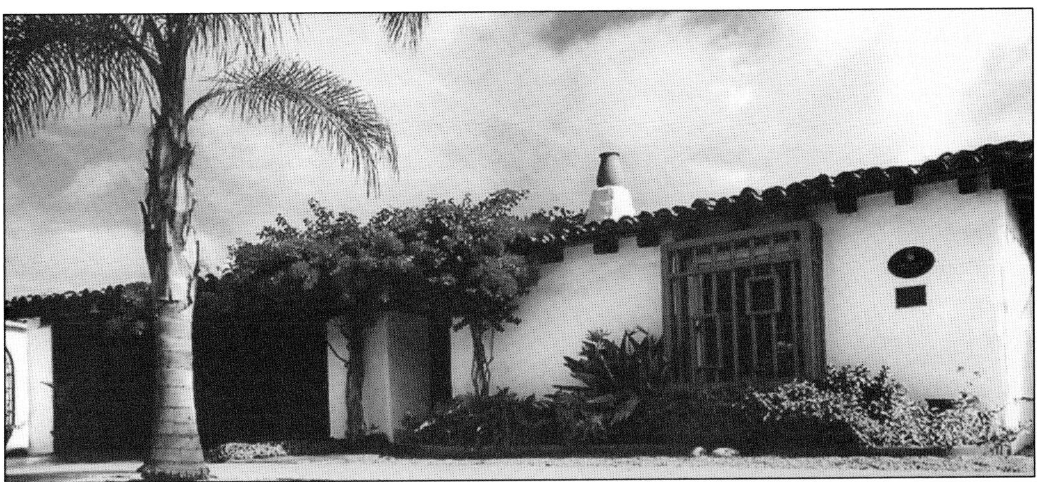

The Lindstrom House is not only a local treasure but also a National Historic Landmark. Located in the Talmadge Park No. 1 subdivision, this is the second house built by noted architect Cliff May. As a sixth-generation Californian, native San Diegan, and member of the Estudillo and Pedrorena families, May was inspired by the family's adobe ranch houses at the Las Flores rancho and the Estudillo house in Old Town. He moved to Los Angeles in 1936, and by 1941 had established a national reputation as the designer of the California Ranch House. (Courtesy of Margaret McCann.)

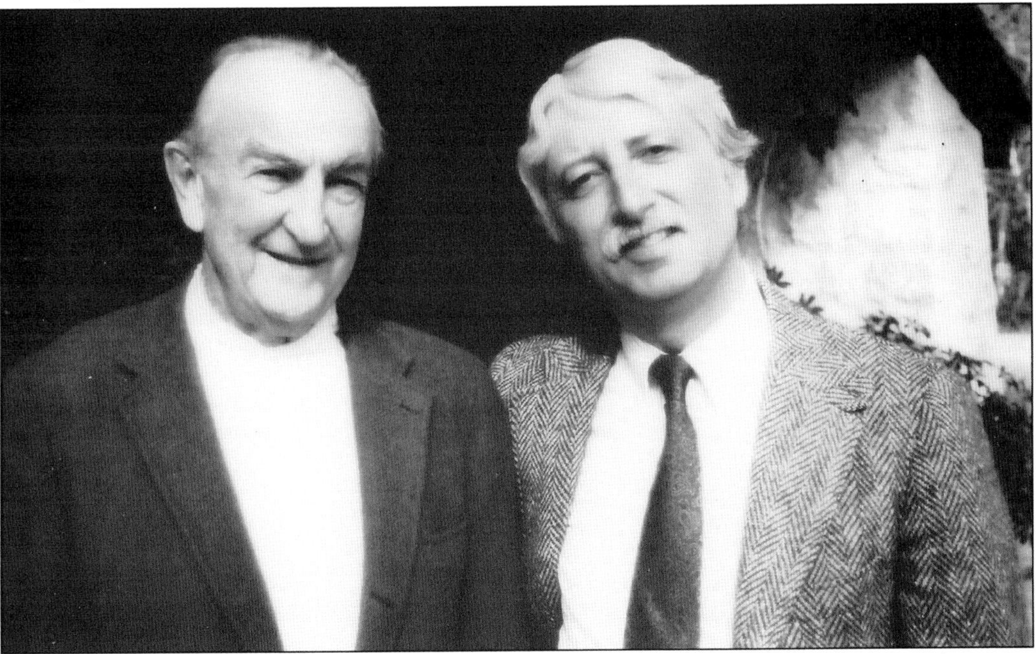

Architect Norm Applebaum (right) and the late Cliff May, father of the California Ranch House, shared a love for architecture and jazz music. Applebaum was invited to lunch at May's home. Cliff had a band at the Hotel Del Coronado in the early 1930s in which he played tenor sax. Norm plays jazz trombone so they had a session together with May playing his grand piano, and the bond between the two architects was complete. This 1983 photograph was taken at Mandalay, Cliff May's home in the Brentwood neighborhood of Los Angeles. (Courtesy of Barbara Roper and Norm Applebaum.)

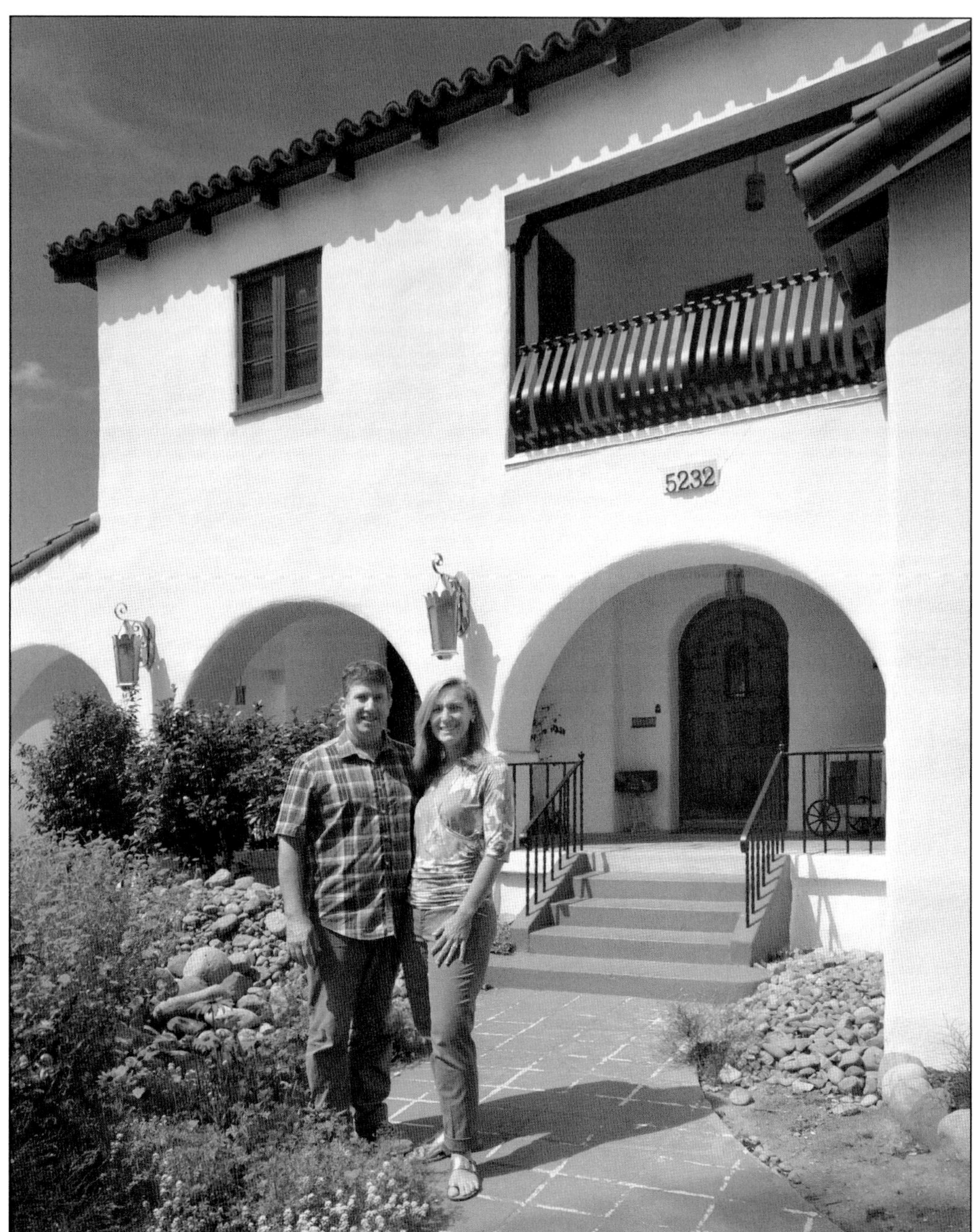

Devin (left) and DeLayne Harmon inherited their 1929 Spanish Revival–style house at 5232 Marlborough Drive and immediately set about a restoration that led to a People in Preservation Award from Save Our Heritage Organisation. They also went through the process of obtaining historical designation status from the City of San Diego and can now call home the Enrique and Esperanza Aldrete/Carl B. Hays House. Meticulously detail-oriented, the Harmons hired top-notch artisans, craftsmen, architects, and contractors for exacting work on the house inside and out. In the process, they became passionate about preservation and are happy to share their home and talk with fellow preservationists. (Courtesy of Sandé Lollis.)

Save Our Heritage Organisation has awarded several Kensington residents and groups with a coveted People in Preservation award. Among the honorees are Robert and Ingrid Coffin, the recipients of SOHO's 2012 award for home restoration. Since 1977, the Coffins have devoted themselves to meticulously restoring and maintaining their Spanish Colonial Revival–style home, which had been the home of former Mexican president Pascual Ortiz Rubio in the 1930s. Pictured here from left to right are Robert Coffin, Ingrid Coffin, and their team of restoration experts, Glenn Carlson, Dionne Carlson, and Jeanne Whalen. (Courtesy of Sandé Lollis.)

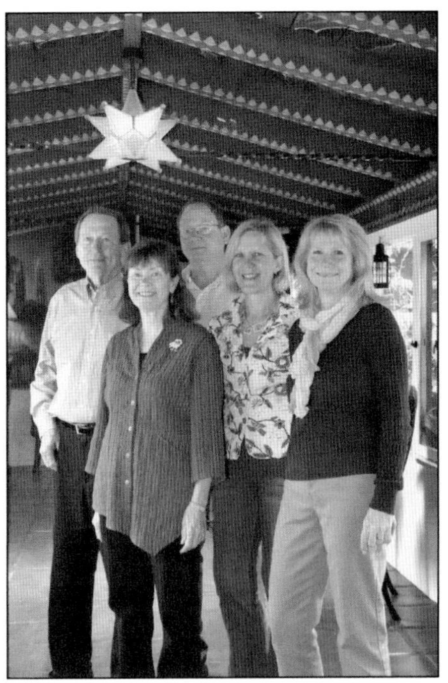

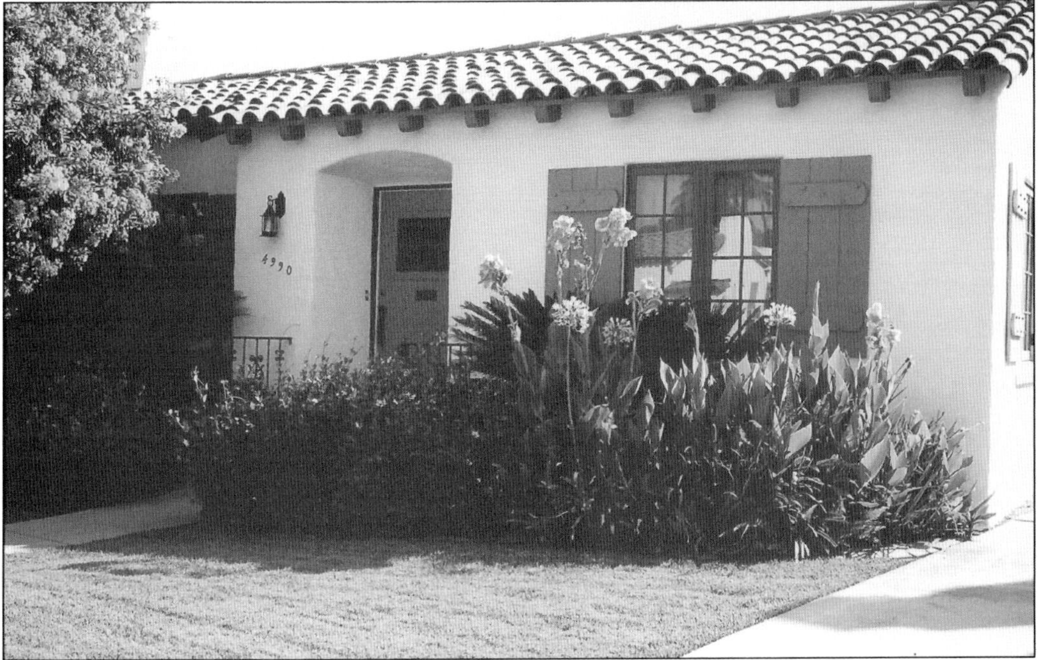

The Cora M. and Cora Lee Wells House, built in 1927, is the home of Priscilla Berge. For many years, Berge served on the City of San Diego's Historical Resources Board, which evaluates resources for historical designation. Retired from her position as lecturer and teacher of Native American studies at San Diego State University, Berge researched and documented the Kensington Manor Unit No. 2 subdivision and submitted a historic district nomination to the city in 2008. If accepted by the city, this would be the first historic district within the boundaries of greater Kensington. (Courtesy of Margaret McCann.)

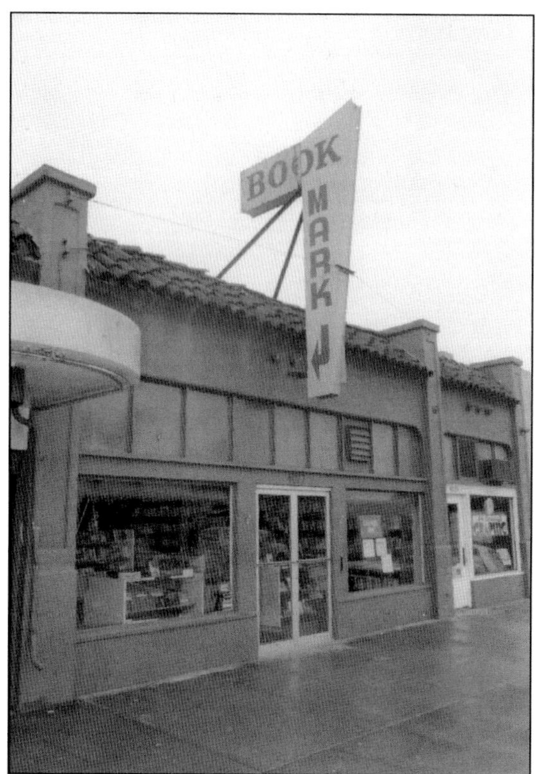

John Richardson owned one of the first bookstores in San Diego to stock gay- and lesbian-themed books and videos. Located at 4077 Adams Avenue, Richardson advertised that his "More Than a General Book Store" offered a "Gay Section." The bookstore began operation at this location in 1976. (Courtesy of Lambda Archives of San Diego.)

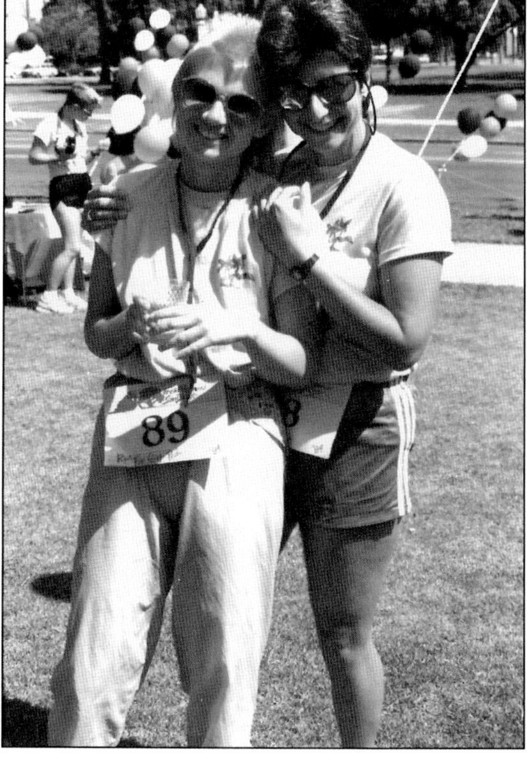

Gabriel Gilbert (front) and Ann Rubenstein share their happiness at finishing the 1984 Run for Gay Pride, held in conjunction with the annual San Diego Pride Festival and Parade. The parade began in 1975, and the event has grown each year since, with more than 200 floats and entries viewed by a crowd of more than 200,000 people representing communities all over San Diego. Together since 1983, Ann and Gabe were finally able to marry in 2008 on their 25th anniversary as a couple. (Courtesy of Gabriel Gilbert and Ann Rubenstein.)

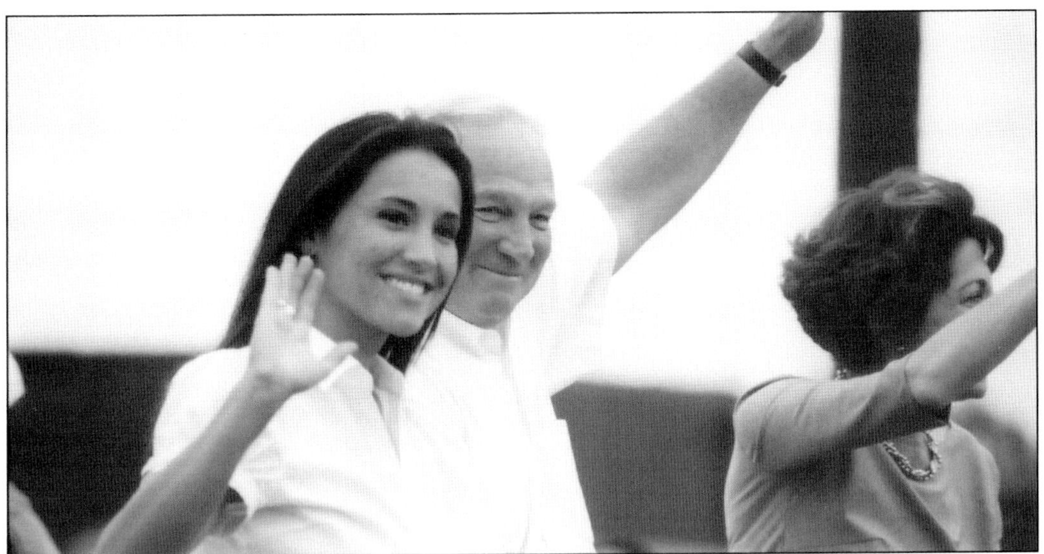

Jerry Sanders is often seen on his daily walk around Kensington and down Adams Avenue. As mayor of San Diego, Sanders vowed to veto a city council resolution to join a lawsuit to overturn a ban on gay marriage. He famously reversed his position on September 19, 2007, when he signed the resolution. In a tearful speech before the cameras, he explained that he wanted his daughter Lisa, who is gay, and other gay people to have their relationships protected equally under state laws. A veteran of many Pride Parades, Sanders (center) is seated between his daughter Lisa (left) and his wife, Rana Sampson, in the 2008 San Diego Pride Parade. (Courtesy of Lambda Archives of San Diego.)

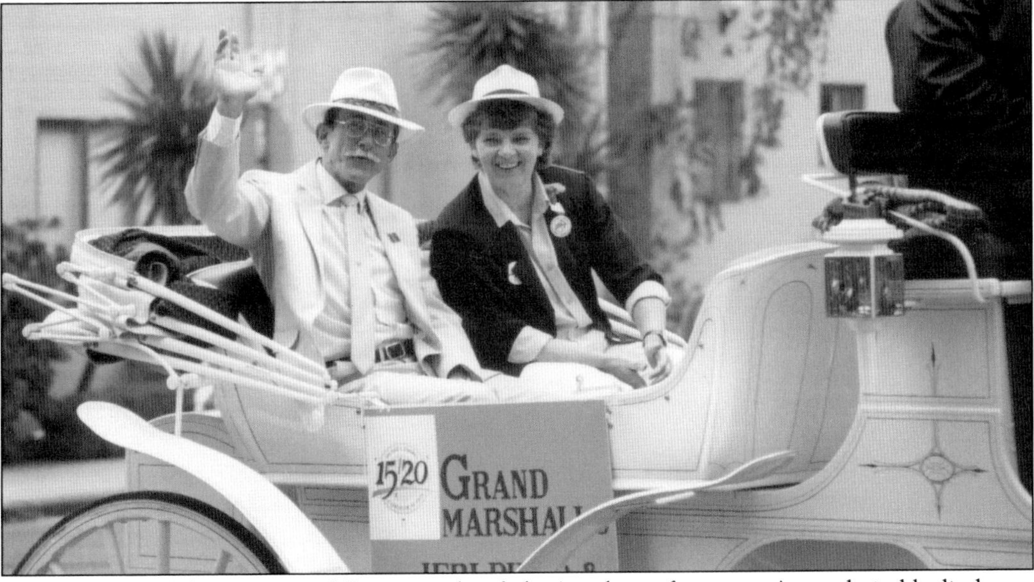

Jeri Dilno joined the Air Force following in her father's military footsteps. An undesirable discharge for being a lesbian in 1961, later upgraded to honorable, was the likely catalyst for her to undertake the role of activist for LGBT equality. Dilno played a key role in the creation of the San Diego LGBT Pride organization and participated in the first Pride Parade in 1975. Among her many honors was being chosen in 1989 as the grand marshal of the Pride Parade. She is pictured (right) along with Jess Jessop on the parade route. (Courtesy of Lambda Archives of San Diego.)

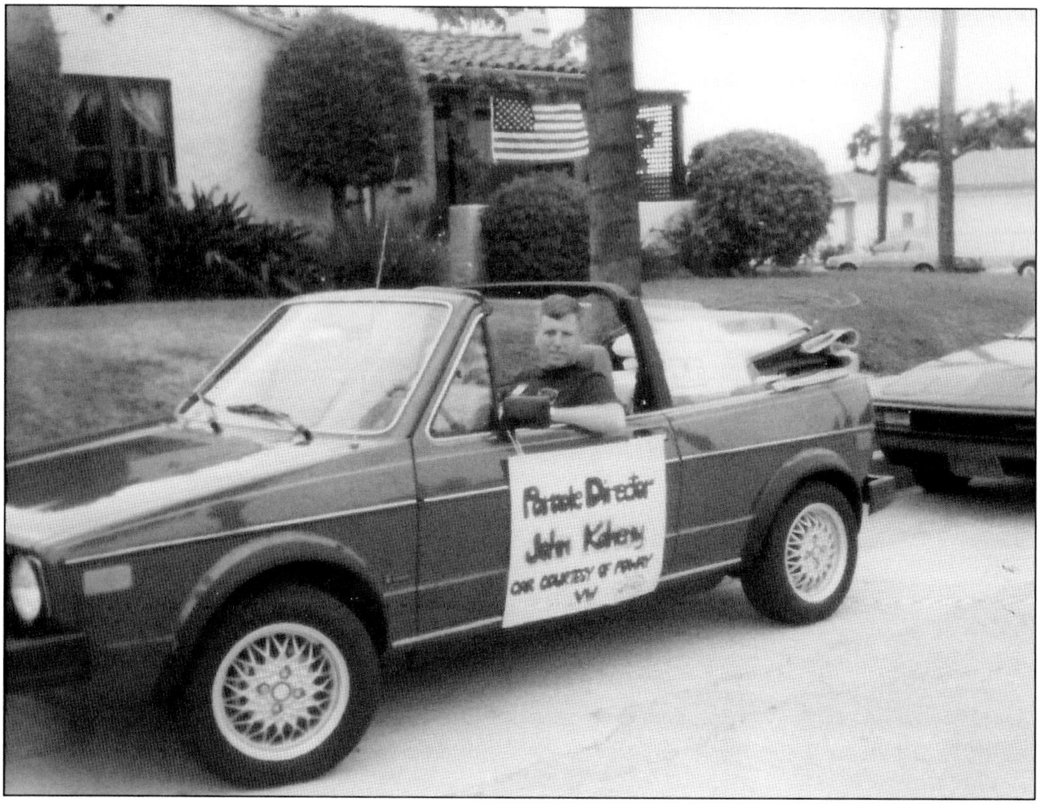

John Kaheny, a retired Marine colonel and former deputy city attorney, assumed his most important position when he undertook the role in 1982 as the Holiday at Home parade director for the Kensington Social and Athletic Club (KSAC). Held annually on Memorial Day weekend since 1982, the parade starts at the north end of Marlborough Drive, heads south, and ends a mile later in front of the Kensington Community Church. In this photograph from 1985, Kaheny is ready to corral tanks, toddlers, and retrievers as needed. (Courtesy of John Kaheny.)

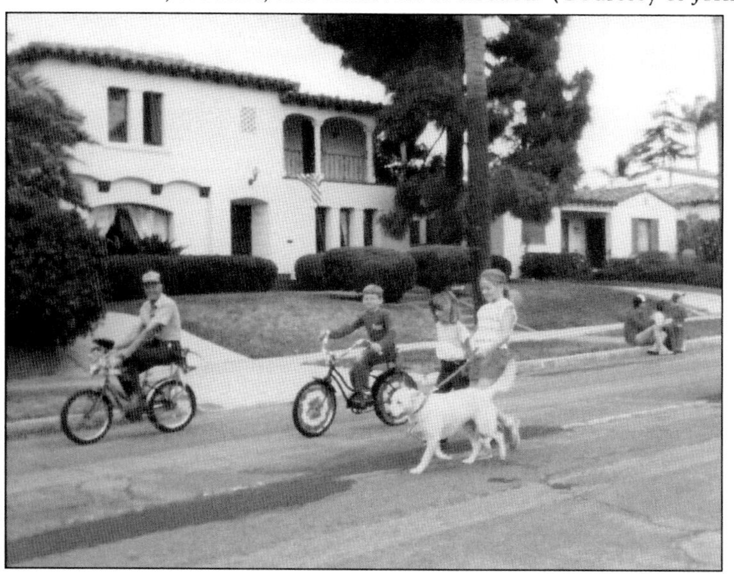

No Holiday at Home parade is complete without kids, dogs, and bicycles, and the 1985 parade was no different. Both houses in the background have been historically designated, with the George and Bertha Cooley/Lois and Benjamin Torgerson Spec. House No. 1 on the left, and the Paul and Nellie McCoy Spec House No. 1 on the right. (Courtesy of John Kaheny.)

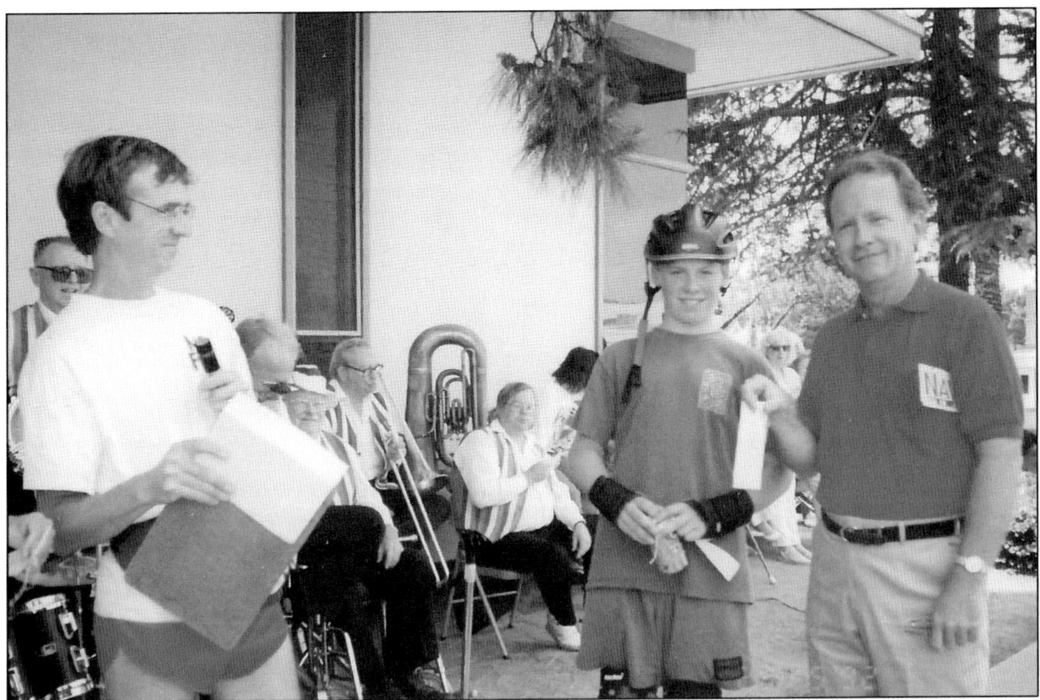

Two icons of the annual Holiday at Home parade events, the late Dale Larabee (left) and Milt Keller (right) announce the winners of the race in this image from 1992, while an unidentified youth looks on. Larabee, a 42-year resident of Kensington until his untimely death in 2014, founded the Kensington Miracle Mile Relay Race and the Kensington Litter Pickers, and cleaned up trash in the neighborhood once a month for over 15 years. Keller, a Kensington native, was the announcer for the parade for 32 years and a leader of the brigade of KSAC members who surreptitiously award ribbons to homes deemed to have the best display of Christmas lights each year. (Courtesy of John Kaheny.)

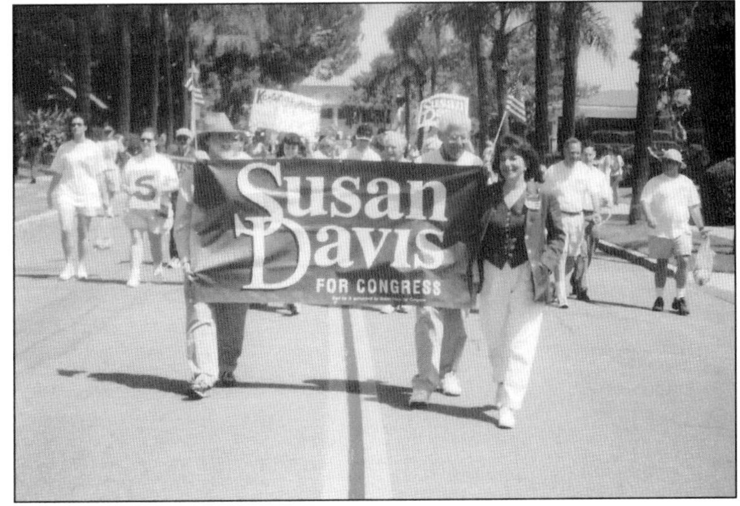

Congresswoman Susan Davis (right) only needed to walk a couple of blocks from her home to assume her position in the 2000 Holiday at Home parade. Regardless of whether there is a (D) or (R) after the name, Kensington residents support their neighbors in the political arena. Davis was earlier honored at the 1984 parade when she was chosen as the grand marshal. (Courtesy of John Kaheny.)

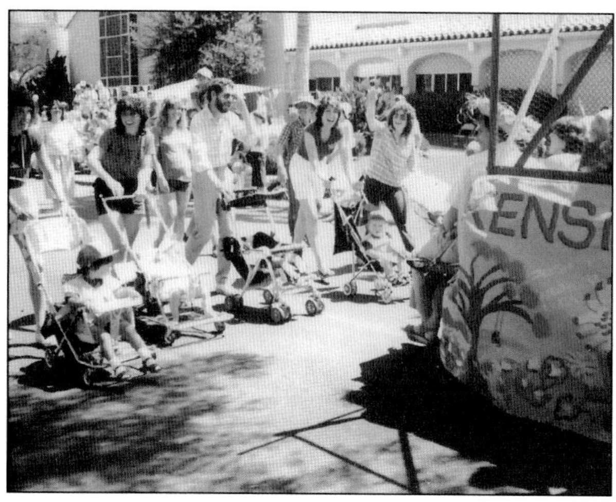

The Kensington Coop, a babysitting co-operative, joined in KSAC's annual Holiday at Home parade on Memorial Day weekend in 1984. Included among the stroller crew is, from left to right, an unidentified woman and child, Cyndi Croff pushing one year old Adrianne Croff, Roger Utt with son Andrew, and Jill Crusey with son Jeff. Adrianne Croff was born on May 30, 1983, the date of the first parade. Twenty-four years later, she was selected as the grand marshal of the 2007 parade in honor of the coinciding birth dates. (Courtesy of the Croff family.)

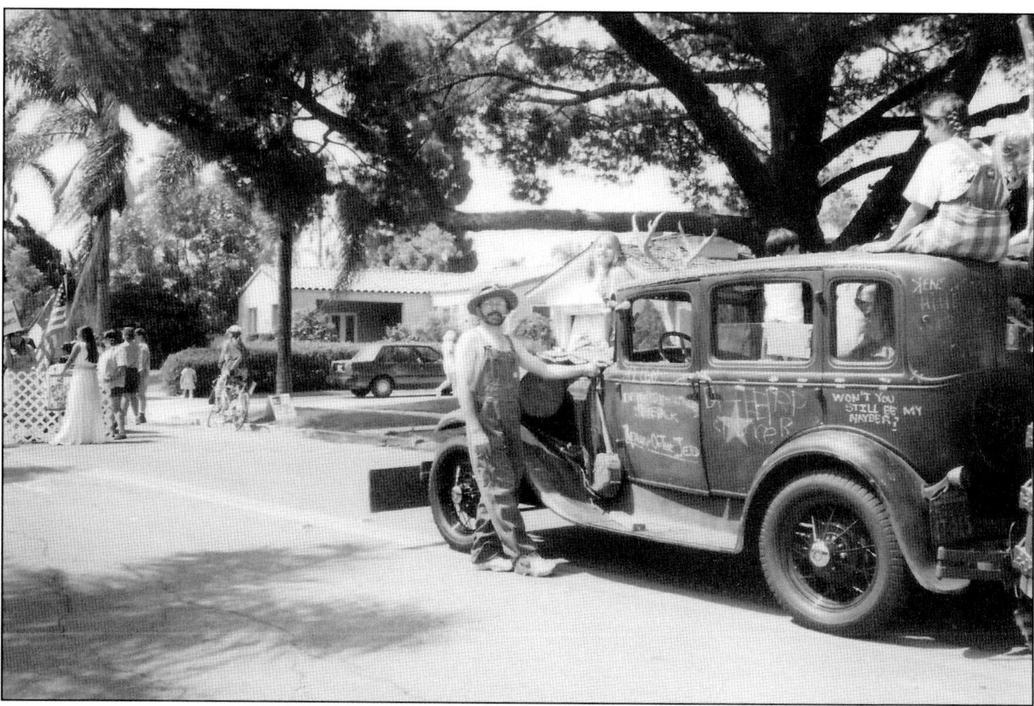

Lover of old cars and houses, small business owner, devoted father, great neighbor, and all-around good guy, Canterbury Drive's Jim Croff never misses an opportunity to put on a costume and get into the act. Pictured here at the 1991 Holiday at Home Parade, the Croff family's entry was "The Kensington Hillbillies." Every year around Christmas, Jim Croff hitches up an old car to a set of reindeer, puts on his Santa suit, and drives around the neighborhood to the delight of young and old alike. Halloween brings the famous Croff Haunted House, with Jim and family providing the thrills, frights, and a different theme every year. (Courtesy of the Croff family.)

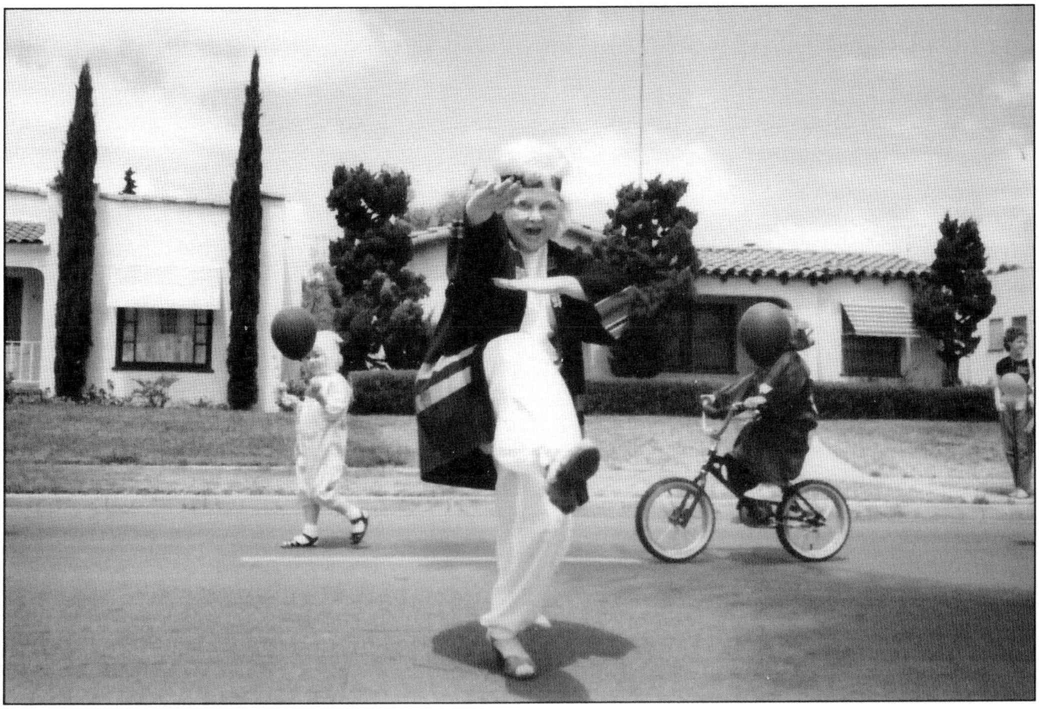

The annual KSAC Holiday at Home parade on Memorial Day weekend has been entertaining Kensington residents since 1982. Featuring at various times marching bands, fire engines, dogs, a tank, chickens, clowns, antique cars, politicians, and local kids, the parade is the main event that also includes a pancake breakfast and a relay race. Each year, a Kensington resident is chosen as grand marshal, and past winners have included Judge Earl J. Cantos, Congresswoman Susan Davis, Ernie Todd, a mail carrier, Police Chief Jerry Sanders, Mary Jane Swann (a resident since 1927), and Adrian Croff, chosen for having been born on the day of the first parade. In this photograph, neighborhood treasure Winnie Hanford shows off her ninja moves as the parade moves along Marlborough Drive. (Courtesy of Winnie and Rich Hanford.)

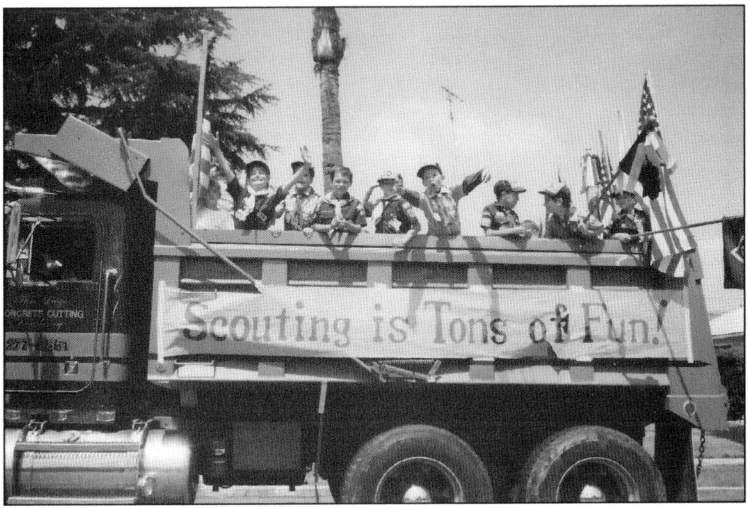

Cub Scout Pack 958, sponsored by the Kensington Community Church, was one of the entries in the 1991 KSAC Holiday at Home parade. Neighbor Jim Croff rolls out his company trucks each year to serve as parade floats, as evidenced by the San Diego Concrete Cutting Company sign on the truck's door. (Courtesy of the Croff family.)

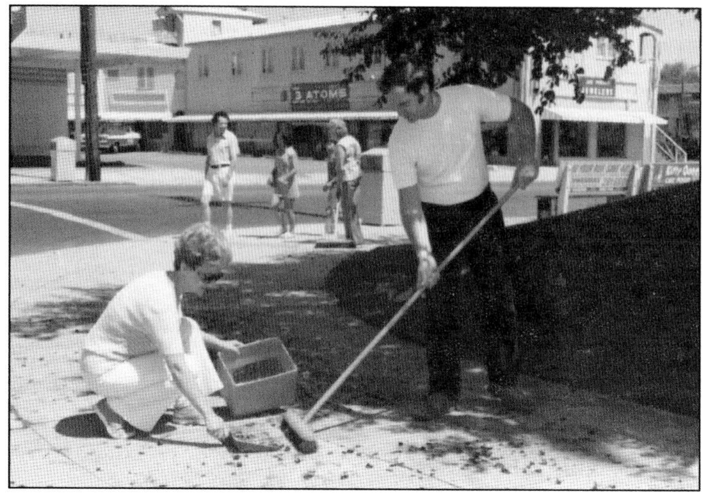

Winnie Hanford and son Guy clean up after a concert in the park in 1972. Across Adams Avenue can be glimpsed the gas station that preceded Clem's Bottle Shop, as well as the former home of 3 Atoms TV Repair, and the original location of Peevey Jewelers. The Hanford family has resided in Kensington since 1963 and are the neighborhood's biggest boosters. (Courtesy of Winnie and Rich Hanford.)

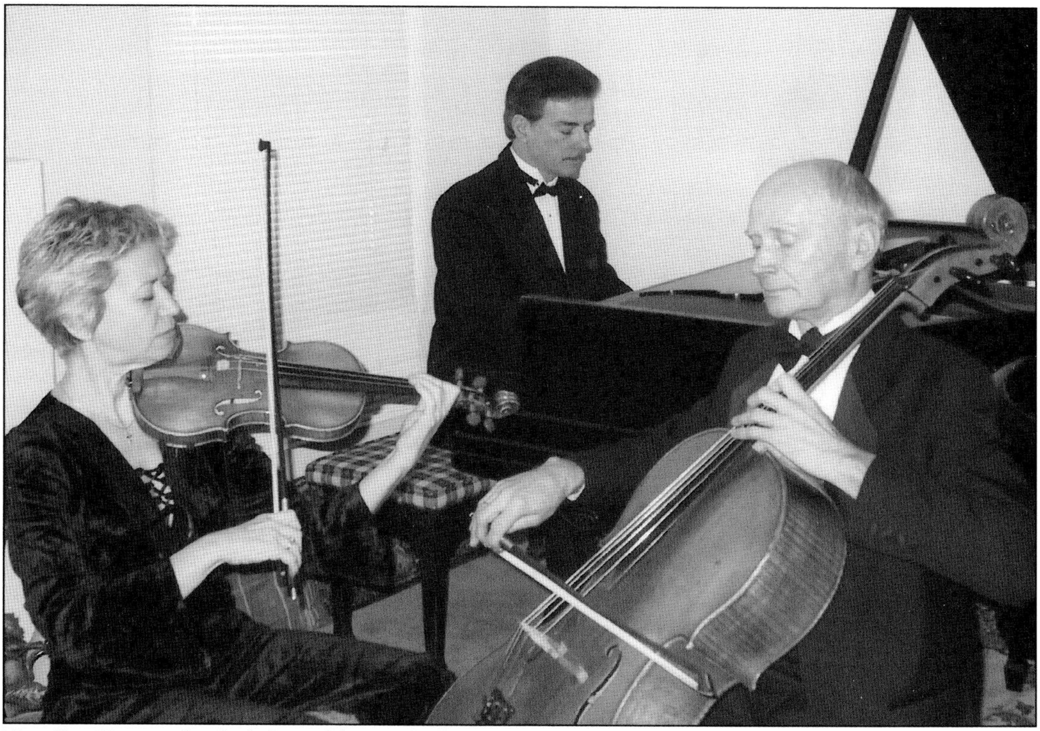

Natalka Kytasty (violin), Ronald Morebello (piano), and Yuri Kytasty (cello) form the Kensington Trio, performing together since 2001. Morebello founded the Kensington Concert Series the same year, and the trio has given superior musical performances at house concerts in local Kensington homes and beyond. All of the net proceeds are contributed to the Friends of the Kensington–Normal Heights Branch Library. (Courtesy of Ron Morebello.)

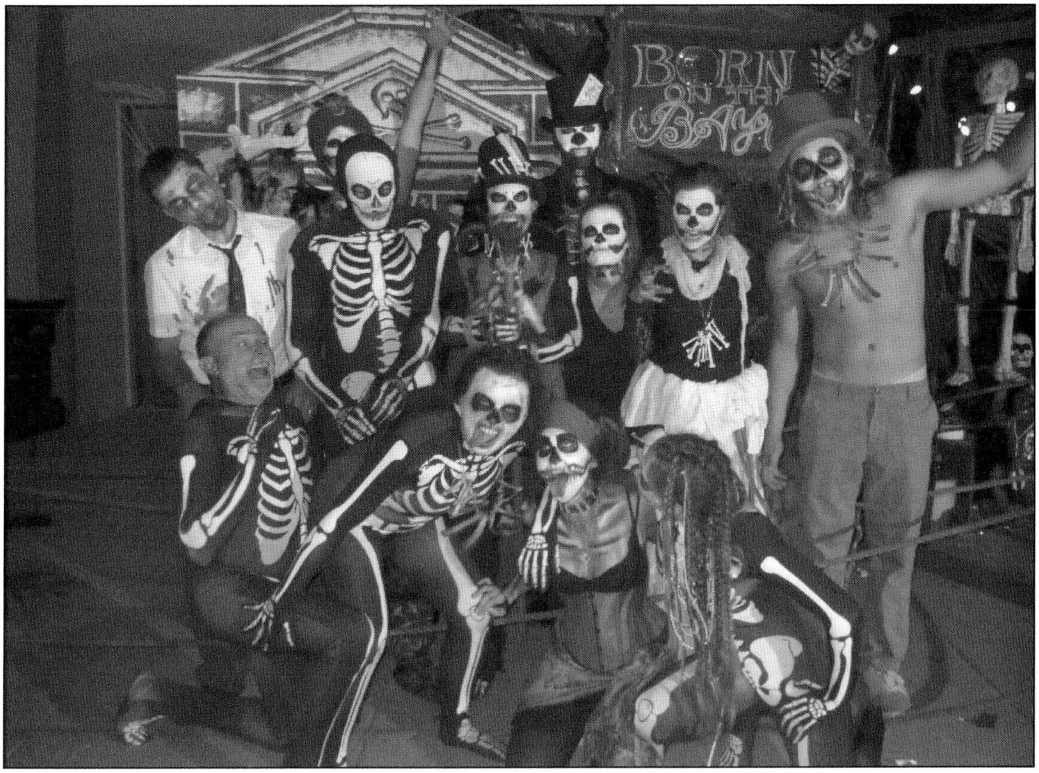

Halloween in Kensington is a big event, with carloads of kids big and small from all over the city descending on the neighborhood known for going all out. One of the favorite houses is the Croff residence on East Canterbury Drive, where the entire family suits up in costume and mans the haunted house, built every year with a new theme. The Croffs and friends are ready for the onslaught in this image from 2013. (Courtesy of the Croff family.)

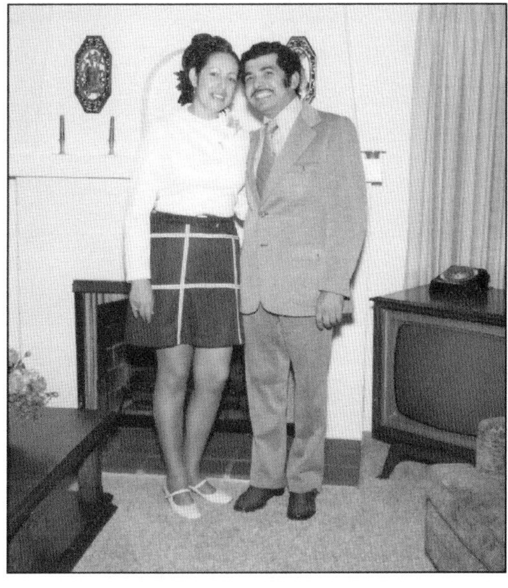

Everybody eats at Ponce's Mexican Restaurant at the entrance to Kensington on Adams Avenue. Ponce Meza Sr. grew up in the town of Talpa in the state of Jalisco, Mexico. There, he learned a great deal about work ethic, family, and community awareness. He moved to San Diego in October 1957 when he began working as a dishwasher at Padrillos in El Cajon and then Nati's Restaurant in Ocean Beach. In 1969, Ponce opened Ponce's Mexican Restaurant on Adams Avenue, where he worked every single day for over 30 years. One of those work days was September 20, 1972, when Ponce Meza Sr. and Maria Guadalupe "Lupe" Ruiz stepped out of the restaurant long enough to get married. Here, the newly minted Mr. and Mrs. Ponce Meza Sr. beam with joy on the day of their marriage in 1972. (Courtesy of the La Familia Meza.)

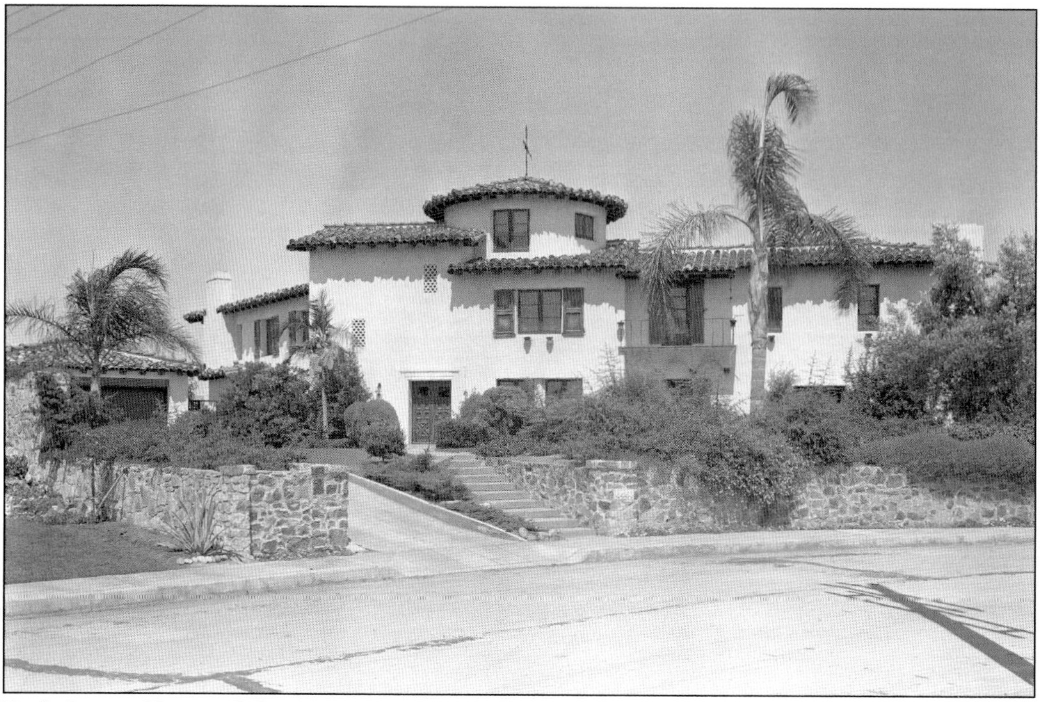

Beth-Sarim: House of the Princes on Braeburn Road brings people from all over the world to Kensington, but not just because the house is historically designated. Its big draw is that it was built in 1930 by the Jehovah's Witnesses as the home of Judge Joseph F. Rutherford, head of the Watch Tower Bible & Tract Society, and for the heavenly "princes," who were prophesied to return to Earth from heaven. Rutherford moved here from Brooklyn, New York, living here until his death in 1942. The house eventually became the home of G. Aubrey Davidson and his wife, Elizabeth, in 1953. Davidson headed the drive to bring the Panama-California Exposition to San Diego in 1915 and was instrumental in the establishment of the Marine Corps Recruit Depot, the Naval Training Center, and the Naval Hospital in Balboa Park. (Courtesy of James and Suzanne Lance.)

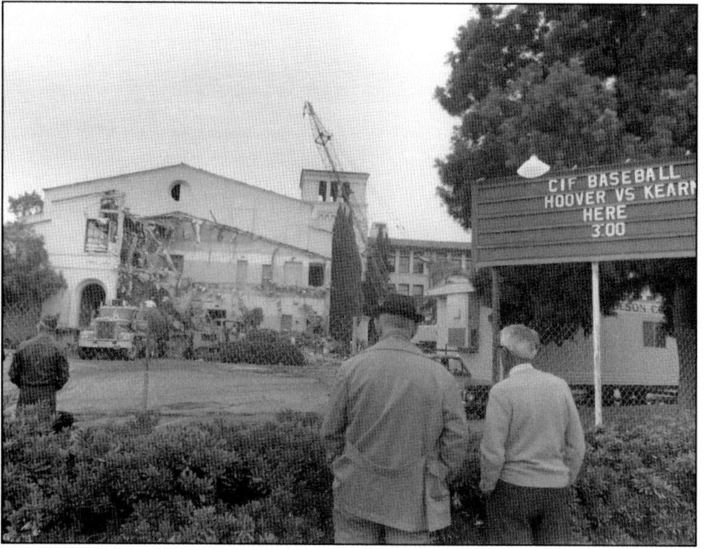

Due to maintenance costs and earthquake safety regulations, most of Herbert Hoover High School's original buildings were torn down, as seen in this photograph from 1976. Students were often housed in temporary structures until the new buildings were completed. As of March 2017, there are plans to again renovate the school, incorporating elements of the original Spanish-style design including the iconic tower. (Courtesy of Herbert Hoover High School.)

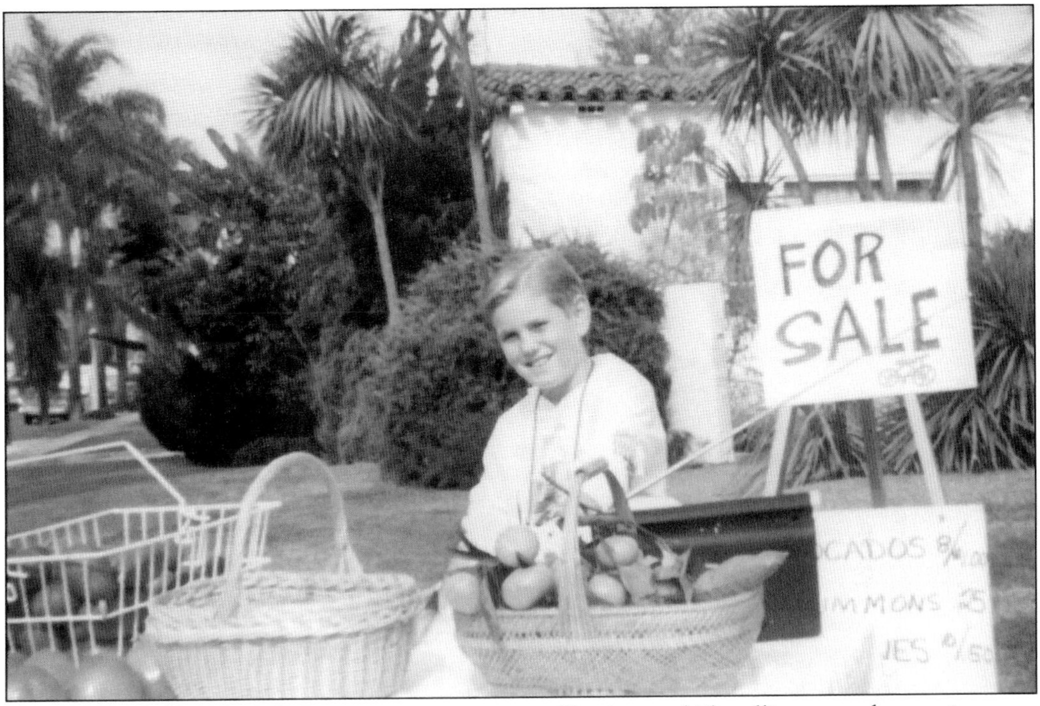

Ryan McMullen engages in a common practice among Kensington kids: selling avocados, persimmons, lemons, and limes from a stand set up in front of his family's home on Canterbury Drive in 1985. Kensington is an ideal place for growing fruits and vegetables year-round in the backyard, and neighbors are known to be generous with their bounties. (Courtesy of Becky McMullen.)

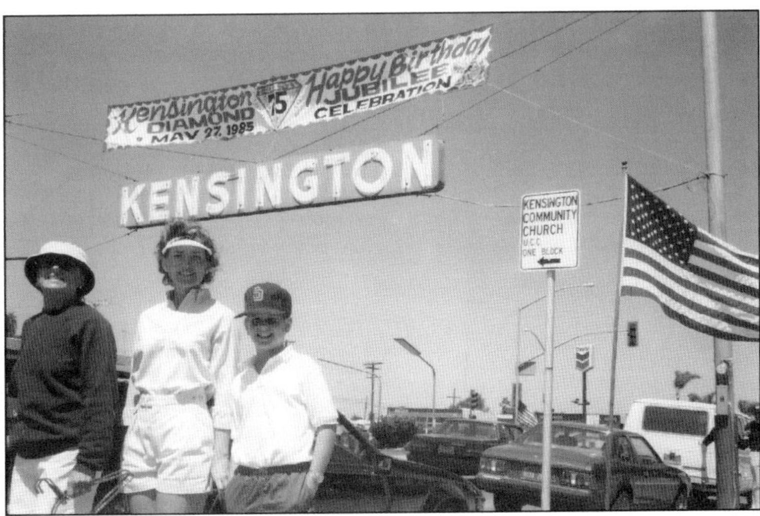

The year 1985 marked 75 years since the founding of Kensington, and the community celebrated with parades, contests, and the publishing of Dr. Thomas Baumann's book *Kensington-Talmadge, 1910–1985*. The Kensington sign in the background is an iconic representation of the community's spirit. (Courtesy of Becky McMullen.)

Consistent with our mission to preserve history on a local level, this book was printed in South Carolina on American-made paper and manufactured entirely in the United States. Products carrying the accredited Forest Stewardship Council (FSC) label are printed on 100 percent FSC-certified paper.

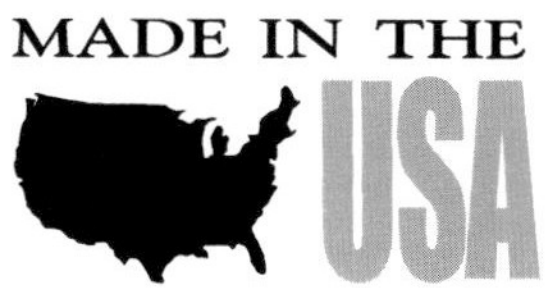